Heinrich Wilhelm Schäfe.

Protestant 'Sects' and the Spirit of (Anti-)Imperialism

Religious Entanglements in the Americas

INTER-AMERICAN STUDIES
Cultures – Societies – History

ESTUDIOS INTERAMERICANOS
Culturas – Sociedades – Historia

Volume 37

Heinrich Wilhelm Schäfer

Protestant 'Sects' and the Spirit of (Anti-)Imperialism

Religious Entanglements in the Americas

WVT Wissenschaftlicher Verlag Trier
Copublished by
UNO University of New Orleans Press

Protestant ‘Sects’ and the Spirit of (Anti-)Imperialism.
Religious Entanglements in the Americas /
Heinrich Wilhelm Schäfer. –
(Inter-American Studies | Estudios Interamericanos; 37)
Trier: WVT Wissenschaftlicher Verlag Trier, 2021
ISBN 978-3-86821-855-8
New Orleans, LA: University of New Orleans Press, 2021
ISBN 978-1-60801-209-1

SPONSORED BY THE
Federal Ministry of Education and Research

The project, on which this book is based, has been funded by the German Federal Ministry of Education and Research (Bundesministerium für Bildung und Forschung, BMBF). The responsibility for the content of this publication lies with the author.

Cover Image: Luis Quintero

Cover Design: Brigitta Disseldorf

Library of Congress Control Number: 2021934052

Publisher: WVT Wissenschaftlicher Verlag Trier, Postfach 4005, D-54230 Trier, Bergstraße 27, D-54295 Trier, Tel. 0049 651 41503, Fax 41504, www.wvttrier.de, wvt@wvttrier.de

Copublisher: University of New Orleans Press, 2000 Lakeshore Drive, Earl K. Long Library, Room 221, New Orleans, LA 70148, United States, 504-280-7457, unopress.org

In memoriam

Julia Esquivel

and Eugene Stockwell

Table of Contents

For of the last stage of
this cultural development
[sc. of victorious capitalism],
it might well be truly said:
"Specialists without spirit,
sensualists without heart;
this nullity imagines that it has attained
a level of civilization never before achieved."
(Max Weber 2001, 124)

Preface

The present book is the result of the cooperation at the Center for InterAmerican Studies (CIAS) of Bielefeld University. At the end of an interdisciplinary research project funded by the German Federal Ministry of Education and Research (BMBF) with the topic "The Americas as Space of Entanglements," a series of long essays on this subject from different disciplinary perspectives is being published in Spanish and English. This book is the English version of the essay, and it is written from the point of view of the sociology of religion. It is thus about the entanglements of religious praxis between Latin America and the USA. Since these interrelations have been and are primarily generated by Protestantism, the book is primarily concerned with Protestants; and since the relationship between the two subcontinents is characterized by the expansion of the capitalist economy and society, the context for interpreting the entanglements should be specified in social and economic terms.

Where capitalism and Protestantism are concerned, Max Weber is never far away either. I will therefore use his study of the United States as a springboard to delve into a history of religious entanglements that is first shaped by the dynamics of the American mission, and then increasingly by the energy of the Latin American Pentecostal movement and the migration of Latin American Christians to the United States.

Those who now expect a dry historical treatise should be warned. It is not only the concept of the essay series that is designed to make some polemical points. As author of this book, after almost 40 years of dealing with religious praxis in Latin America and the USA, I also cannot claim to be free of experiences that can hardly be put down on paper *sine ira et studio* – other than with an occasional polemical passage.

At this point, I would like to thank my colleagues from the Inter-American Studies Department for their initiative and incentive, first of all Olaf Kaltmeier and Wilfried Raussert; and also the Rectorate of Bielefeld University for its support in many ways. I am also pleased to thank the translator, Michael "Mike" Pätzold, whose translation perfectly matches the German original, even in its ironical passages.[1] Once again, I would also like to thank my assistant Sebastian Schlerka for his excellent, reliable and humorous support in all technical matters. If there are still any errors or ambiguities, the author is responsible for them.

HWS, Bielefeld, October 2020

1 An exception is this preface, which the author himself presents with the support of the helpful gnomes, the electronic Brownies of DeepL. At this point, I would like to say a few words about the capitalization of church names. We distinguish between names of institutions (Catholic Church, First Baptist Church on main street, No. 23, etc.) and generic terms (Mainline churches, Historical churches, Protestant churches, Black churches, Hispanic churches etc.). Furthermore, in this book I do not document interviews, interlocutors and other sources in a separate appendix, but only in the footnotes. This piece is just a long essay, already overloaded with footnotes and bibliography. As our theoretical approach is praxeological, based on the sociology of Pierre Bourdieu, we substitute the English word "practice" by the concept of "praxis," in distinction to "practice*s*."

1. Introduction

Weber's Journey

On his journey to St. Louis in 1904 Max Weber was able to gain a much clearer idea than in Germany of how his distinction between "church" and "sect" – a difference he had elaborated himself – worked out in reality. On the one hand, there were the firm institutions of the European Roman Catholics and Lutherans: *Heilsanstalten* (institutions of salvation) and *Gnadenanstalten* (institutions of mercy); on the other – besides the sedate German Lutherans of the Missouri Synod in St. Louis – the "sects"[2] of Baptists, Methodists and others, which were based on voluntary membership and easily played a leading role in the USA. One could also speak of "Free churches" in the sense that they were (and are) free of governmental administration. In his study "Protestantische Sekten und der Geist des Kapitalismus" (Weber 1946a), Weber made a few observations that are also of interest from an Interamerican perspective. The difference between the "Heilsanstalt" with an almost obligatory membership and the "brotherly community" of like-minded people is also of importance for the reflection on the religious entanglements between the USA and Latin America. If what you are after is the trust of other people, or public recognition as, e.g., politician or businessman, membership of an institution into which you are born is of lesser importance. Membership in a voluntary community, by contrast, which demands your conversion and a certain amount of esprit de corps, is significant: in the circle of brothers and sisters it lays the foundation of creditworthiness, for example. Further, once the community of like-minded people has spread to a substantial part of the population, say 25%, religious creditworthiness can be converted into political capital. Weber reports a Baptist group baptism of a relative, who draws his attention to a young man and predicts his baptism – which the young man then duly under-

2 We use the term "sect" in the strict sociological sense. No theological evaluation is therefore linked to it in the present work.

goes. How does the relative know this...? "Because he wants to open a bank in M." Now that he is baptized, he will attract "the patronage of the whole region and he will outcompete everybody" (Weber 1946a, 305). The mere fact of his membership in a Baptist church is taken in M. as proof of his ethical qualities, which guarantees him the approval and trust of the local people.

Bolsonaro

Jair Bolsonaro has certainly not read Weber, but is very likely to have received from one of his friends on the religious right – maybe from Silas Malafaia – a reference to the effect just illustrated. About 30% of the Brazilian population are Protestants and politicians of the religious right are hoping for a corporatist "voto evangélico:" "Brother votes for Brother." In this way, the far-right Catholic Bolsonaro had himself baptized in the river Jordan in 2016 by Pastor Everaldo – a well-known member of the Pentecostal right. This news was distributed in the media of the religious right and has stuck in the public's mind. As the situation in Brazil is different from that in the USA, and the Catholic hierarchy and the religious right still exert a marked influence in the country, Bolsonaro has assured people time and again that he is still a Catholic – even after his baptism. Of course, this did not show up on the small screens of the Protestant media of the right but appeared more likely on pages two or three of the secular press. This apart, the theological view of Anabaptism behind this act and the partial denial that followed is highly significant, as is the non-appearance of a reaction from the Catholic hierarchy. At the time of the waning Middle Ages, Anabaptists were shoved into sacks and drowned. That would no longer be adequate today, although excommunication would seem to be appropriate. Be that as it may: his action is likely to have gained Bolsonaro some of the votes of members of Evangelical, Pentecostal and Neopentecostal churches. He was assured in any case of the support of the "bancada evangélica," the cross-party camp of conservative Protestants (and Catholic charismatics) in Congress and Senate.

Break-Up of the Catholic Hegemony

In brief, the spread of Protestant churches from the USA into Latin America broke up the Catholic hegemony on the continent, which brought about various effects. For a start, there was now competition, which established a religious field in the first place. The Catholic Church, which already suffered structurally from a shortage of priests and – depending on the country – from the consequences of laicism, had now got a potent competitor for members. A further effect was that Protestant actors were now active in the political arena, running either as individual candidates or Protestant parties. Whereas – to put it very roughly – three poles had previously constituted the political field with parties of the old oligarchies, parties of the modernizing Liberals and the organized left, new actors were now appearing who were oriented above all to corporatist self-interests and today are tending rather to the right – that is, to power! This puts pressure above all on the Latin American left.

Migrants in the USA

Conversely, the partly Catholic, partly Pentecostal migrants from Latin America in the USA set the religious field in motion, which meanwhile has also impacted politics. In 2016 Donald Trump was elected into office polling 81% of the vote of the white Evangelicals. However, all statistics indicate that this will not be enough in the future, since the weight of the white Evangelicals is declining. For the 2024 election it has been calculated (Wong 2018, 96) that the Republicans will end up at least 3% below the majority even if they achieve 100% of the white Evangelical vote. This changed relation is due not least to the fact that the Latino migrants entitled to vote – and non-eligible Latinos probably even more so – have a positive attitude towards big government, state health care, increased taxation of the rich, and climate policy. In addition, the Black churches are even more progressive than the Latinos, which, however, has nothing to do with Interamerican entanglements, but with the overlapping ethnic[3] and social discrimination of the African-American population.

Weber: Classes, Capitalism

Back to Weber. He is concerned with the connection between Protestant "sects" and the development of capitalism and democracy. For example, he sees connections between the organization of social, cultural, ethnic and religious differences in voluntary clubs, associations or sects and the development of democratic structures (Weber 1946a, 310-311). He also draws attention, however, to the fact that different class affiliations imply quite different attitudes towards religion and uses of religion – an argument that he develops in detail in his chapter on "The Religious Propensities of Peasantry, Nobility and Bourgeoisie" (in Weber 1978, 468ff.). Multi-millionaires, for example, do not need a religion for their self-understanding and social ascent (Weber 1946a, 309-310) – it would be more true to say that they use it, especially when you look at the Americas of today.

Weber's view of the differentiated social classes also prohibits a one-sided reading of his approach from the point of view of modernization theory. Weber does not see capitalism as the paradise at the end of social evolution. One would be well advised to read the last pages of his book on Protestantism (Weber 2001, 102ff.), which is often used for the modernization thesis. Industrial capitalism, he says, determines the lives of all individuals "who are born into this mechanism ... with irresistible force" and is likely to keep determining it "until the last ton of fossilized coal is burnt. […] [T]he care for external goods should only lie on the shoulders of the 'saint like

3 We will use "ethnicity" instead of "race" as the latter concept is not the scholarly precondition but the effect of racism, see Deutsche Zoologische Gesellschaft: Jenaer Erklärung, September 2019 (https://www.uni-jena.de/unijenamedia/Universit%C3%A4t/Abteilung%20Hochschulkommunikation/Presse/Jenaer%20Erkl%C3%A4rung/Jenaer_Erklaerung.pdf, accessed 22 September 2019).

a light cloak, which can be thrown aside at any moment'. But fate decreed that the cloak should become an iron cage" (Weber 2001, 123).

Victorious capitalism has made human beings "specialists without spirit, sensualists without heart," who, moreover, deceive themselves into thinking that they have "attained a level of civilization never before achieved" (Weber 2001, 124). Which brings us to the problem of American exceptionalism.

Puritanism

That Puritan Protestantism in the New World and with it also the United States as a state are something very special is the nation's birth story that has been cultivated since the Puritan colonies. The Puritan project on the new continent – inhabited by "Indians," but nevertheless empty of real human beings – is the new Zion, the city upon a hill from which will come the salvation of all mankind. This exceptional status obliges the people of the settlers to keep pushing the boundaries of the sacred community, as Madison later noted in his interpretation of the new state: it can only operate meaningfully in an "extended sphere" that must be extended further and further. In complete contrast to many independence fighters, Madison turns against "Montesquieu's principle that liberty could exist only in a small state. Madison boldly argued the opposite: that empire was essential for freedom" (Williams 1980, 45). Thus, the enlightened, secular father of the constitution transforms the Puritans' religious mission and civilization project into expansive secular aims and objectives. In his presidency he pursued corresponding goals with the Louisiana Purchase and the British-North American War of 1812. Under his successor, James Monroe, expansionism was extended to cover the entire western hemisphere by the Monroe Doctrine and used by President Polk to legitimize the war against Mexico. "Giving the world law and freedom" – as the title is in German –, that is what is at stake (Williams 1980).

Spheres of Influence

For our purposes, it is important that law and freedom in the USA have a strongly religious undertone and that the expansion of the spheres of influence is accompanied by a collusion between the religious missionary zeal of the Protestant churches, the interests of the trading houses and ultimately almost the entire economy as well as the political-military actors. It would, however, be mistaken to simply assume that there was a concerted action between the economy or the military and the missionaries. On the other hand, one cannot rule out cases of close cooperation between, say, missionaries and secret services. Different social operations and processes follow similar courses not only because individual planners make arrangements with each other – which of course can also occur. They usually proceed in similar ways or in the same direction because the actors follow homologous practical logics that they have taken on board due to similar socialization. Thus, certain identities of interests also arise and lead to similar – but not identical – results. The territorial extension of the spheres of influence in the practical logic of these different actors operates according to their own respective laws, specific types of legitimation and motivation, special kinds of semantics and interests – but in the same direction: after the boundary of settlement, the frontier, was closed in the West, expansion turned south.

Conservatives and Liberals

It cannot be said, however, that there was nothing in the South. When the first organized Protestants set out in the 1830s, shortly after the proclamation of the Monroe Doctrine, from the North to Latin America, the states there found themselves fighting the Spanish crown for their independence or had achieved it recently. Of special relevance is the fact that their fight for independence continued as a conflict between conservative and liberal elites, with the one party firmly anchored in the colonial hacienda system and allied with the

Catholic hierarchy, while the other was anticolonial, republican and without religious representation. It is obvious that the latter, especially in northern Latin America, orientated itself by and large more often to the USA than Europe and so turned into "natural" partners of the US American missionaries. (Special influence was exercised in Argentina, Uruguay and Brazil by France.)

Disposition for Hierarchy

It is, however, necessary not to underrate the Catholic Church in Latin America. A pre-Tridentine, ritualist and magic Catholicism had already left its mark for 300 years when the anticolonial rebellions erupted. What determined the societies' character was not a Puritan colony, but monarchy by means of its impenetrable hierarchies and the structures of the hacienda economy, while at the same time establishing contexts of corporatist responsibility and making plausible arguments for a strong state. These interrelations were protected in the religious field by the Catholic Church. But above all, this social structure has left its mark on the habitūs of most Latin Americans. These have survived rapid structural change and have contributed to the establishment of the new structures in the mode of Big Government as strong states, in part also dictatorships under the rule of the Liberal elites. The orientation towards strong states and strong corporatist structures is continued in the family, economy, religion and politics, as is the centrality of the relations in extended families instead of individualism in both upper and lower social strata, and the imperviousness of class boundaries for social advancement. When we were looking at the migration of Latin Americans to the USA, we noticed that the dispositions mentioned determined the migrants' political options while exerting political influence in the process – much to the displeasure of white Evangelicals and the religious right. These dispositions leave their marks also on the Protestantism in Latin America. In most cases – with the exception of Brazil – we are dealing in the end with missionary Protestantism from the USA. But the amalgam of this type of Protestantism with Latin American everyday life has produced in many cases new practices and even new formations of religious actors who strike out in new directions and impact, for their part, Protestantism in the USA. In this context we would like to mention the influence that socially committed Latino-Evangelicals or Liberation Theology had on the rise of an Evangelical left in the USA during the 1970s.

In short, the religious relations between the USA and Latin America have been characterized over the course of time by a pronounced reciprocal entanglement. One is almost tempted to speak of a symmetrical exchange. This first impression should not, however, deceive us about their real nature – the entanglements are still asymmetrical.

Literature 1

The literature on Interamerican religious relations has been less interested in entanglements than one-sided influences from the North on the South, and migration in the opposite direction. The former relate above all to the Protestant mission in Latin America. The interpretation of the Protestant presence in Latin America is, moreover, a hotly debated topic, as is that of influences on religious policy. There are, roughly speaking, four interpretations.[4]

The first is clearly polemical. As early as the first half of the 20th century public pronouncements of Catholic dignitaries became known in which Protestants were called agents of "Yankee neocolonialism" and "imperialism," as "traitors to their country" as well as supporters of atheism, free masonry, spiritism and communism. Almost prophetic – and indeed long before the phenomenon had arisen – would appear today the explanation by Josef Peters (1927), a Catholic scholar of religious missions, that Protestantism in Latin America was spreading "a Puritan spirit with a utilitarian bent" (cf. Prien 1978, 838, my translation). His assessment would

4 Cf. Escobar 1994, from whom we differ on several occasions; B. Smith 1998, 3-4; Prien 1978, 837ff.

not, in fact, become correct until 50 to 60 years later. This line of criticism was continued in the 1980s by representatives of Liberation Theology and the political left under pressure from military regimes and the perception of Protestant collaboration with dictatorships. The "sects" were widely taken to be the CIA's moles. Though this is too sweeping a judgment, it cannot be rejected out of hand. For there has indeed been cooperation time and again of missionaries with the US secret services as was shown by the Frank Church Committee of the US Senate (1975), the Iran-Contra affair and military-missionary cooperations in Guatemala during the 1980s.

The second interpretation is a sociological one. Its main exponents are the German-Brazilian Emilio Willems in Brazil and Chile, and the Swiss scholar Christian Lalive d'Epinay in Chile with their work during the 1960s and early '70s (Willems 1967; Lalive d'Epinay 1969; 1975). These authors offer sociological studies of the Protestant praxis, taking as their starting point congregation members in the context of industrialization processes. According to the sociologists, conversion to Protestantism took place as a by-product of the changes hitting the poor people, especially migration, and the loss of traditional lifestyles and loyalties (for example, the hacienda system). These losses were compensated for in their congregations, and through this action Protestantism could function as an agent of modernization. A special role was played by the ecstatic Pentecostal movement, which combined a highly integrative congregational praxis with charismatic legitimation through direct "revelations" for illiterate people, who protested in this way against the system. The diagnosis of protest results from the investigation of microprocesses like glossolalia, and stands in contradiction to the affirmation of the dynamics of modernization.

The third interpretation follows dependency theory. It dates back, as Escobar (1994, 122 ff.) points out, to the anti-imperialist thinking of the type represented by the Peruvian Marxist José Carlos Mariátegui, which was confirmed by an ethnological analysis of indigenous Adventists by Luis Valcárcel (1927). The current interpretation of Protestantism from a dependency-theoretical point of view is shaped largely by the Argentinian Methodist theologian Míguez Bonino (1995). In this approach, US-American Protestantism is above all an agent of US-American culture in Latin America. It is especially when adopting a historical perspective that Miguez sees historical (or "Mainline") Protestantism as an option of the liberal elites in the 19th century. The alliance is continued in history by circulating a positive image of the USA in Latin America. The Pentecostal movement is appreciated from this historical angle as a step in the indigenization of Protestantism in Latin America, accompanied however by the blemish of having a socially alienating effect. The political commitment of Historical Protestantism or its remains hardly justifies such an assessment. For the Pentecostal movement, important differentiations must be made: some Pentecostals wait for the next world, others seek to apply God's law, while others again teach (successfully!) how to employ management strategies to gain riches and political power.

A fourth approach, adopting the way the Evangelical missionary tradition sees itself, attempts to present Protestantism and "the" Pentecostal movement as the solution to all the problems of civilization of Latin America.[5] David Martin, in his treatment of the political role of the Pentecostal movement in Latin America during the Reagan era, adopts a position that is decidedly in favor of US foreign politics. This leads him to a positive bias toward "the" Pentecostal movement, which bias he sees confirmed in undiluted form in his results. He utilizes a "Weberian thesis" cut down to a trivial sort of modernization theory in order to subject Latin American Protestantism to a much-reduced form of the theory. As we will discuss Martin's ideological stance below, we will concentrate here on the general use of this "thesis," which surfaces also in other work (for example in Sherman 1997). According to Martin, the "Weberian

5 Escobar finds the same approach in Stoll 1990 and Martin 1990. I fail to see how Stoll's work, an ethnological study critical of all approaches and largely free of theory, can be considered on a par with that of Martin, full of prejudices as it is.

thesis" can be proved in Latin America by the fact that Protestants there generally experience social "betterment" by dint of their asceticism in the "Methodist" tradition. He goes on to say that Protestantism, and not least the Pentecostal movement, favor democracy. To be sure, his social-betterment thesis is correct as far as it goes. But it is not limited to Protestant believers because convinced Catholics of the middle class or the charismatic movement also exercise asceticism in the sense intended by him: they don't smoke, don't drink, or only rarely and in moderation, they don't go to brothels, they don't gamble away their money… If the "Weberian thesis" is used to open up more or less of a difference between Latin American (or US-American) Protestants and Catholics, then it must be considered not only trivial, but wrong. The denomination is not what matters, but the existence of strong religious beliefs in the context of an ethical religiosity, whether oriented to Catholic social teaching or the Asambleas de Dios. There is, moreover, another qualification to be made. The prosperity-prophets' religiosity directs attention to monetary riches as the magical result of large donations to religious organizations and of the belief in the miracle of the hundred-fold monetary recompense by the Lord. The legitimation of prosperity finds a home in the upper-middle class for a special feeling for pleasurable enjoyment in the former ascetic Protestantism: SUVs, long-distance travel with the family, holiday homes, expensive clothes, etc. As for democracy: a look at the strategies of the Protestant right in Latin America and the USA – especially at the Neopentecostals, who are oriented to a management logic – demonstrates something else, namely that they subvert democratic processes, and drive and legitimize a refeudalization (Kaltmeier 2019). It can hardly be claimed that the support of the Brazilian military dictatorship and the Bancada Evangélica's election support for Bolsonaro, let alone the cooperation in Guatemala with the dictatorship of Ríos Montt were acts of support for democracy. An expressly democratic attitude can at best be recognized in the Historical Protestantism of the 19th century and some of the corresponding churches of today, like Methodists, Lutherans or Presbyterians. Also mentioned can be the – by now fading – liking of Evangelical Christians for left-leaning political parties like APRA (Peru), PT (Brazil) and PRD or PRI (Mexico), which came about primarily because of their championing freedom of religion. Of the historical and Evangelical actors just mentioned, some are now part of the ecumenical movement and promote democracy in these cooperative contexts – the reason why they are hated by those actors who use the broad "Weberian thesis" to hype them up into spotless democrats.

Literature 2

The opposite direction of the flow, from Latin America to the north, is far less important with respect to religion, as I have hinted at above when I mentioned an asymmetry. Catholicism experienced a gradual growth in the southwest – its present-day center instead of Rhode Island – through the arrival of mostly Mexican workers in the *bracero* program during the 1940s and '50s. The social sciences, using socio-demographic methods, did not take note until the *Immigration and Naturalization Act* (1965). However, religion did not come into the view of the sociology of migration and transnationality until the 1990s (Vasquez and Marquardt 2003; Alba, Rabouteau, and DeWind 2009; Juergensmeyer 2005). Clara Buitrago (2021) distinguishes between two analytical approaches, the first is the *incorporation* one, which considers the role played by Latino-Pentecostal congregations in the integration of migrants into US society. However, the functionalism utilized by proponents of the approach takes into account mainly non-religious factors. The second, the *religion-on-the-move* approach, considers the role played by transnational missionary enterprises for the maintenance of durable relations between migrants and their homes, while neglecting the part played by religious convictions, which field is the focus of Buitrago's work. She finds a connection between social position, convictions of faith, and the re-definition of religious identities and strategies through the mission in the North. In this way, migrants in need of help turn into *expatriates* who offer spiritual help. This change in position and strategies brings in its wake other effects in the receiving society: Latino-Protestant preachers are able today to pack stadiums while Latino-Catholics shift US Catholicism in a different direction. Religious praxis occurs here precisely through the effect of religious articles of belief in a mode of authentic entanglement.

Collective Actors

The focus of the present study is entanglement, which is why the central theorems of entanglement history (Werner and Zimmermann 2002) determine the direction of our observations. For the sake of simplicity, we will concentrate on two collective actors, US-American Protestants, such as missionaries, and Latin American Protestants. The inductive approach of this investigation of the relation naturally takes into account contextual factors like the Catholic Church and social class structure. This makes it not only admissible but necessary to consider different investigative yardsticks and units. As "the" Protestantism does not exist, the literature on the history of the denominations designs a taxonomy according to different group memberships: historical and Mainline Protestants respectively, Evangelicals, Pentecostal churches and Neopentecostal churches. This taxonomy is, however, only partially useful. Our research has shown that, depending on social class, there are further differentiations to be made. Above all, it is of little help with the study of the political mobilization of religious actors. We will, therefore, distinguish between these relevant political actor formations, which are, *cum grano salis*, active both in the USA and Latin America:

Formations

- Those who hope for salvation in the afterlife and are not politically active are often recruited from the classic Pentecostal movement and Evangelical groups, and frequently belong to the informal lower classes (HOPE FOR AN AFTERLIFE);

- Those who want the values of the Kingdom of God to show to best advantage through social service in this world belong mostly to historical and Mainline Protestantism respectively, Evangelicalism or churches of *indígenas*, and come from the lower middle or lower classes (VALUES);
- Those who want to valorize God's law by legal means also come from Evangelical or Pentecostal groupings, and frequently can be assigned to the downwardly mobile (lower) middle class (LAW);
- Those who want to dominate the political system on the basis of ideals of prosperity and management frequently belong to Neopentecostalism or classic Pentecostalism, and can be placed in the rising upper middle and even upper class (MANAGEMENT).

As a rule, the last two formations make up the religious right today, while the second forms the religious left. In the current political climate, this polarization is of some importance.

Experts

A further differentiation must be introduced between believers and religious experts. The latter produce the salvation goods (Weber) of which the former stand in need. These experts compete for followers and through this competition shape the religious field. Those with the most, and most affluent, followers dominate the field: in Latin America this is the Catholic Church, in the USA the most important actors of the MANAGEMENT and LAW formations – clearly not a cluster of homogenous institutions. Followers are involved in the religious field only in so far as their options prefer certain experts and strengthen them. This does of course not mean that the believers are not religious. On the contrary, it can be assumed that they live their religiosity in the most different social spheres: in the economy through hard work and application, in the world of fashion through reserve, in legal relations through honesty, and in politics by voting for politicians who are bishops in their church, like Marcelo Crivella, a member of the religious right, in the Igreja Universal do Reino de Deus in Brazil. Religious capital (recognition of an expert as religious expert by his clientele) can in conditions of a formal democracy be transformed into political capital (votes of electors) by influencing how religious electors cast their votes. For the study of politico-religious praxis it is of primary importance to observe the experts, while the laymen have to take a back seat.

Containers

The history of entanglements seeks to avoid treating nations as "containers," nevertheless we will speak here of the USA in contradistinction to Latin America. We will do this simply because this is the only way in which the historical phenomenon can be captured. For it was missionaries from the USA who, in the context of a Pan-Americanism conceived by Protestants, undertook the mission in "Catholic Latin America," and in the process confirmed the said contrast through their praxis, using it as the starting point of their program. And conversely, Protestant and Catholic Latin Americans judged the missionaries as ambassadors of a country whose interventions in the internal affairs of the Latin American countries were plain to see, and who in addition could be clearly identified by their language as people who did not share the collective Latin American habitūs. We will therefore not treat the two regions as containers. Having said that, we will not rule out categorically the use of comparison and transfer as working tools. Given that the Protestant mission in Latin America transferred religious dispositions that arose in US Calvinism, which have absolutely no correspondence in Catholic socialization, the investigation of the starting conditions in the USA compared with Latin America and the processing of dispositions in Latin America are the precondition for an understanding of the entanglement of US American and Latin American habitūs into new forms of praxis.

Transnationalism

The present slim volume would be overloaded if transnational praxis of religious actors in general, beyond the Interamerican entanglements, were to be examined.[6] Relevant actors will of course be mentioned in passing, like the Vatican, the World Council of Churches or the World Evangelical Alliance, but an investigation of these and similar actors – such as the web of aid organizations like ActAlliance – are beyond the scope of this book.

Imperialism

To assume symmetry here would be misleading – as is also stressed by Werner and Zimmermann. There is no symmetry between the two regions either in terms of collective political and economic actors or missionizing Protestantism and locally rooted Catholicism, which is also bound to the Roman universal church. This theoretical statement finds its correspondence in the course of history in the imperialist grasp of the USA on Latin America. A table of military interventions of the USA in Latin America since 1800 provides sufficient evidence of this fact – it lists almost 100 cases – and also makes manifest the Latin American attitudes that result from them. Here, however, it is crucially important to look closely in order to find out for which actors the interventions evoke negative and for which positive connotations. As concerns the entanglement between the USA and Latin America we are thrown back to an analytical similarity between two theories, that of imperialism and that of dependency – unless one wants, as does Martin (1990), to bury the praxis of the Latin American actors under a US-American prejudice. So, it is precisely the framework of a history of entanglements that vindicates our transformation of Weber's essay title. Admittedly, we are talking only of a similarity, and that for two reasons: first, religious convictions cannot be imposed and, second, even religious be-

6 For transnational aspects see Schäfer 2016. See also Juergensmeyer 2005.

havior imposed by imperialists undergoes a process of resignification in the actors' praxis, which is nothing but a religious entanglement. On the other hand, one must not lose sight of the fact that certain social situations – for example, a counter-insurgency war – can produce a religious demand, which can in its turn be easily manipulated; but that, too, is entanglement.

An especially sensitive situation in both regions – this is made manifest through a comparison – comes about whenever the hegemon of the respective religious field is reciprocally placed under pressure. In the USA the hegemon is white Anglo-Saxon Protestantism, which is weakened relative to Hispanic Protestantism, Catholicism and agnosticism to such an extent that it will not be able to determine the formation of a government in the 2024 election, even if all white Protestants voted for the same party (Wong 2018, 96). In Latin America it is Catholicism, which is dominant and equally under pressure, in this case from a Protestant share of the population of up to nearly 50% (Guatemala), depending on the strength of the laicity of a country and various other factors.[7] We have already quoted the confused comments of the Catholic hierarchy against Protestantism; similar comments can now be found in the USA from the Protestant right against immigrants from Latin America, whether Catholic or Protestant.

Observer

There is also a reflexive element to the history of entanglement, namely the entanglement of the respective scholarly observers of this topic. This should be thematized so as to find out about a possible change in a scholar's position over the course of an investigation. It shall be stated here that the present author has been concerned with issues of religion and social change in Latin America since the late 1970s. His first major field research in 1983, 1985 and

7 Admittedly, the percentage in Mexico is a low 9%, with most of the other countries in between.

1986 took him to Guatemala, Nicaragua and the USA. In over 200 in-depth interviews and recorded sermons he focused above all on the praxis of Protestant believers in counter-insurgency wars as well as on the impact on missionary organizations and the interested public in the USA.[8] Between late 1994 and 2003 he was Professor of Theology and Sociology at the Universidad Bíblica Latinoamericana, Costa Rica, and worked with Protestant students in various Latin American countries on smaller field projects. As Professor of the Sociology of Religion at the University of Bielefeld he took part in, and led himself, after 2006 a series of field studies in religious actors, especially a large-scale study between 2012 and 2014 in Nicaragua and Guatemala. In addition, the author is the only European member of Red Latinoamericana de Estudios Pentecostales (RELEP). All this work has contributed to a basic positive feeling on the part of the author as regards Protestant actors. A 2008 comparative study of US-American and Islamic fundamentalism, however, dampened his mood somewhat (Schäfer 2008). A new study carried out over the last few years on the political activities of Protestant experts in the USA and Latin America has fully confirmed the author's worst former fears and revealed a bottomless pit of abuse and corruption. The corruption of the Bancada Evangélica in Brazil, for example, is surpassed only by its abuse of religious convictions. The religious right in the USA uses deceitful statements on purpose. Its leading actors, it is true, must not be mistaken for average Protestant believers – and vice versa.

For an investigation of the religious entanglements between Latin America and the USA it is, therefore, imperative to distinguish strictly between experts and laymen and avoid a bias against experts. Conversely, results found in the studies on lay people should not simply be projected onto experts. As experts usually command a much larger social agency, they have a different percep-

8 A 600-page study has not been published up until now due to adverse circumstances. Its essence has been distilled in Schäfer 1992a, with an abbreviated German version in Schäfer 1990.

tion of their social environment, see things differently and act differently from lay people. A further difference exists between actors of the religious right (LAW and MANAGEMENT) and the religious left (VALUES). Because of his earlier research and his long-standing experiences with Protestants in Latin America and a European view, the author has a left-wing bias. This must be born in mind when writing and reading. From a European perspective, as far as I can see, the post-secular question appears to be, following Habermas (2004), really a two-fold one: first, whether religious actors are willing to translate their positions into ethical tenets that can be communicated to and debated by the public at large, or whether they want to universalize religiously legitimized claims. Second, what results will be obtained through the post-secular translation of religious discourses into ethical ones? The author's studies so far have demonstrated that the actors of the religious left strive to achieve precisely this translation, whereas those on the religious right seek to impose their religious claims to power through political means.

Structure of the Book

This book is an essay, although quite a long one. This means that it is not intended to deal with a problem from all possible angles, as in a scholarly treatise, nor, on the other hand, that a disordered collection of aphorisms will be presented. We will operate a temporal and thematic frame: the starting point will be the US-American missionary convention in Panama in 1916, and the end point a critical review of this convention at a conference of Latin American Pentecostals in Panama in 2016. This will be the frame within which we will highlight a few episodes of the history of the missionary entanglements between the Americas. The treatment of the Panama convention is followed by a review of the development of Protestantism in the USA, because it is only against this background that entanglements to the south can be understood. A centrally important chapter will deal with the entanglement of religious dispositions, which will demonstrate how fundamental narratives of US Protestantism in Latin America are shaped into religious dispositions of varying meanings.

Our sole object of study is Protestants, understood in the widest possible sense. We could have included different aspects, in particular the part played by the Catholic Church in the context of the Hispanic immigration into the USA or the counter strategies against Protestants in Latin America. Further interesting episodes might also have lent themselves to treatment. But this is always the case.

2. Panama 1916 and What Happened Before

The Catholic archbishop of Panama was well prepared for the convention that US Protestants wanted to stage in 1916 in the city of his see. So, he threatened all those hotel owners with excommunication who wanted to put up Protestants.[9] The congress was to coordinate, and direct to important topics, the 100-year old US-American mission in Latin America. This raised two difficulties. On the one side, the organizers sought to preserve a Pan-American perspective, on the other they did not want to make an implacable enemy of the Catholic Church. Catholic observers, though invited, did not attend, perhaps because they were afraid of their colleague's threat. The Panama convention marked the beginning of coordinated and structured work of historical missionary churches of the Mainline and of the Evangelical tradition in Latin America, which was continued in further regional and continental meetings.

As this effort cannot be understood without its past history in US-American Protestantism, we will first offer a few reflections on the missionary congress and then insert a historical review.

2.1 Panama 1916

The Congress on Christian Work in Latin America (CCWLA), which the Committee on Cooperation in Latin America (CCLA) organized because of the bishop's ban in the Canal Zone from 10 to 20 February 1916 and not in Panama City, was the result of a disappointment. Its past history in the USA was massive in as much as the missionary movement at the end of the 19th century was running at full steam. Various missionary societies had been founded on the model of commercial companies, and the "Ecumenical Missionary Conference" of 1900 in New York was the largest event ever of its

9 Cf. Prien 1978, 914. On the Congress on Christian Work in Latin America (CCWLA) of the Committee on Cooperation in Latin America (CCLA) cf. i.a. Prien 1978, 914 ff.; Salinas 2017.

kind with its 200,000 participants. From the people associated with the Protestant revivalist preacher Dwight Moody, John Mott, a young activist, struck out on his own and had founded in 1888 the revivalist Student Volunteer Movement for Foreign Missions (SVM) with the motto *Evangelization of the world in one generation*. This was also the motto of the World Missionary Conference of 1910 in Edinburgh, which was organized for 1,200 delegates by the World Missionary Conference, and whose plenary sessions were chaired by Mott. To carry the gospel to all non-Christian peoples was a program that smacked of colonialism, but excluded, at least in the minds of most delegates, Latin America from the Protestant mission, as the Catholic Church had already done a thorough job there. For the US-American delegates, however, who had by then started missionary work there, this was inacceptable. This is why special US-American measures were adopted in a meeting at the fringe of the congress, with Robert Speer in the chair.

Back in the USA, it was decided to set up the Committee on Cooperation in Latin America (CCLA) in 1913 with the explicit task of "Latin America." It was not to work against the Catholics, but was expected to make God well known more efficiently on the "neglected continent." In the CCLA there were missionaries who had a sound knowledge of Latin America, and who sought to make a peaceful impression. This was the reason why the convention planned in Panama was not to be called "Latin America Missionary Conference" but CCWLA because that would be "more acceptable and better understood by our Latin American friends."[10] Nevertheless, very few delegates attended from Latin America. It was a conference of missionaries. What was explicitly addressed was the *social* problems of Latin America, to which "the Gospel" is seen "as the only adequate solution" (ibid.). Blessing and money for the preparation of the conference came not only from the missionary societies and churches, but also from diplomats and businessmen.

10 … from the August 1915 information leaflet of the CCLA (Committee on Co-operation in Latin America 1915).

One of them, "president of one of the largest banks in North America," quite correctly saw the conference in the context of "Pan-Americanism," and appreciated the missionary activities as a means to promote friendly relations.

> The peaceful intentions of this nation and our worthy national ambitions have been impressed upon our southern neighbors as never before. They are seeing that the motives underlying our relations with them are not imperialistic (ibid.).

Together they could succeed in improving the religious and educational standards of those countries. The conference's preparatory papers and reports are imbued with the spirit of a well-meaning educator. The conference was prepared down to the smallest detail by a 215-strong team, which processed reports from 600 correspondents in Latin America. On top of that, Speer undertook a 12-month research trip through Latin America. According to the scholarly standards of the time, things could hardly have been done better.

In the reports of the Panama Conference can be detected the cautious and self-critical hand of the Social Gospel Movement. Committee 1, "Survey and Occupation," states that the call of the churches is "to evangelize, not to Americanize" (Committee on Cooperation in Latin America 1917, 130). Incidentally, the latent as well as manifest racism in the relation of US-Americans to Latin Americans is sharply criticized, and the Pan American Union is praised as a tool to overcome it. Even so, when compared to racist remarks of Committee 2 (Comission on Cooperation in Latin America 1916, 11ff.), the ambivalence of American Protestantism shows up where race is concerned. Even in the Social Gospel there are manifest racists, for example Josiah Strong, one of the movement's leaders.

For a study of entanglement, the report of Committee 2 on "Message and Method" is the most interesting (ibid.). It uses a very modern way of placing the missionary task in the frame of a detailed analysis of those conditions in Latin America that pose a challenge to the mission. The "relevant facts" concern first "racial complexity," then the "Latin spirit," the religious heritage, political isolation and finally democracy. The report says that a great problem, apart from the indigenous genes, is that the *conquista* produced at first a "racial admixture" from indigenous blood and that of "adventurers, freebooters, soldiers, – unprincipled, lawless, contemptuous of moral restraint, desirous only of gold," with "higher Castilian culture" being added only later. Even so, the report goes on, the Hispanic tradition in Latin America is heavily influenced by the laws, religions and arts of Spain and Italy, as well as the rationalism, socialism and poetic feeling of France. And it was only in the very recent past, it is claimed, that the "Latin spirit" began to adapt to the "utilitarian realities of Anglo-Saxon, Teutonic or North American commerce." It is, the report stresses, the French influence that needs close analysis. In so far as the missionaries are Anglo-Saxons, the greatest difficulty of the "missionary enterprise" is seen in the "sympathetic penetration into the Latin-American spirit." A particular challenge is posed by the religious heritage, it is said, because the Catholic Church has not managed to eliminate the pagan religions and that it – notwithstanding the many good aspects of its work! – clings to a wrong interpretation of Christianity; its only remains are compulsion and institutionalization. Scientific analyses, the report continues, show that the Catholic Church is in a state of gradual decline, which precludes the possibility of speaking of a Christian Latin America. The Catholic Church, it is conceded, is still de facto the state religion in many places despite the freedom of religion which was introduced by the Liberals, and presents therefore an obstacle to the Gospel. Catholicism, so the report's conclusion, is a complete failure. As a reader, one can't help getting the impression of a continent devoid of all religious truth, so that the late-comer Protestant missions need to be united, so the report's advice. Reading this paragraph, one is reminded of the polemic against Catholic immigrants to the USA. Furthermore, the influence of the colonial system is held responsible for a political isolation which blocks relations with non-Latin countries – principally the USA. In addition to the control of trade, politics and intellectual life must be added the purposive neglect of education. This last criticism corresponds with the missionaries' explanation that underdevelopment is due to a lack of education and their own predilection for educational programs. And a final point in the report: Liberalism is to be praised as beneficial to democracy because it represents – though often with violent means – the Latin Americans' striving for equality, fraternity, liberty, individualism and thus democracy. Knowing very well that that many of these democrats were agnostics, the chapter ends with an interesting argumentative twist. Its authors refer to Lamartine, a French (!) Romantic poet of great significance for Liberals, and note that he gets his political ideas from the New Testament and that one can use it to define democracy as "'the direct reign of God,' the application of Christian principles to the problems of the world." Clearly, Protestant sermons have to take a positive attitude towards the idealistic efforts of the Liberals' leaders and make it clear to them that

> through the acceptance and application of the gospel of Christ, the highest hopes of the leaders can be fulfilled wherein they are right and transcended wherein they are imperfect; and that the true welfare of the republics can be realized in the establishment of what Jesus meant by the kingdom of God. (Committee on Cooperation in Latin America 1916, 33)

Consequently, the church is tasked to preach the pure "essentials" of Christianity without Catholic or ultra-sectarian[11] Protestant obfuscation. "Back of this evangel is the assurance that the true Christian Church is the home and the propelling force of true democracy."

From the point of view of the Committee, the essential content of the Christian faith is more or less unambiguously that of the Historical Protestantism of the last but one turn of the century with an admixture of Evangelicalism. The latter is manifest from the stress on the Bible as the ultimate source of truth. This holds true, says the Committee, for the "poor and unlearned, as well as … the rich and

11 Here comes through the controversy about fundamentalism in the USA.

learned." Yet, in the debate of how to reach the "educated classes," a much less strict interpretation of the Bible is proposed. In agreement with the conservative Evangelicals, Christ's godhead and his death as expiation of human sins are held convictions necessary for redemption. From this, a spiritual life grows that breaks the "tyranny of priestcraft," as the report puts it with a sharp anti-Catholic cut. The stated goal is typical of the evolutionist variety of the Social Gospel: the Kingdom of God on Earth – an extremely flexible concept, which today is used for theocratic tendencies of the religious right. For the missionaries of the Social Gospel the concept is not linked to the wish for a totalitarian theocracy. If at all, the first steps towards the attainment of the Kingdom of God, they believe, can be taken instead through moral actions based on a moral value system. And so it is not surprising that the concept acquires political connotations that one would associate more often with the moral left: refusal of injustice and support for the "deliverance of the poor from injustice and oppression" (41). In sum, the program as a whole amounts to the following amalgam: personal salvation, fatherland, love of one's neighbor, purification of political and industrial life from cruelty, of trade from dishonesty and of social life from vice and immorality (42).

After the description of the Latin American problems and its own religious program, one would have expected the Committee to proceed to different topics, but the Committee takes up again the social program, dealing this time with the expected industrial revolution in Latin America, and the special audience it wants to address, the "educated classes." Its reflections see the beginning industrialization from the aspect of resource utilization, the building up of a manufacturing industry (this is therefore not extractivism, as it would be nowadays) and the raising of the necessary capital, and urban consumption. A second aspect is the new social problems caused by abrupt social change, such as ideological conflicts, socialism, labor unions and the mass exodus of the workers from the churches. Latin American elites, says the report, have little knowledge of these problems, but have abilities of a different kind. England, Germany and Italy have gained more relevant experiences, but have sadly also businessmen who (with some praiseworthy exceptions, of course) exert a bad moral influence. More suitable are Evangelical clergy, the YMCA, and people from other nations who want to establish better relations with Latin America. This help with industrial development should pay attention to prevention, an area where the experiences of the USA with industry (a stance against child labor, for example) are especially fruitful. This setting is where missionary social work comes in. The missionaries' "business is not only to win souls to Christ, but to create a Christian civilization" (49). The presumption that Latin American countries lack a "common sentiment" lead the authors to declare that the Latin Americans, once they have gained their independence, "must be trained for their duties". The corresponding enlightenment of their minds as well as purification of their morals is seen as a genuine task of the Gospel, which would in this way advance democratization (51). Many examples of this can be found in the USA and the Protestant missions in Latin America, it is said, and Jesus has laws, which only need to be properly applied to fulfill God's will on earth as in heaven, so that the Kingdom of God will become reality (57).

Of this program, the Committee estimates, only the inherent evolutionism will be understood by the "educated classes" – in their majority agnostics – rather less so the religious component because of a "widespread hostility to the Christian faith" (58). For this reason, the missionaries receive special preparation for intellectual debates with the Liberal elites. They are to give a Christian explanation, with a "modern bias," of the theory of evolution, offer an interpretation of the Bible with some light historical touches, present a plausible explanation of religion as an anthropological necessity, and the church as a community. Liberty, equality and fraternity are to be co-opted in such a way that they can be read as Christian ideals in origin, which need strengthening through religious argumentation. To put it differently, the missionaries make use for their own purposes of the fact that the modern liberal state has no other justification than its mere existence to offer themselves as specialists for non-Catholic transcendental justification. The force behind this proposal may well have been experiences like those of the Presbyterian mission in Guatemala, where the President had explicitly invited the mission in 1883; the work that Protestant missionaries for the Mexican urban revolution under Carranza; or the introduction of the Lancaster School by Presbyterian missionaries in Columbia.[12]

Objective and subjective entanglements of the interests of liberal Latin American elites with those of Protestant missions have occurred time and again over the course of the 19th century. The Panama Congress was meant to transform them into a systematic Pan-American missionary program. The motto of the Edinburgh Congress – "Evangelization of the world in one generation" – has sometimes been given over-sophisticated interpretations. The one most shared was the trivial, literal one: in one generation the world was to be flooded with a North Atlantic, mainly Anglo-Saxon "Gospel" so as to speed up Christ's second coming on the clouds of heaven, or, in a different version, to generate heaven on earth. The Panama Congress turns this motto into a civilizational program for the hemisphere, in whose center is the Bible and a Christology with a narrow focus on Christ's death as expiation of human sins. Civilizational this approach is not through its theological direction, which can easily be combined with a retreat from the world. No, it gets its civilizational force through the projection of a religious and social ideal state – the Kingdom of God on Earth – which contrasts with concrete deficiencies in missionary regions. The necessity of the expansion of one's own convictions and institutions is provided from the very beginning through religious motives: the "great commission" and the expected totalization of North Atlantic Christianity as obedience and expectation of God's reaction. As a civilizational project, however, the expansion needs to be justified, independent of US imperialism and approaching it from the social conditions in

12 In Mexico should be named, in addition, at least Juárez and Cárdenas; in Venezuela Guzmán Blanco; in Columbia Hilario López; in Ecuador Eloy Alfaro and Leónidas Plaza. Cf. Damboriena 1963, 20-21.

Latin America. The analyses of the state of Latin America, carried out with great care and attention to detail, show a recurrent line of argument and one result only. Latin America, its inhabitants and the Catholics get a certificate that they have great potential and that some individuals have indeed demonstrated that fact; but that – more's the pity – on the whole the race, the culture, the economic activities and its religion will be the social ruin of the subcontinent. This assessment demands, according to the report, the pure Gospel and Protestant know-how to help the subcontinent out of the difficulty. So as not arouse their Latin American friends' suspicions, it is necessary to distance themselves from military and economic imperialism – which, given the USA's political and military praxis in the 19th century, will have been inevitable with such an apparent civilizational program. So, the missionaries arrived not to Americanize, but to evangelize – at least that is what they said. They came, really, in order to help. This contains an implicit rejection of Theodore Roosevelt's big-stick diplomacy. They were closer to the imperial friendliness of their contemporary Woodrow Wilson, who preferred instead to convince the whole world of the American way of life by means of multilateral diplomacy under the leadership of the USA (Williams 1980, 133ff.).

Notwithstanding the many verbal disclaimers, American captains of industry were fully aware of the general and objective benefits of the mission to economic enterprises abroad, not least because of the missionaries' interest in education and technological support. To strengthen this synergy John D. Rockefeller Sr (Standard Oil), for instance, donated large sums of money to the mission. Frederick Gates, his advisor and property administrator, is quoted with the reflection that the "heathen nations" will be "honeycombed" through the mission "with light and with civilization, with modern industrial life and applications of modern science..." The greater "productive power" of those countries "will enrichen us as importers of their products. We are only in the very dawn, with all its promise, to the channels opened up by Christian missionaries." Nelson Rockefeller, the senior's grandson and author of the *Rockefeller Report on the*

Americas (1969), extends the cooperation with the Summer Institute of Linguistics/Wycliff Bible Translators (Hvalkof and Aaby 1980; Arbeitskreis ILV 1979), which had a highly controversial status owing to its collaboration with US authorities and damaging influence on indigenous cultures. The cooperation served the purpose "to secure resources and 'pacify' indigenous peoples in the name of democracy, corporate profit, and religion" (cited after Blanke 2003, 3-4). Finally, together with the American way of life the American way of belief was also meant to become obligatory the world over. That even Historical Protestants, despite being under the influence of European hermeneutic thought on their theology, could not break the mold of expansionist thinking is very likely to do with the fact that the US nation identified with the religion of the Pilgrim Fathers.

2.2 Puritan Perfectionism: Law, Expansion, and "Liberty"

The origin of the US state and the role of religion in it – especially that of Protestantism – can hardly be compared with corresponding processes in Europe and Latin America. The US state rose from the history of a European religious minority which saw in the "new" continent the place to realize a religious utopia, the New Jerusalem. A modern age came into being of a religious – not a secular – stamp. The institutions of this modern age *sui generis* arose not from a transformation of existing structures (as was the case in Europe) but from the myth of a complete new beginning in an empty continent, from the factual conquest of the land from the Native Americans and through a revolutionary liberation from the colonial power, which helped at first with the conquest. Here is a concise summary of the most important difference: in the strongly anti-clerical European and Latin American modern age, religion disappeared from the public discourse about politics, while contracts of cooperation were signed, or denied, between the state and heavily institutionalized churches. In the USA, in contrast, an institutional separation of state and church was brought about through Jefferson's interpretation of the First Amendment, while religion determined the public political discourse, that is to say not just any religion but that of the Puritans.[13]

On the occasion of the arrival of a group of dissenters in the newly established colonies (from 1611), John Winthrop, the founder of the Massachusetts Bay Colony, developed in his sermon "A Model of Christian Charity" (1630) the program of a "City upon the Hill" (sic) (Fea 2020, 78ff.). The ideal of a New Jerusalem and the idea of God's exclusive covenant with the Puritan community of settlers was accompanied by a high standard of proving oneself through good moral behavior and missionary zeal. This was, and still is, the basis of the dogma of American exceptionalism. If the faithful were to fail to live up to this standard, they would incur God's punishment. Quite similar to that of Calvin's in Geneva, an oppressive internal social regime developed out of the theory of the chosen people. As a yardstick of good behavior, the concept of sin was reified and listed in a catalog of verifiable vices, like loose language, crimes, sloth, and rebellion against authorities, excesses, gambling and adultery. Though a theological absurdity, reification worked, and still works, as a disciplinary tool that could be made to easily fit the respective religious, social and political common sense. This collection of threats was linked to apocalyptic or otherworldly beings and places, like devils, witches and hell (cf. Fuller 1995) – late medieval concepts which have been cultivated by the religious right up to the present day with the same social intention. The religiously motivated internal repression came to a head with the burning of 160 "witches" and sympathizers in Salem (1692). Of the religious idea behind this, a sermon of Samuel Perris (1692) gives an account: the world is in a state of war between the "Devil and his instruments (and) Christ and his followers"; there are only two "parties" in the world, that of the Lamb and that of the dragon (Samuel Perris, 11.9.1692; Fea 2020, 83).

This also laid the foundation for external demonization, which was applied to the aboriginal American people. Cotton Mather (1663-1728), a former Harvard professor with an honorary doctor-

13 For more detail see Hochgeschwender 2007; Schäfer 2008, 91ff.

ate from the University of Glasgow and a Puritan minister, stated in his history of the American colonies[14] that the *Indians* had been thrown into this world by Satan as a first line of defense against the gospel of Lord Jesus Christ. On this basis, or simply because of dehumanization, numerous massacres of the indigenous peoples were legitimized. Mather envisioned, incidentally, in his "Essay to convey religion into the Spanish Indies" (cf. Prien 1978, 794 ff.; further Rosenberg 1999) already the extension of his model of civilization beyond the Gulf of Mexico. How radically racist the Calvinist position was becomes especially apparent when one compares it with, respectively, the deist and Unitarian-Universalist views of the Fathers of the Constitution, Franklin, Jefferson and Washington, who advocated for ethnic recognition and/or cultural assimilation of the *natives* on the continent, even if they stopped short of opposing territorial expansion.

A second characteristic feature of US religion is emotionalism. While the frontier was being pushed farther and farther westward, ever new churches came into the USA that were less bound to the colonial regime. The acquisition of land furnished the context for massive missionary campaigns, the so-called Great Awakenings of 1734. At first, there was a mixture of a Puritan program (Jonathan Edwards) with Methodist emotionalism (George Whitefield): the City upon a Hill, chosenness by mercy, the realization of the millennial kingdom in the process of history through moral and religious betterment and emphatic spirituality. The ideas of awakening and the subjective decision for a pious existence were, however, in tension with the Calvinist objectivism of being chosen by God. In the long run, i.e. over the course of the Modern and Post-Modern era, the subjectivism of individual decision was to be used more and more to generate legitimacy and truth claims in internal relations with fellow believers, while in external relations with non-believers of all kinds the attitude of the Calvinist soldier of faith with a sense of mission remained in vogue.

---

14 *Magnalia Christi Americana*, 1702, cf. Fuller 1995.

Demonization became more established in foreign politics during the War of Independence against King George III of England, who was declared an agent of the Antichrist (Fuller 1995, 68ff.). Demonizing your political opponent has a long history, in which the underlying basic dualistic scheme has seen multiple transformations. In a social situation that is not determined by state churches, dualism takes on a special function: adopting a religious understanding of the *foreign* political situations as a battle between the Devil and God, the religious actors as representatives of the USA at the same time also achieve a position as representatives of the *entire* respective nation. In a quite related vein Billy Sunday, millionaire and preacher of the Great Awakening, wanted to make himself into the nation's religious representative when he strongly advocated for the USA's entry into the First World War. The legitimizing strategies of the religious right did a similar job for the secret service actions in Central America under Ronald Reagan and in G.W. Bush's Iraq War.

Do such actions not violate the principle of the separation of powers? First: the constitution of the USA is neither completely laicist nor puritanical. Its preamble is couched in the simple words of contractual theory (United States Senate 1791). In 1789, when the Constitution came into effect, George Washington's inaugural address lent it, or rather the government under it, a slight, deistically restrained splendor of eternity – as it were a *diet* deistic religiosity. It would be inappropriate, according to Washington, to forgo the fervent prayers to the "Almighty Being" which "rules over the Universe" and which presides in the "Council of Nations". More than any other country the USA was obligated, he claimed, "to acknowledge and adore the invisible hand, which conducts the Affairs of men." Each step the country had taken in the direction of independence allowed the observer to catch a glimpse of the working of Providence (National Archives and Records Administration 1789). In this way the President laid down a sort of minimum standard of religiosity for governance: an almighty being who ruled over the universe and the nations, and, as Providence, conducted their political fate with an invisible hand – that much civil religion[15] there had to be. In view of this openness and the continued influence of the East Coast churches it would seem advisable to make a few remarks on the relation between state and religion, which is precisely what the First Amendment (1791) was designed to do. It established no laicity in the strict sense after the French model, which protects the state and to a degree also public life from the influence of religious activists. Rather, it merely prohibited the formation of a state church and protected the freedom of religion from interference from the state.[16] The Amendment says that Congress "shall make no law respecting an establishment of religion, or prohibiting the free exercise thereof..." (United States Senate 1791). Nothing, then, is said about interference in the opposite direction, i.e. interference from religious activists in the affairs of state. Thomas Jefferson, it is true, saw the Amendment in 1802 as a "wall of separation between Church & State" (Jefferson 1998 [1802]) with the interest to exclude interference in political matters by established (colonial) churches. This formula captured the tension between church activists and deists and characterized the public debate even more than the Amendment itself. Even today it provokes high tension between Universalist laicism and the religious right, which is intent, in the Puritan tradition, on building a "Christian Nation". Religious campaigns of fear, already against Jefferson (Fea 2020, 13ff., 75ff.), demonstrate clearly that the Liberal program of the separation of state and church came under the fire of the religious protagonists of a Christian Nation. Later court judgments (1947, Everson v. Board of Education) and the Johnson Amendment (1954), however, confirmed Jefferson's interpretation. The prohibition of political adver-

15 On civil religion in the USA cf. the classic treatment by Robert Bellah 1967.

16 Significantly, the freedom to practice one's religion completely free of any restriction by the state was first laid down in writing in the colony of Maryland in 1634 on the initiative of the *Catholic* Lord Baltimore and can be regarded as a forerunner of the First Amendment.

tising formulated in the Johnson Amendment against religious activists explains why in evangelization campaigns before elections the word "Republican" is not used but "red" – said straight out like that. In sum: it is precisely the separation of state and church laid down in the Constitution that has led to an even more vigorous presence of religion in social and political discourse (Noll 2008, 28-29; for a similar view see Prätorius 2003, 61-62).

In contrast to many Latin American and European states, it should remain clear that the non-Puritan position, too, was not anti-religious. Already in his inaugural speech, mentioned above, the first President understood the perfectionism, the striving of the people of the USA for liberty and happiness as blessing on the part of God's Providence. There is also an implicit reference to exceptionalism when he says that no people is more obligated than the USA to recognize the invisible hand of Providence.

As for religious entanglements between the USA and Latin America, the deistic-religious orientation of supposedly secular politicians shows a partial agreement of their religious dispositions with those of the Puritans. Following Robert Bellah, one can speak of a wide-spread deistic-Christian civil religion.[17] Puritan religiosity took up civil religion in certain respects while also radicalizing it. Exceptionalism and the linked obligations towards less well-off people – people south of the Rio Grande, for instance – was no longer grounded only in a vague Providence but in a law-giving and punishing God, who finds himself in a struggle against the Devil. Through this homology of habitūs, the Christian foundational myth of the USA together with its obligation to carry the "light of peoples" in fact to the peoples became, over the course of time, a highly efficient operator in the political field. This operator also generated homologies between political, military, economic and religious-missionary expansion.

---

17 On *civil religion*, see Bellah 1967.

Perfectionism and Expansion: The 1st Half of the 19th Century

In the first half of the 19th century up to the Civil War there was far-reaching agreement about the utopian project of the US modern age: the creation of the New Jerusalem on the basis of the nation through the conversion to a consciously practiced Christianity and moral improvement. The Methodist idea of individual as well as societal improvement through moral action combined with the postmillennialist expectation of a thousand-year Kingdom on Earth. As we have seen, this expectation was shared in a weakened form by most of the missionary churches that gathered in Panama. But these churches were far from making up all of the churches that were active in missionary work in Latin America. The argument about the correct interpretation of the Bible in US-American Protestantism led to the rise of Evangelicalism in contradistinction to the Mainline churches.

The difference between a reading of the Bible as a law book where every word is to be understood in the literal sense, and the Bible as historical document – but even then it was still the word of God (similar ambivalences could be found in the documents of the Panama Congress) – this difference must be explained by the social situation of the actors. Baptist and Methodist congregations on the frontier had nobody with a formal education in divinity, and the smaller settlements rarely had any legal institutions at their disposal. Law had, therefore, to be dispensed by those who could read from the one legal document which was available at least in church – the Bible. The Bible created public order, communitarian common sense, and local autonomy. As a law-making agency it had to be given a literalist interpretation and had to lay claim to public prestige. This was vital for the community of settlers. Legal judgments oscillated between the law, morals and religion, and even reasons of state had to be legitimated in moral and religious terms (Huntington 1982, 241 f.). On the East coast, theologians of already established Protestant churches (Presbyterians, Episcopalians, Congregationalists and some Methodists) in urban middle-class society were quick to adopt a historical interpretation of the Bible, influenced by European ideas. But in rural North America this could only be considered an attack on public order and, in the end, the word of God and God himself. This split erupted in full force not until the second half of the 19th century, not least in the development of literalist fundamentalism and independent conservative-Evangelical mission societies. For the entanglement between US-American missions and Latin American converts of a different social class, this difference has been relevant till today.

A second religio-cultural development of great importance is perfectionism, which was promoted primarily by the Methodist-driven Second Great Awakening (around 1837-1838, Charles Finney, Henry W. Beecher, Richard Allen). The Methodists were concerned with sanctification, which manifested itself in moral action and contributed to individual and collective perfection. Over the course of time, this idea amalgamated with that of the Fathers of the Constitution about the "pursuit of happiness" and resulted in a civilizational idea of perfection. In this way, the habitus of striving itself became a cultural good, a prerequisite for the command to reinvent oneself again and again, and thus also a strong expression of openness to the future. It was no longer the Methodist social ethic that could be striven for, but any given goal, above all the individual "pursuit of happiness." The religious tradition has since strengthened the idea of the American Dream, and its socio-religious teleology was a forerunner of the further development of Darwin's theory of evolution into the social Darwinism of the Gilded Age in the 1880s. The religious pursuit of economic prosperity also has its origin here. Social optimism, and self-confidence gained through religious activities belonged together in this phase.

Correspondingly, the religiosity of the Great Awakening proposed – in contrast to the Calvinist doctrine of being chosen – that everyone is personally responsible for their own salvation. This religious voluntarism taught that individuals choose their salvation and take care not to lose it – or that they reject it. Everyone was, so to speak, the architect of their own salvation. Success or failure were taken as due in any case to one's own efforts. This perfectionist thinking was translated into the individualist economic will to achieve, which fits seamlessly the economy's organization based on individual property. The idea that property is vindicated through successful striving was part of the same package. To turn the argument on its head, it means that those who are poor have not exerted themselves sufficiently.

The voluntarist turn of the revival did not mean, however, that the objectivist tradition of Calvinism (chosenness by God, special covenant with the USA, orientation to the law) became completely obsolete. Both religious habitūs amalgamate easily if covenant theology and exceptionalism are seen as a frame for individual striving. In this way the motif of perfection also impacts external relations.

Exceptionalism, Foreign Policy and Mission

External relations were first concerned with the frontier in the West. The literature rightly sees a connection between exceptionalism, the theology of the covenant, millennialism, Monroe Doctrine, manifest destiny and Pan-Americanism. The lack of connection described by Huntington (1982, 240ff.) between isolation and crusade manifests itself in the tension between isolationism ("entangling alliances with none," Jefferson 2006) and the actual development, already begun by Madison, in the direction indicated by the Monroe Doctrine. The foreign other could be met with indifference, or could be seen in an almost hysterical way as questioning one's own identity and existence, or as confirmation of one's sense of mission. This caused the self to be transfigured: Christian religion became an element of a utopian project of the modern age. The Monroe Doctrine (1823) – formulated, as it happened, precisely at the time of Latin America's struggles for independence and after a series of military operations in the Spanish colonial area – had an ambivalent character from the very beginning. It was a doctrine meant to protect from colonial interference, but it represented at the same time a claim to the hemispheric hegemony of the USA. In politics, it was quickly linked to the USA's manifest destiny to take possession of the entire continent. This was the sense in which President Polk used it offensively to justify the Mexican War – and missionaries were later to distribute Bibles in the occupied parts of Mexico.[18]

The "New Jerusalem," according to Marcia Pally (2008), grew into a nation with the experience that violence, liberty and God's blessing stand in a positive relation to one another.

To find a place for the Protestant churches in these developments, the Calvinist theologian Lyman Beecher designed in his widely distributed treatise *A Plea for the West* (Beecher 1835 – almost a decade before the occupation of half of Mexico) a strategy for expansion in which he links the Protestant world mission with the expansion of the US-American model of "liberty." The triumph of the Protestant mission is treated as equivalent to the spread of the civilization of liberty on the order of Providence. "But if this nation is, in the providence of God, destined to lead the way in the moral and political emancipation of the world, it is time she understood her high calling, and were harnessed for the work" (Beecher 1835, 11). Beecher set his sights already at Latin America, where it was a matter of abolishing the forces of superstition against the Catholic Church's despotism (Beecher 1835, 117 f.).

While Beecher was busy writing, two things happened in Latin America, the fight for independence and the rise of the Liberals, and in the USA the Calvinist American Board of Commissioners for Foreign Missions (ABCFM) had been active since 1810. One aspect of the ABCFM's work with Native Americans is of interest for the question of entanglements and occurred several times during the 1970s and '80s[19] also among US-American missionaries in Latin America. The missionary work with the indigenous groups led to the missionaries fighting the removal policies (such as the Removal Act of 1830). Obviously, an identification with the addressees could

18 The Louisiana Purchase 1803 and the end of the war against Cuba etc. were understood as providential acts.

19 Ross and Gloria Kinsler, Irene and Robert Foulkes, John and Irene Stam and others.

occur as well as a role reversal. This logic can even be intentional in modern religious cooperation, as e.g. on the part of the Global Ministries, USA.

Over the course of the 19th century through 1916, most of the churches of the Historical Protestants founded denominational missionary societies which took up their work still in the first half of the 19th century.[20] A new form of organization developed a little later from the Evangelical Revival Movement in the second half of the 19th century. Theme-oriented organizations arose on the model of commercial societies, that is to say practically Non-Governmental Organizations (NGOs): Young Men's Christian Association (1844), Student Volunteer Movement (1886), Central America Mission (1890), Latin America Mission (1921), and over the course of the later 20th century an almost uncountable number. The stance of these mostly new organizations was not as cautious as that of the missionaries at Panama. Prien (1978, 797f., my translation) quotes from the 1913 Mission Conference in New York: whether the churches in the mission countries were Christian or not, was completely unimportant. What mattered, however, was that "millions and millions of their inhabitants are robbed of the Word of God and do not even know what the Gospel is."

Money is needed for organizations without ecclesiastical links to take the Gospel to unbelievers. The Laymen's Missionary Movement (1906, Speer and Mott were among its members) was one of many examples of institutionalization and professionalization through modern business techniques (Rosenberg 1999, 32f.). Another was fundraising, which had a considerable influence on what the work of the organizations was about. The more the situation of people under the reign of poverty, violence, self-hatred, stupidity, backwardness, etc. was depicted as terrible, the better the donors could be portrayed as saviors, knowledgeable and capable people, and superior representatives of the species in order to elicit a larger

20 1825, Presbyterian Church USA in Argentinia; 1824 in Columbia and 1827 in Mexico, at the invitation of Liberals.

sum of money. A legendary example is the "pageant of darkness and light" (Cambridge Tribune 1911) at the fringe of a missionary exhibition in Boston in 1911. There, in their darkness, natives, Eskimos and Africans were handed the message of light by missionaries. The brutal othering and declassification of the mission addressees could be used profitably as a financing technique because racism had not been overcome even in the ranks of the Social Gospel. Josiah Strong (1847-1916) was one of the founders of the Social Gospel and at the same time a proven racist. In addition, in his book *Expansion*[21] he wrote on the economy and world domination of the USA and developed a cunning theory of the relation between the freedom and independence of underdeveloped peoples, in his case the Philippines. Real freedom meant living under US-American law, whereas independence would mean remaining in backwardness etc. A missionary, cited in Rosenberg (1999, 43f.), sees expansion as an objectively efficient function of Christianization, for "blindly and unworthily, yet, under God, surely and steadily, the Christian nations are subduing the world, in order to make mankind free."

Economic efficiency made the fund raisers look increasingly for large donors. Like Strong, they brought into religious play their own ideas which were heavily influenced by the economy. Conversely, Protestant missionaries came to realize over the course of the 19th century that trade posts had their uses, while it dawned on traders and investors that missionary activities of the most varied kind could be useful for their activities, e.g. in ports. Similar considerations will have applied to the military. The YMCA, in any case, grew after 1898 primarily on Cuba and the Philippines (Rosen-

21 Rosenberg 1999, 44. Cf. Strong 1900, 284ff. Strong developed here a theory of legitimation for the USA's world domination on the grounds of its economic and ethnic supremacy. Developed capitalism, he claimed, needed foreign markets (72ff.). Regions taken into account were i.a. the Panama Canal and the "Anglo -Saxon" Mediterranean Sea. The "village world" (214) was in need of a new politics and ethic, a global police force which was to be able to exercise well-meant force, and a clear distinction between freedom and independence.

berg 1999, 31). Samuel Capen of the Laymen's Missionary Movement is quoted with his claim that a pagan, once he has been converted, will also want Christian clothes, house furnishings and tools and "the other things which distinguish Christian civilization from the narrow and degraded life of the heathens" (Rosenberg 1999, 32). This constitutes a subjectively perceived objective identity of interest between the missionaries' and the traders' activities in the Christianization of the world, with the traders' interest directed to profit and that of the missionaries aiming at the spread of their faith – which also means their position in the religious field.

In Latin America the main adversary of the Protestant mission was the Catholic Church. At home in the USA the Protestants had had to deal, since the colonial days of the "French and Indian War" (1754-1763) with the Catholic French for instance, and from around 1812, with beer-swilling immigrants from Ireland and Germany, but not with a hegemonic power. Lyman Beecher (1835, 61) nevertheless criticized, as did the Panama Committees, the Catholic system as "adverse to liberty". Individual Catholics needed not be feared because of their faith nor to be discriminated against. But the Papists, he continues, fall like "locusts…from the hills and plains of Europe" onto the "green pastures" of the USA. To keep the Catholics from being led to the "altars of demons" they have to be converted (Beecher 1835, 72f. and 78).

Civil War, Questions of Class, and Religion: The 2nd Half of the 19th Century

The Civil War and its consequences caused a deep split not only in the 19th century but also in the people of the USA. It was waged about the issue of slavery and ultimately also about which of the two economic models was to dominate, the agrarian-patriarchal one or the urban-capitalist one. The historian Mark Noll (2008, 1) maintains that race and religion together count among the most important political factors in the USA. Racism certainly left its mark on the theory and praxis of missions. In the praxis of Latin America, however, it played at best a minor role. The Black churches were very important to US Protestantism, but in contrast to white Protestantism not for their missionary activities as they did not see any reason for a civilizational expansion. We will therefore throw light only on those aspects that are important for the entanglement.

Social Question and Millennium

Very important for the entanglement of different types of mission with Latin American actors is the emergence of two very different religious conceptions of time as a reflex of the social division created by industrialization in the Gilded (not a golden) Age. The old idea of realizing a national Kingdom of God on Earth through moral perfection was tied to action spaces that made it possible to launch corresponding actions. These "*post*millennialist" plans were thwarted by the Civil War. Under the conditions of industrialization, the idea of earthly perfection could at best be considered only for the upper classes and could be easily combined with secular evolutionism and even social Darwinism. From this tradition developed – nonetheless! – the so-called Social Gospel, which shaped the program of the Panama Conference. Its most influential branch, represented above all by the socially engaged Baptist theologian Walter Rauschenbusch (1861-1918), put its money also on structural changes, above all with regard to capitalism, nationalism, militarism and individualism. According to him, the Kingdom of God was not to be realized, however, only its first beginnings were to be experienced by the faithful. Today these positions are shared by, among others, Evangelicals of the political left in the USA and Latin America.

The proletariat, however, and workers in the informal economy even more, had hardly any prospects for action in their situation. The old idea of time no longer corresponded to their living conditions. Remedy was provided by the idea held by conservative revival preachers – such as Cyrus Scofield and Dwight Moody – that "in reality" everything was heading towards the end of the world and was getting worse and worse till the Lord would take the true believers into heaven and only then himself proclaims the thousand-year Kingdom. Thus, the construction of the Kingdom is beyond human responsibility and no longer a national project, but the conversion to the right faith was all the more important. Since the turn of the century this "*pre*millennialism" was the seed of the activity of the Evangelical "faith missions," which were directed at conversion and the building of churches and showed little interest in changes in civilization. Like the labor unions, the premillennialist preachers espoused social grievances in the proletariat, but came up with more "American" answers; or at least answers without structural perspectives of change. The individual, it was said, must make a conscious decision for Christ and master any social crisis through moral self-discipline and church-based activity. This compensated for social deprivation through religious activity. In addition, the organizations offered charitable help. In Latin America, too, it was the simple, Evangelical positions that resonated with the *lower* classes, who were both oriented towards the immediate environment and authoritatively grounded in a Scriptural verse. Only certain parts of these new Evangelical "faith missions" were represented at the Panama Congress.

2.3 Puritan Perfectionism: Emotion, Charisma and Power

The Pentecostal Movement

What was not represented at all at the 1916 Congress was the Pentecostal movement. This religious movement arose in the black and white underclass and broke away from the entrenched fundamentalist dispute at the beginning of the 20th century by cultivating ecstatic practices from the Evangelical sanctification movement and giving them a name: the descent of the Holy Spirit at Pentecost. The "Pentecostal movement" achieved its first official foundation of a congregation (Azusa St., Los Angeles) in 1906 under the black preacher William Seymour. It spread extremely quickly among marginalized black and white people as well as abroad, and via the regular border traffic of migrants also directly to Mexico. The movement's major selling point was its charismatic legitimation "from below," which granted even illiterate people divine authority, recognizable by an ecstatic form of language (glossolalia). In addition, its emphasis on miracle healing met an important religious demand of the marginalized. The ethnically mixed community in Azusa St. split after a few years into a black and a white community (whereby the whites were said to have made off with the community chest). The emerging black Pentecostal movement engaged in no foreign missionary work; and even today this happens only on a small scale. The White Pentecostal Movement[22] – especially the big Assemblies of God – soon resorted to the fundamentalist scriptural principle, sought hierarchical organization, and set up foreign missions, before long using the radio and adopting for its missionary activities the model of free religious enterprises.[23] The missionaries, who were charismatically (i.e. by claims of divine revelation and their recognition) and legally (by training and certification) legitimized, were interested only in conversion missions, ecstatic worship celebrations and the enlargement of their congregations. In the USA the white Pentecostal movement established regular procedures, rose to the lower middle class and became more and more similar to the Evangelicals. The ecstatic religious impulses had a much stronger impact in Latin America.

Neopentecostalism

A development that pointed the way to today took place in California in the 1950s with the founding of the Full Gospel Businessmen's Fellowship International (FGBMFI) by the millionaire Demos

---

22 Above all: Assemblies of God (1914), Church of the Foursquare Gospel (from 1923), the Pentecostal Church of God of America (1919), the Church of God, Cleveland (ca. 1907), and Church of God of Prophecy (1923), Pentecostal Church of Christ (1917). The Pentecostal Fellowship of North America was founded as roof organization in 1948.

23 Jimmy Swaggart, Oral Roberts, T.L. Osborne and Manuel "Yiye" Avila (Puerto Rico).

Shakarian. The Fellowship quickly made its way into the upper and upper middle classes counting numerous politicians, industrialists and military men among its members. In the early 1960s the new trend spread to Historical Protestantism with the so-called Charismatic Movement; in the 1980s, finally, to Evangelical churches with the so-called "Third Wave." In a parallel development, Kenneth Hagin and the Copelands, a married couple, left the Pentecostal Movement to set themselves up as "health and wealth" preachers with huge religious entertainment businesses. Their message was perfectly compatible with that of the esotericism of the 19th century (Phineas Quimby) and its updated version through "positive thinking" in the motivational industry from the 1950s onwards (Norman Vincent Peale, the young Trump's pastor and personal friend of Richard Nixon).

The movement is organized less after the pattern of traditional churches, than as the clientele of well-known preachers. Among many others these were in the 1980s, each with their own television channel: Pat Robertson (Christian Broadcasting Network, CBN), Jim Bakker (Praise the Lord, PTL) and Paul Crouch (Trinity Broadcasting Network, TBN). They were all active in the religious right. In the 1970s, authoritarian-theocratic movements also formed around the Dominion Doctrine, Reconstructionism with its program of Old Testament law as constitution, and the authoritarian doctrine of Discipleship.

Today, this tradition is represented above all by newer Prosperity businesses (such as that of fashionable Paula White, with direct access to Donald Trump) and the postmodern, more casual Independent Network Charismatics in easy-going California. Crucially, the new movement is oriented toward the religious needs of the modernizing upper middle and upper classes. It combines the charismatic legitimation of its own positions and strategies with the social and political ability for action of privileged social classes and channels them into support for the religious right.

All these actors are by no means lost to the Puritan cause. On the contrary, they propagate the puritanical core concerns with the most modern means and a high degree of manipulative competence, and go even further: theocracy, exceptionalism, expansion in the interest of dominion, the demonization motif as Spiritual Warfare, and well-being in the capitalist form of individual prosperity – all of course in the neo-liberal mode of the Republican Party.

Max Weber noted a kinship between the radical Calvinism of the New England colonies and radical Islam. Their "salvation aristocracies" obligated the respective believers to "tame the world of sin" for God's glory and to produce for this purpose the figure of the "crusader" (Weber 1946b, 336; similar statements also elsewhere). The question is what is left of it in the entanglement with Protestant praxis in Latin America, or is perhaps even strengthened.

3. Entanglement of Religious Dispositions

Entanglement occurs in conditions that precede it, which makes it important to be clear about the differences between the respective actors and regions involved. On this basis it will be possible to gain an overview of the most important agents of entanglement and the changes they underwent in the process of entanglement. For reasons of historical facticity we will primarily be interested in the entanglement dynamics of US-American Protestantism in Latin America, and as we have discussed the USA already, we will first briefly ponder conditions in Latin America. Then we will take up again the most important religious dispositions of US-American mission Protestantism and sketch its transformations through the entanglement process.

3.1 Conditions of Religious Entanglement

Protestantism, as we have seen, played a decisive role in the colonization of the USA and represented the *raison d'être* of the new polity: the New Jerusalem, the City upon a Hill. Puritan Protestantism stands for successful liberation from and accomplished revolution against their colonial master, so that the conservative Protestants of today fantasize about a reform of the political system as a return to the original state of a "Christian Nation" of the whites. The ethnic ("racial") split is central here. In Latin America, by contrast, the Catholic Church has traditionally been the religious and societal hegemonic power. Protestantism was in consequence at first a subaltern invader, which could only over the course of time build up a relatively strong position, at the price, however, of a series of changes that came about through its entanglement with Latin American reality.

Hacienda

In Latin America the Catholic Church has a similar civilizational role as Protestantism does in the USA. But this role is filled differently. In connection with the European, pre-modern colonial powers it stabilized a hierarchical social structure oriented to the system of estates by a likewise hierarchical organizational structure and a ritualistic religious praxis. The hacienda, its hierarchy, its corporatist relations of responsibility, its religious protection through direct legitimation by the Catholic Church (every hacienda has a chapel) as well as the homology of this structure to the overall social power structure stands as *pars pro toto* for the colonial society of Latin America. The hacienda disappeared in the late 19th century as an institution or *dispositive*, respectively; but the dispositions shaped by it continued to have an effect for a long time to come:[24] the orientation towards hierarchies and strong corporatist structures in family, economy, religion and politics; the centrality of large-family relationships instead of individualism in the upper as well as in the lower class; and class boundaries impermeable to social advancement. In today's processes of refeudalization (cf. Kaltmeier 2019) such dispositions are combined in a completely new way with neo-liberal logic to form a modern authoritarianism. For politics, it remains to be noted that in Latin America – unlike the USA – the strong state is a matter of course. For religion, the affinity of hacienda dispositions to hierarchically organized Catholicism is obvious. With regard to the Pentecostal movement, it was already established in the 1970s (Lalive d'Epinay 1969; 1975) that congregations or churches take over the social functions of the lost hacienda in a capitalist economy. In Brazil one can see a similar effect in the role of the *pastores presidentes*, who lead their churches like *fazendas*.

24 Kaltmeier (2016) understands the hacienda according to Foucault as a "dispositive," i.e. a distinct social unit that consists of institutionality, recurrent practices and the corresponding dispositions of the actors. If one assumes that habitūs can last beyond the end of corresponding structures (hysteresis effect, Bourdieu), it is reasonable to suppose that the attitudes and behaviors of the Hacienda can still be found even in altered societal structures.

Liberalism

The second structural factor is the liberalism of the independence movements. The Criollo elites, born in Latin America and betting on trade with the USA and freedom from the European monarchies, primarily strive for economic liberalization and republican constitutions. Economic liberalism, however, excludes neither dictatorship as a form of government (Guatemala) nor the possibility of social revolution (Mexico). The Liberals weaken the Catholic Church – to varying degrees, depending on the country (least in Costa Rica and Paraguay, most in Mexico and Uruguay) – through the nationalization of church goods, laicist constitutions and the opening of the religious field by means of religious freedom. From a religious angle, then, there is an objective affinity to Protestantism. Of central importance is the laicity of the state and thus the removal of the Catholic presence from the political field. Laicity in Latin America is the result of a bloody struggle to end the colonial regime and the object of ongoing, sometimes violent clashes between two factions of the ruling class. It is thus to a much greater extent a political issue than is the case in the USA, where the First Amendment was an object of political debate between a strongly and a slightly religious group; it was constantly undermined by public debate anyway, and has only at present become again the object of conflicts through fundamentalist attempts at religious manipulation of the constitution.

Fight of the Elites

The conflict with the representatives of the colonial system in Latin America, to be sure, has not been finally dealt with through the establishment of liberal republics. The tension has continued to the present day between, on the one side, at first colonially oriented, conservative and pro-Catholic forces and, on the other side, anticolonial, economically liberal and capitalist ones. It takes the form of fights between different factions of the elites, as mirrored especially in two-party systems like the Colombian. The old oligarchies tend to be pro-Catholic and linked to the traditionalist Catholic right – Opus Dei, the Legion of Christ, etc. These are the only people who look back to colonial times as a golden age. The neo-liberal and technocratic social climbers, by contrast, used to be close to Historical Protestantism – today to the Prosperity Gospel – and not infrequently look forward in a positive and evolutionist way to an "Americanization" of society. Using Pareto's concept of the circulation of elites (Pareto 1916), according to which combinatorial "foxes" take turns with persistent "lions," it can be observed that the chances of different religious actors to influence politics either rise or fall, as the case may be.

Evangelical Left

This mechanism does nevertheless not mean that the impermeable separation of the social above from the social below is finished. The hierarchical structure of society has turned out to be stubbornly long-lasting even today. The fact that it received the blessing of the Catholic Church before the 2nd Vatican Council has contributed to the development of non-religious or anticlerical resistance movements from below. Significantly, this was not the case in the USA. Werner Sombart (1976 [1906]) found in 1906 that there was no socialism in the USA, but that it was likely to develop soon. He obviously did not expect a large part of the industrial workers in the 19th century to be co-opted by the Evangelicals. On the other hand, stable socialist and Marxist movements and parties developed with anti-Catholic verve in Latin America, both in the cities and countryside. This had various effects on the religious field. The strongest was probably the change of Catholicism through Liberation Theology and its grassroots organizations. In Protestantism, by contrast, there were, beginning in the middle of the 20th century, on the one hand affinities with political parties of the left (e.g. APRA in Peru, PRD in Mexico), presumably because of the homologous positions of the two marginal actors relative to the ruling classes and the Catholic Church. On the other hand, the similarity of the positions also resulted in objective competition, for instance between the workers' movement and the Pentecostal movement in Chile (not least about how much time members invested in the respective organizations). The rigid social structure and the social plausibility of socialist alternatives in Latin America have led Latin American Protestantism to the formation of social reformist and revolutionary groups, such as the student-based, ecumenically oriented Confederação Evangélica do Brasil (CEB) under the leadership of the Presbyterian Waldo César as early as 1934. As a result of these developments the Social Gospel was "shifted to the left" in the Latin American way. Even the conversion piety of the Evangelical and Pentecostal US organizations was fully caught up by this development at the beginning of the 1970s.

Account must, nevertheless, be taken of the fact that in Latin American Protestantism – in quite a different way from US-Protestantism, as I have shown in earlier studies (i.a. Schäfer 2009) – the political transformation of religious convictions cannot be taken for granted. This is manifest especially in the political charge of apocalyptical ideas and a political use of the doctrine of Spiritual Warfare in the USA. In Latin America, on the contrary, Protestantism is firmly based in everyday life, above all in its Pentecostal form. Although political activities by Protestant actors have gained increased attention from the modernizing upper middle class only over the last few decades through Neopentecostal groups, they make up for that by their greater aggressiveness.

Comparisons of Value Systems

Regarding the differences between the USA and Latin America as conditions for the entanglements, Protestantism in Latin America is often identified with certain values projected onto the USA, which are said to be diametrically opposed to Latin American ones. These value comparisons, mostly made from an US-American perspective, are based on a grain of truth and a grain of naive self-perception. The USA, for example, has freedom and equality ascribed to itself and is associated with the philosophical principles of Locke, Madison and Jefferson, which are of course given only a positive interpretation, although one could certainly take a critical view of Madison's preparation for global expansion (cf. Williams 1980, 48ff., 59ff., 70ff.). Seymour Lipset depicts the USA as a society of free farmers, while he sees profound inequality at work in Latin America due to the contrast of *latifundium* and *minifundium*. According to this picture, an undemocratic form of state based on inequality is postulated for Latin America, and the opposite for the USA.[25] As a consequence, the Protestant mission in Latin America is automatically handed the role of bringing freedom and equality to the Latin American continent. In a particularly naive application of "Weber's thesis" it is – as already noted in the introduction – occasionally also assumed that the Protestant ethic (of the Methodist stripe) gives a tremendous impetus to Latin American progress and brings the Latin American people betterment. Such assumptions about the role of Protestantism have a grain of truth in that there are indeed habitus differences between traditional Catholics in Latin America and Protestants in the USA, which of course also have to do with different social structures, religious forms of organization and religious practices. They fail to recognize, however, that Protestantism from the USA cannot simply be transferred – just as democracy cannot be transferred by military regime-change politics. Even a brief look at the development of Protestantism in Latin America shows that, already in the first generation, the discourse schemata of what is on offer from the Protestant religion combine to form a strong amalgam with religious and cultural dispositions from the Latin American context, and undergo a change in the encounter with the changed

25 On this cf. the brief observations in Krumwiede 2002, 26ff. What these arguments leave out, however, is that the plutocratic political two-party system of the USA is made watertight against the chance of anybody running for President who is not financed by huge sums of money from commerce and the economy. Similarly disregarded is the achievement of democratic procedures in Latin America, which has led, respectively, to a period of social-democrat or socialist administrations.

context of action. Already the look back to the Puritan age, constitutive of the White Anglo-Saxon Protestantism of the USA, can hardly be understood by a Latin American Protestant – even an Evangelical one. What should he or she look back to? The Catholic colonial period? The liberal revolution? Or the Puritan colony in Massachusetts? It is also connected with this condition that the majority of Protestants in Latin America soon after the liberal period in the 19th century became apolitical and preferred to turn to everyday piety. This in turn means that the jealous view of doctrinal purity and the categorical rejection of non-Protestant religiosity by the Puritans cannot simply be transferred from the USA to Latin American praxis. On the contrary, doctrinal discipline tends to be softened by an increase in charismatic forms of piety in Latin America. This is emblematically represented by the judgment of a Latin American pastor passed on the statement of an Evangelical Christian from the USA that salvation can only be achieved by faith in Jesus Christ. The pastor, a Pentecostal (!), simply said: “This man is a fundamentalist.”

USA: Hegemonic Protestantism

In other words, as a result of English colonial history, Puritan Protestantism in the USA is hegemonic and has developed into a civil religion. In Latin America, on the other hand, a ritualistic Catholicism occupies this position as a result of Spanish colonial history. This means for Protestantism, which interests us here, that in the USA we have an unbroken tradition of highly political, strongly Calvinist Puritanism – even if it has been transformed in the last few decades by neo-liberalism and Neopentecostalism. The intervention of Protestant actors in political debates and decisions with religious arguments is in any case – despite the First Amendment – considered normal by the public. The tension between the religio-political collective and the duly orthodox individual can only be guaranteed by the collective’s rigorous control of both orthodoxy and the lawful praxis of the individual. In this process, strategies of exclusion and the setting up of hard differences are of particular importance, as is the accompanying orientation towards ethnicity (race), which is particularly manifest in the strategies of white Evangelicalism. In the course of the last century the corresponding religious habitus also clearly stamped the white Pentecostal movement in the USA, which is why it was hardly able to build up an attractive unique selling position in comparison with Evangelical hegemony. Whether Pentecostalism or Evangelicalism, Protestantism in the USA (especially that of the whites) is determined by a logic of either/or.[26]

Latin America: Hegemonic Catholicism

In Latin America, on the other hand, Protestantism was at first a very marginal religious option relative to hegemonic Catholicism. Until the second half of the 20th century, the religious habitus of the majority of the Latin American population was characterized by the magical-ritualistic piety of traditional Catholicism, which is particularly clearly seen in popular Catholicism and its amalgamation with indigenous religion. The practical logic of this Catholicism is inclusive and hierarchical. Its interest is to baptize irrespective of what ethnic or social group a person may belong to. What is at stake is the extension of the civilizing presence of a hierarchical model of society to the greatest possible number of physically present people. Of course, there is always exclusion, especially of insurgent indigenous people. Nonetheless, the principle of differentiation of this practical logic is the classification of social actors into a hierarchy, at the top of which stand the Catholic Church and at most one more, if at all possible, royal – thus dependent on God's grace – representative of secular power. In the praxis of popular Catholicism endless variations are possible of veneration of saints as well as multiple religious affiliations provided the individuals are officially placed in the Church's hierarchy. In this context, ethnic belonging or race are seen as a continuum, which is reflected in terms like the Brazilian *morenidade*.

---

26 For this and what follows cf. Vazquez and Marquart 2003, 30.

Latin America: Marginal Protestantism

The US-American mission Protestantism presented a sharp contrast to these cultural conditions. This was especially the case with Evangelicalism and the Pentecostal movement. But its role was not hegemonic as in the USA, and not even dominant. It entered a foreign Catholic culture and played a marginal role until about the 1980s. So, it was far from important in the political field, but had at first to struggle to find a tolerably significant position in society through successful conversions and quantitative growth. Accordingly, what is still central for the greater part of Latin American Protestantism in search of new followers today is the conversion of Catholics. The resulting tension between Protestantism and Catholicism in the religious field can only be overcome selectively, for example in cooperation on political issues such as the fight for restrictive abortion laws or social justice. Protestantism seeks to combine its conversion mission with the revaluation of its own political significance by claiming that social problems would solve themselves if only as many people as possible converted to Evangelical or Pentecostal Protestantism. The boundary line with the social environment is thus drawn in religious terms, by belonging to a very clearly defined religious group. This sharp, religious demarcation has been softened in recent times, however, by two processes. On the one hand, Historical Protestantism, changed by ecumenical impulses and led in part by *indígenas*, takes up more and more initiatives of the interreligious dialogue. On the other hand, the Pentecostal movement – over time and to a much greater extent than in the USA – has developed its ability to allow and cultivate diversity. The more the Pentecostal churches put down roots in Latin America, the more they diversify and the more often it is the case that one and the same person practices in different religious places of worship. An important informant of our scientific partner in São Paulo, for instance, is organized in the Pentecostal Assambléias de Deus because they do good community work; she goes to the Catholic Church to achieve a meditative distance from the stresses of life in the city; and she goes to the priest of the Candomblé when she is seriously ill.

Racism

We have already identified racism as a decisive factor in the explanation of religious conflicts in the USA. The same goes for Latin America. However, in the USA, for example, through the quasi-destruction of the indigenous population, slavery and institutionalized discrimination, a much more brutal segregation took place until the 1960s than in most Latin American countries. In addition, racial difference was long, and still is, constitutive for the membership of Black churches. For all the racism in Latin America, a much stronger *mestizaje* took place which was based on biology and culture and partly was of a programmatic character (Mexico, Brazil, and Cuba).[27] Although the Catholic Church still has a predominantly white hierarchy, it has also developed integrative pastoral work (*pastoral indígena*) and symbolism (Virgin of Guadalupe). As lower and middle class people, the majority of Protestants are anyway mestizos or blacks; only in some Neopentecostal churches can an racial difference be found objectively, which is however only of small importance, if any. Nevertheless, one must speak at least of subliminal racism towards the indigenous and African-American population, which the indigenous people for their part have answered over the last few decades by founding independent indigenous churches. They generally combine religious praxis with social and cultural work, often also with political participation in matters of indigenous interest.

Neocolonial Dominance

A very important framing condition for the Protestant mission in Latin America, which mainly comes from the USA, is the neocolonial dominance of the USA over Latin America in almost all fields of social praxis, but particularly in the economy. In continuation of the hemispheric policy of the Monroe Doctrine and in the interest of

27 … however much euphemism may be behind it.

unfettered access to cheap raw materials, there have been countless military and political infringements by the USA on Latin America since the 19th century. This objective dominance still had impacts in the late 20th century on the public perception of Protestantism as a "submarine" of US secret services or at least US-American culture. For Latin American Protestants, however, replicating American culture is not of greater interest than for their society as a whole. The exception are Neopentecostal organizations of the modernizing upper middle class, for which American models of self-management, positive thinking and professional careers determine their identity. The masses of Latin American Protestants in their majority reject the cultural and other dominance of the USA tacitly, but sometimes also in loud protests. Of particular importance for the development of Protestantism in Latin America were conflicts with missionaries. Since the beginning of the 1960s, younger national leaders have distanced themselves from the control, authority to issue directives and programs of US missionaries and often also from the US-American cultural model. This led to the foundation of domestic churches, often in the Pentecostal tradition (such as the Unión Evangélica Pentecostal Venezolana, UEPV), which developed their own programs, often oriented towards social commitment. The UEPV, for instance, is clearly composed of members of the lower class and is equally clearly on the side of Bolivarian Revolution.

Binary and Continuous Identities

Finally, and with all due caution, another important difference between the USA and Latin America can be noted in terms of the construction of collective and individual identities. There is a difference only in the strength of the tendency, and exceptions are found in both regions. Even so, it concerns a central structure of identity construction and we think it therefore helpful to mention it as part of this general orientation. Vásquez and Marquardt (2003, 30) draw attention to an observation by Néstor García Canclini (1999, 108ff. esp. 117; see also 2001) on the construction of identity in connection with ethnic (that is in this case racial) classification. In the USA, they say, due to the sharp segregation and the corresponding binary coding (black / Caucasian), identities are perceived as "autonomous units," which makes negotiations about gradations or shades difficult if not impossible. In Latin America, especially in Brazil, although the cultural framework is still hierarchical and Eurocentric, the "subjects reserve to themselves the chance at different affiliations, they can move between identities and mix them" (García Canclini 1999, 117, my translation) – as in the case of the Catholic Candomblé Pentecostal woman from São Paulo mentioned above. So, the essentialist reference to a certain ethnic group as core of one's national culture does not apply either. This open and variable form of identity formation corresponds to a conception of ethnical differences as a continuum of different degrees of mixture. While the model attributed to the USA is clearly associated with the praxis of slavery, the Latin American one has its counterpart in the *mestizaje* – which does not mean, however, that it does not also hold racist potential. But the identities, or rather their value in social exchange, are repeatedly renegotiated in everyday praxis, influenced by power relations and the changing times, and are thus subject to constant change.

If one looks at religious praxis with the question outlined above in mind, similarities can be found. The assumption of the chosenness and uniqueness of the USA creates a strong internal-external contrast, which can operate both by expansion and isolation. Both are known from the history of the USA. The external is traditionally identified with old Europe, the Pope, feudalism, church hierarchy, exogenous control, etc. Internally, however, operates the freedom of the individual's decision for the true religion. The internal is ruled by true Christianity, the external by something else, whether atheism or a foreign religion. In any case, the external is neither chosen nor American. In the case of the expansion option, the logic of world mission develops – which, interestingly enough, was never considered by the Black churches! – in the same direction as the logic of manifest destiny, the Monroe Doctrine, the merchant and commodities fleets as well as the military interventions.

The identity construction described for Latin America in terms of continuously emerging differences is associated in the religious field above all with Catholicism. This limits openness, especially when one takes into consideration the attitude of the Catholic Church, widespread in colonial times, towards non-Catholics. But the development of Catholicism to this day has shown that it is capable of becoming open to other religions. However, this opening is also always subject to the condition of hierarchical logic. Catholicism can be inclusive, because it is hierarchical – if you want to be precise, this started with God (the first mover), continued with the Pope and the priestly hierarchies right down to the individual believer. And that means that Catholicism asserts its own theologically constructed universality (which is strictly speaking paradoxical). Placed in this great pyramid of being is the continuum of ethnic groups, whose individual representatives, as parts of the pyramid's ordered elements, are of course fully accepted depending on their position. This is quite similar to the way the representatives of different religions are accepted in principle as capable of certain theological truths, but with differing positions – closer to or more distant from the center of a truth continuum imagined as a concentric structure. It also corresponds to the fact that Latin American Catholicism no longer knows an external other after the completed or no longer necessary Christianization of the *indígenas*. It is part of a universal community, the World Church. A similar world picture also seems to have found its way into the habitūs of most Latin American politicians, which could partly explain the low number of international conflicts on the continent and the complete renunciation of extra-continental expansion. There are local saints among Latin American Catholics (the Virgin of Guadalupe, the Virgin of Aparecida, etc.), but there is no religious theory of the chosenness of any one nation. What is left is the position in a hierarchy at whose apex is Rome.

Large parts of Latin American Protestantism are therefore forced to find their way in a complex situation once the US-American missionaries' ideology of chosenness has been sloughed off – which after all only highlights its own unique role and has relegated the Latin American activists to the cheap seats in history's theater, for the Promised Land is, strictly speaking, in Massachusetts. As hinted at above, some Neopentecostals of the upper middle class dream of assimilating their countries to the USA, of re-sacralizing laicist politics and of thus solving all their problems (strangely enough also those of the economic dependence on the USA). Most Latin American Protestants, however, are busy trying to fix an identity of their own for themselves, as authentic a one as possible. In as much as this identity is to be made up of Protestant religious dispositions, they have to fall back on the discursive inventory of Protestantism, giving it a new profile with their local community in mind.

What are the most important elements of this inventory and how can Latin American Protestants utilize them?

3.2 Religious Dispositions: Transformation through Entanglement

Part of the specific conditions of the conquest and settlement of the North American continent is that the Puritan immigrants brought with them the religious discourse of a marginal European group that had been forced to emigrate. As is usual in sectarian discourses, there is a logic at work, also in this one, of hard separation, an either-or attitude and the opposition of internal-external. Due to a lack of competitors, this discourse became prevalent in North America so that exclusivist schemata were now used from dominant positions. Over the course of US-American history and from new religious impulses (Methodism, for instance) as well as political ideologies (e.g. manifest destiny), a series of partially contradictory religious convictions developed from the Puritanical discourse which were the expression of how different formations of US-American society saw, and still see, themselves. These religious dispositions have generated in their turn the discourse which the missionaries take with them into the "field."

In Latin America, this discourse met religious, political, economic, cultural etc. dispositions and institutions which had taken shape in colonial times and the anti-colonialist fights of the Liberals. In the most important period of entanglement so far, the 20th century, two competing positions became dominant, Catholicism and Liberalism. Depending on the degree of national laicism one of the two positions was dominant while both represented quite different operational conditions for Protestant churches. But even if these conditions were good, e.g. under liberal rule, freedom of religion and a low degree of laicism (as in Guatemala, for example), Protestantism was always subaltern. And it has remained in that position in most countries till today, even if, for various reasons, it finds good political operational conditions, as in Brazil or Guatemala. From this subaltern position missionaries and national experts offered at first a religious discourse after the US-American model. But this was received under different conditions and modes of judgment and perception than were established in the USA. It was heard, so to speak, with "Catholic" ears. Religious dispositions of a highly exclusive nature (redeemed parishioner/pagan condemned to hell) encountered tolerance of diversity; a strictly individualist notion of salvation (personal acknowledgment in public of Jesus Christ as Lord) was confronted with a habitual collectivist idea of salvation (child baptism and sacramentalism). Even if Protestant missionary discourse asserted that conversion radically changes lives and produces a completely "new man," it is our observation that many of the old dispositions tend to continue in the new identity, sometimes with new content, sometimes not even that. This is the case as far as we can see when – as we will show in the next chapter – Latin American Protestants confront US-American individualist salvation with the social responsibility of the Christian man.

The question must therefore be asked what becomes of US-American Protestant religious discourses in the formation of religious dispositions in Latin America.

Uniqueness

The religio-political imaginary of American exceptionalism is constitutive of the Pilgrims as well as today's religious right. And you can be taught even on train journeys with educated and widely travelled Americans that the USA has undergone such a superb development in terms of democracy and technology that it now bears the responsibility of making such a development possible for all other nations in this world. The Pilgrims clothed the idea of uniqueness of the new country in the metaphors of the "City upon a Hill," the "New Jerusalem" and the "Light of the Peoples" (Winthrop). The underlying Old Testament and Zionist idea of an apocalyptic Zion as power center over the peoples of the world is here transferred from the Jewish to the US-American context. In the course of history – especially since the beginnings of Christian Zionism in the late 19th century – this notion gave rise not only to the claim to uniqueness but also to an ambivalent relation with Judaism. The notion of uniqueness combines with that of an exclusive covenant with God and that of manifest destiny to shape the project of a *Christian Nation*. During the conquest of the continent, the project of "Light of the Peoples" linked up with a strong motif of mission and expansion, which was first directed towards the conversion of the Native Americans but was extended shortly after the founding of the state to other sovereign territories. The idea of God's covenant with the US-Americans is also borrowed from the Old Testament. The theological concept of an exclusive alliance with Israel was transferred or extended to Christendom. Early Calvinism applied the theory as "federal theology" for self-legitimation purposes, while the Pilgrims soon applied it to themselves.[28] The covenant with God confirms and reinforces the US claim to exceptionalism through the religious concept of chosenness. Besides, one should not forget that the narra-

28 This conceit has seen a luxuriant offshoot in the British-Israel theory, which had many followers in the 19th century. It stated that the 10 tribes of Israel had migrated to Europe and founded Great Britain. Even Jesus Christ was said to have been seen there.

tives of the alliance with God in the Old Testament belong with the account of the preparation for Israel's warlike settlement in Canaan (Book of Joshua). Expansionism was, then, part of their mental make-up.

It is also the focus of the transfer of the idea of chosenness to political ideology in the metaphor of the manifest destiny of the US-Americans. The term *divine destiny* is also used, for the idea is grounded in religion, so that one finds again and again that the goal is the salvation of mankind. God's Providence, it is claimed, has entrusted the USA with a special mission, at first in the context of the advancing settlement frontier, but then on a hemispheric scale and finally on a worldwide one. The concept had its origin in the first half of the 19th century under the impression of these developments: increasingly frequent military operations in the Spanish, French and British colonial areas;[29] the development of Pan-Americanism since Jefferson (with a first conference at Panama in 1826); the hegemonic interpretation of Pan-Americanism through the Monroe Doctrine (1823), which proclaims the protection of the recently independent Latin American states from European attacks – and thus presupposes of course the military hegemony of the USA in the Western hemisphere. If one reads one of the earliest documents of manifest destiny – the article "Annexation" by John O'Sullivan in the *Democratic Review*, 1845 (O'Sullivan 1845) – the usefulness of the narrative for religious overdetermination of territorial claims becomes immediately clear. O'Sullivan vehemently advocates for the separation of California and Texas from Mexico and their admission to the Union. The Anglo-Saxon settlers in these areas, he contends, have a greater right to it than Mexico's "artificial tide of sovereignty".[30] He also opens up the prospect of the annexation of British Canada and

29 1798-1800 naval war against France; 1806 Interference at the Rio Grande; 1810 West Florida; 1812 East Florida; 1813 West Florida; 1814-25 various Caribbean islands; 1822-23 Cuba; 1824 Puerto Rico; 1831 Falkland Islands; 1833 Argentina; 1835 Peru, 1844 Mexico …

30 Sullivan on Mexico: "Imbecile and distracted, Mexico never can exert any real governmental authority over such a country."

Spanish America. There is no real population growth there, he states, unlike the USA, which is why the millions of Americans who gather against European bayonets under the Star-Spangled Banner have every right to settlement and annexation. One was not going to be prevented by the Europeans from "the fulfillment of our manifest destiny to overspread the continent allotted by Providence for the free development of our yearly multiplying millions." This politico-religious motive was in fact used to legitimize the war with Mexico and the annexation of the Mexican territories.

Clearly, all this shows immediately why Latin Americans had their difficulties with the idea of the expansive uniqueness of the USA. As a result of the war with Mexico, the working conditions of US missionaries in Mexico deteriorated for a long time. The ideologies of uniqueness and manifest destiny are not simply transferable to Protestantism in Latin America. The divine mission is that of the USA, not Latin American countries, which are merely the addressees of the USA's claim to power. The civilizational claim of the early Protestant missionaries in Latin America resonated with the idea of the manifest destiny of the USA, but only as the motivational background of the missionaries, not the missionized. Today, one can at best speak of a subordinate identification with the US-American claim among the Neopentecostals of the upper middle class. They identify with the cultural model of the USA, especially neo-liberalism, present themselves in the national context as ambassadors of the North American Protestant way of life and thus seek to transfer the symbolic capital of the USA to themselves. The idea of a national manifest destiny with the aim of dominating the entire hemisphere is not even expressed in Bolsonaro's Brazil. Accordingly, there is no need for a decision between crusade and isolation, which occasionally haunts US-American Protestantism.

Latin American Protestants can, however, transfer the motif of God's covenant with his people to themselves. But then it is no longer the covenant with the USA, a nation with territory and power structures, but with a collective religious actor in a subordinate position in a society consisting primarily of refusers. In special situations, the motives of chosenness and covenant can also be claimed for Latin American nations. This was the case during the one and a half years in which Guatemala was dominated by the Neopentecostal dictator Ríos Montt. Guatemala was selected as the chosen country by the Neopentecostal churches of the spiritual MANAGEMENT formation, and the dictator as King David. One could also understand in the same way the establishment of the New Jerusalem Temple in São Paulo by the Igreja Universal do Reino de Deus, the Templo de Salomão, merely because of its symbolism. Then we would have the claim that the rightful election of God by the people of Israel – who failed to rebuild the Temple and thus did not fulfill their spiritual obligations – has passed to the billion-dollar event company of "bishop" Edir Macedo. The criterion for election would then no longer be the divine power of decision, but how fat one's wallet is.

Law and Revelation

The concept of the Bible as God's law which he had dictated word for word was very useful in the living conditions of settler communities (whether Puritans in New England or the later settlers on the frontier). Where secular legislation is weakly represented in particular, biblical law functions as a moral and social principle of order. This fact explains the appreciation of the Bible as such in the USA. Biblicism, however, goes hand in hand with a non-hermeneutic, a-historical and reifying concept of Scripture. In the 19th century, this conception competed with the historical hermeneutics imported from the European academies, which understands the Bible initially as a historical document. Historical hermeneutics was simply a threat to the naive but practical approach to Scripture for the settlers and later the rural population in general, but the Evangelical university theologians made a counterproposal with an ingenious, positivist theory of induction. The Bible, according to their theory, simply depicts transcendent realities. From this seed of biblicist fundamentalism developed, in the 1970s and '80s, the Moral Majority of Jerry

Falwell as the most important actor of the religious right. True to biblicist principles, the then leaders of the religious right would, frequently and in an authoritarian way, utilize quotations from the Bible. Falwell himself, based on his exegesis, even predicted the Lord's return in the mid-1980s. However, the arbitrariness and frequency of the use of Scripture as well as the quarrel over the "correct" interpretations of the verses blocked the movement's capacity for political action. In the years after President Reagan it was therefore given a general overhaul by strategists like Ralph Reed and provided with a new source of revelation by Neopentecostals.

The idea that God gives direct revelations in the form of visions, auditions or (good) ideas is as old as religion itself and a classic form of charismatic legitimation. In the USA this access to divine truth developed from Methodist emotionalism and the subsequent sanctification movement. Such open-mindedness attained a key function in the early Pentecostal movement, where it helped people from the lower classes, the marginalized and illiterate to dignity and self-confidence. This form of revelation was adopted into Neopentecostalism with a corresponding change in social position. While it was a form of religious compensation for the marginalization suffered in the early Pentecostal movement, in the Neopentecostalism of the upper middle class – especially among its experts and entertainers – it became an instrument of arbitrary pretense, legitimation of power and, where necessary, of distinction. Now everyone – provided they had a sufficiently large microphone – could claim that God had spoken to him directly and that he or she now had the mandate to carry out the divine commands. Pat Robertson, for example, said in his television show *700 Club* in 2005 that God had told him – probably during the morning wet shave – that Venezuelan President Chavez should be killed by a CIA commando in order to avoid an otherwise necessary war against Venezuela because the government there was sitting on US oil deposits. (After public critique, he confirmed this once again.)

If you ask yourself now about the divine conception of international law, you have another think coming. For God is, according to the prophets of the religious right, against international law and for theocracy. What is decisive is that the pious television audience, and if possible also the government, implement the divine will as proclaimed by the entertainer. This logic of revelation is obviously much more practical for religious mobilization than the tiresome interpretation of Scripture. In the medium term, the legitimacy of the messages will be determined by audience ratings, donations and the private assets of the Prosperity prophets, in short by economic capital. The place of fallen prophets – like Jimmy Swaggart for sexual and the Bakkers for sexual and financial reasons – is quickly taken by new infallibles. And the coordination with interested politicians – mainly Republicans – is easy. With increasing mediatization, and event technology becoming more and more perfect, the potential for manipulation also increases. Today, the exercise of religious leadership through the pretense of direct revelation, and of religious allegiance through the belief in such claims has become a widespread basis of an almost unlimited authoritarianism of religious leader personalities.

Where detailed information about God's will can be given, you also know what He does *not* want. The concept of sin has been a central instrument of religious life and authoritarian rule over people for Protestantism in the USA since the times of the Pilgrims. Here it is crucial that sin is understood as a concrete act. Sin is not, as in theological Lutheranism, an abstract concept, a disturbance in the human relationship to God. Instead, sin occurs in the plural, which is why concrete deeds can be defined as sins. For Puritanism this was, besides a dissolute lifestyle, the consumption of alcohol, and witchcraft – the reason why the "witches" of Salem could also be punished with death. The reification of sin in the form of clearly defined actions is usually tacitly oriented towards social common sense. Sins are then deeds that do not conform to the commonsensical ideas of a group about virtue and vice. In this way, the reified concept of sin serves to incriminate concrete actions and to impose social discipline on the behavior of people for the sake of the collective. The current debate on the family, abortion and homosexuality is largely conducted in these terms by the religious right. The Evangelical left in the USA does not differ fundamentally: it reifies sin only in other areas, such as ecological behavior.

The motif of the law plays an important role in Latin America in everyday life and the political projection of Protestantism. In Evangelicalism especially, Scripture is assumed to have ready the appropriate regulations for social and political affairs. The MANAGEMENT formation draws the rules also from direct revelation. The Bible is central in Latin American Protestantism, except for Neopentecostalism, and is generally interpreted in the tradition of US-American Biblicism. However, the fight between scientific (theory of evolution) and biblical truth (creation in six days followed by a day of rest), which has been raging in the USA since the late 19th century, hardly plays a role in Latin America. What is at issue here is more the practical application of biblical discourses as divine guidelines for behavior in society. This function plays an important role insofar as processes of rapid and confusing social change as well as the unplannable existence in the informal economy of the very poor are experienced as disorder calling for a power to put things in order. Between the Protestant believers and their Catholic counterparts can, in addition, be detected a functional homology in terms of the use of the Bible as law (Protestants) and the order-creating power of a bishops' conference (Catholics). In the Pentecostal movement, and especially in the Neopentecostal movement, the acceptance of direct divine revelation plays at least as great a role as Scripture. While in the lower strata of the Pentecostal movement direct revelations, for example by "prophets," are mostly used in the context of pastoral care and healing practices, in the middle and upper strata of the Neopentecostal movement they are often used also as a guarantor of truth for the assessment of political situations and the recommendation of political strategies. This is similar to their use in the USA, but because of their tension with Catholicism they face bigger problems of being accepted as plausible.

As a rule in Latin America, the concept of sin is as strongly reified as in the USA. After a thorough comparison of the respective discourses, however, we have the impression that it is used with less doggedness than in the North. This is probably due to the following reasons. First, there is no need for pseudo-scientific legitimation in Latin America since there is no pronounced conflict between fundamentalist conceptual realism and hermeneutics. Second, the internal/external contrast between believers and people of a different faith is less sharp. Third, the socially dominant religious dispositions of Catholicism relativize the factual sins through the sacrament of penance. Furthermore, a socio-structural differentiation of the concept of sin can be observed in Latin America, which is less pronounced in the USA. In the lower class, for example, the consumption of alcohol is a sin, which has to do with the socially destructive effect of alcoholism and the small income of families. In the Neopentecostal groups of the upper middle class, on the other hand, moderate social drinking is not a problem. Political factors also play a role: depending on the government, it can be a sin (not) to do military service.

Since the First Great Awakening (1730-1740) led by Methodism (George Whitefield), emotionalism has become more and more important in the USA. It gave individualism a subjective emotional touch and prepared the ground for the triumphal march of charismatic legitimation, which found its first organizational framework with the Pentecostal movement (from about 1900). However, due to the strong influence of the ethnic factor, the black Pentecostal movement in the USA amalgamated with black Protestantism; and the classic white Pentecostal movement moved relatively quickly into the (lower) middle class and changed to Evangelical ritual forms. In the Neopentecostal movement, emotionalism is today the generally accepted ritual form of expression. Emotions present a similar case to the claim to direct revelation. Emotional experiences and religious feelings are regarded as the yardstick of religious legitimacy: the more ecstatic the experience, the more true it is. Thus there is a seamless fit both between the current emotionalism in the Prosperity Organizations or in the Independent Network Charismatics under Millennials, and the intellectual laissez faire of postmodernism and the populist mixing up of discursive truth by drive-controlled feelings of superiority. If the feeling in the event is good, then the electoral advice of "Red" is also correct.

In Latin America emotion finds itself in a social context that resembles that of the original context of the Pentecostal movement in the USA. In the churches of the lower class, emotionality plays an important part in the compensation for social marginality and the experience of being branded as inferior. In addition, ethnicity plays no role in social segregation. Despite processes of embourgeoisement with classic Pentecostal churches also in Latin America, compensatory emotionality of the lower class is as widespread as it ever was. As for Neopentecostalism in Latin America, the situation is similar to that in the USA: the degree of the laicity of politics determines how far the manipulation of religious emotionality can be pushed by the leaders of this religious current. Mexico has imposed strict limits to this praxis, but in Brazil it is untrammeled and can spread far and wide, employing all sorts of corruption, acceptance of advantages, lies and defamation.

Devils and Demons

The satanization of political opponents is a widespread technique of disqualifying others. Devils and demons played an important role in the religious imagination of the Puritans, serving to discipline internally and conquer externally. Both the witch hunts (Salem) and the satanization of Native Americans adopted this dualistic logic. And as a rule, communicative force legitimizes physical force. This scheme has been applied with only slight changes till today. Biblicist fundamentalism of the 1980s spoke relatively unspecific of the devil and hell, and the future in the next world is still an important point of reference because what is ultimately at stake is salvation. This underwent a change, however, in the 1980s and '90s with the charismatic Neopentecostals, who were concerned with the present and the promotion of theocratic approaches (dominion) in politics. They painted a scenario of a cosmic battle of angels versus demons,

Spiritual Warfare, in which human beings were involved, whether they wanted to or not, either on the party of the demons or the angels. This allowed any individuals to be diagnosed with possession by demons and, where necessary, have exorcisms performed on them. In the vast army of highly imaginative litterateurs,[31] C. Peter Wagner was preeminent, a former Evangelical missionary and later mission scholar. As professor at the renowned Fuller School of World Mission at Pasadena, he added new fuel to fundamentalist propaganda of fear with his polished demonology. In his teaching, he even instructed his students to exorcise the demons from the luggage they had carried with them on their visits to indigenous religious sites in Latin America. This was not all, however: he became notorious through his invention of territorial demons. These guys, he asserted, were capable of bringing under their control whole districts, nations or world regions, which would make the leaders and ultimately the citizens of these regions possessed by demons. The least one could do in this case, he contended, was to send a mission there, but a regime change would be best. But above all, one must be on one's guard not to be deceived by the satanic leaders about their intentions. It does not take a lot of imagination to grasp that what he had in mind was not only indigenous people in Latin America but also the Palestine issue and the whole Islamic world. Between this theory and the seemingly somewhat more serious project of 10/40 Window the boundaries are fluid. 10/40 uses military jargon to describe, in terms of degrees of latitude and longitude, a "window" above the Muslim and East Asian world which stands in bad need of missionary activities.[32]

In early missions and Latin American Protestantism the devils of Puritanism were at first of secondary importance. In particular, they were not utilized in political discourse. If at all, demonic possession was relevant only in Pentecostal folk religion in places

31 In terms of theology, these treatises cannot be taken seriously, at best only as products of modern heresy.

32 Accessed on 29 September 2019.

where there were no physicians or where they were at a loss what to do about a psychic disease like bipolar disorder. If such a "treatment" was to be carried out in the context of a congregation, this involved as a rule the assistance of the patient from a pastor or deacon during the acute phase of the illness. In contrast to Wagner and his followers, this procedure was not concerned with telediagnosis or across-the-board satanization of merely disliked sections of the populace. For the latter purpose, the ideology of Spiritual Warfare was, however, made widespread use of by actors of the MANAGEMENT formation. In Guatemala it was employed, in times of war, for the satanization of the guerilla and the entire left; or later in presidential campaigns as an ideology to mobilize voters and the demonization of the indigenous cultural heritage. In Brazil, it was the foundation and precondition of the entire propaganda and discourse of the religious right. The whole construction serves the seizure of political power.

In the USA, the so-called Dominion Doctrine stands for the religiously underpinned claim to exercise a "Christian" control of state and society.[33] It shares this claim not only with Puritanism, but has its roots in the Calvinist tradition. One of the chief ideologues of this Neopentecostal mindset that emerged in the 1980s, Rousas Rushdooney, strove for a reconstruction of the original state in Paradise (Genesis 1:28) of man's dominion over everything that exists. With the only difference that "man" here refers to himself and his followers, and that rule will be achieved by Spiritual Warfare when "God's people will [...] have a long reign over the entire earth, after which, when all enemies have been put under Christ's feet..." (Rushdooney 1986, 24; quoted after Diamond 1989, 139). The ideology amounts to a religious totalitarianism that radically denies legitimacy to all other religious and political positions. The head of the Coalition on Revival, Jay Grimstead, worked out a 10-year plan on how to completely "Christianize" Orange County (a place of a lot of armaments industry) and Santa Clara County (where Silicon

33 Cf. Diamond 1989, 136ff.; Schäfer 1992c, 80ff.

Valley is situated) in California. The main goal was to control leadership positions and build chains of command. The hard core of the movement pursues the reintroduction of Old Testament law with the death penalty for homosexuals, socage for debt and abolition of the credit economy. The politically more cooperative of the activists are satisfied with neo-liberal capitalism, tax cuts, privatization of social services, rearmament and imperial warfare, and support of terrorist forces in the Third World, such as the Nicaraguan Contras in the 1980s. The hard core of the movement did not last long enough to experience the long-lasting rule over the world. The basic idea of the movement – to exercise religious, theocratic control over politics – has, however, found broad support among the religious right in the US. The television star and Republican pre-candidate for the presidency, Pat Robertson, has worked with this logic since the 1980s. Today it is represented as Seven Mountain Dominionism by the rapidly spreading Independent Network Charismatics. The ties with the right in Congress are close. This ideology is, however, met with skepticism by missionary Protestantism, which is dominated by Evangelical ideas.

So it is not Evangelical missionaries in Latin America who spread the ideology but leaders of the of the MANAGEMENT formation, well-read enough to pay attention to this possibility of politically re-arming religious praxis. Persons suspected of secret service activities also help at times with the spread of the ideology. Guatemala is again an example, where the Dominion Doctrine granted the dictatorship of Neopentecostal Ríos Montt major orders as a new King David. The former minister of the exterior Harold Caballeros, is a specialist in the deployment of the doctrine against his political enemies. The bottom line is that the political engagement of the MANAGEMENT formation as a whole tends in the theocratic direction.

Time: Millennialism

The concept of time plays a decisive role in the political use of religious convictions. This aspect manifests a structural difference between the neo-Puritanical direction of US-American Protestantism and Protestantism in Latin America. The white Protestantism in the USA sees the ideal society in the Puritan past. It understands the reform or revolution of contemporary society, therefore, as the purge of the present from the slagheaps of history and its return to the ideal state of the pure Puritan society. A similar historical construction is impossible for Protestants in Latin America. It is instead cultivated by reactionary Catholic groups like Opus Dei or the Legionaries of Christ, whose ideal is baroque society with its almost unlimited rule of Catholicism. An example can be found in architecture with new churches in the baroque style built in cooperation with Opus Dei, as is the case in Guatemala in the gated community of Cayalá. Latin American Protestantism, on the other hand, does not deign to make a positive reference to the colonial period. All it can do is to resolutely look ahead: on the one hand to positivist ideas of social evolution, on the other to millennial projections of a near end of the world or a theocratic empire in the future. The latter option lays the foundation for the attractiveness of dominionism for the upper middle and upper classes in Latin America. This moves forward the reconstruction of an ideal state – Adam's prelapsarian rule or the good old days of the Old Testament – to the future. And it raises the question of time construction in the millennialist model.

Millennialism, the expectation of a millennial Kingdom of God, is closely linked to the program of the New Jerusalem. There are, however, two variants of millennialism.[34] Postmillennialism (Christ will come *after* the Millennial Kingdom) aims at the realization of the Kingdom in history. This view prevailed in the USA until the Civil War. Postmillennialism was later able to amalgamate with secular, evolutionist ideas of progress and to influence both religious social Darwinism and the social work (Social Gospel) of Mainline Protestantism. The other variant, premillennialism (Christ will come *before* the Millennial Kingdom) aims at the hereafter. The Kingdom will come only after the victorious Christ has de-

34 On the practical logic cf. Schäfer 1992c, 46ff. and 52ff.

scended from the clouds and gathered the waiting, politically passive church to himself. This view became predominant after the Civil War as a reaction to the critical break in national history, to the failure of the entire national project, and to the plausibilization of the extreme class antagonisms that had arisen in industrialization. The present appears here as a time of decline into chaos, and the corresponding perspectives for action are either religious or fatalistic. Premillennialism has influenced especially the white Evangelical movement. A conservative variant of premillennialism is so-called dispensationalism, which divides world history into periods of time and brings order and certainty of expectation in this way to the premillennialist theory of chaos. In conservative mission Protestantism, which is focused on eternal salvation, this variant plays an important role, even if the motto of the "evangelization of the world in one generation" is in a certain tension with its program for the hereafter. At present, dispensationalism has lost ground relative to other, charismatic patterns of legitimacy and the postmillennialism of the Dominion doctrine.

In Latin America, millennialism is practically unknown to the Catholic Church apart from a few messianic movements in Catholic folk piety. In Protestantism, by contrast, it performs an important role. It does explicitly not link up with indigenous, African-American or folk-Catholic messianism or millennialism. Rather, it seeks a sharp delimitation, whereas dispensationalism has more or less succeeded in connecting to Latin American dispositions with indigenous believers. The assumption here is that this may be due to the similarity of the historical phase model with indigenous ideas about historical periods taking turns (in Guatemala *baktún*). However that may be, the dispensationalist Central America Mission enjoys a rapid spread in the highlands of Guatemala. A similar development seems to have taken place in the member churches of the Protestant-indigenous FEINE organization in Ecuador. Dispensationalism or open premillennialism determine the convictions of the entire Evangelical and Pentecostal movements, which agree on the central aspect: they place the church in a position of passive waiting for societal events and the concentration on inner-congregational religious activities. Premillennialism responds with this attitude to the demand for a compensatory religiosity in a societal situation that makes social action impossible, and political action even more so. It follows that it is a religiosity typical of the lower class, a "theodicy of suffering" (Weber).

"Runaway religion does not make armies" is what supporters of theocratic concepts are in the habit of saying about premillennialism. If religious actors have at their disposal sufficient space for political intervention, it makes more sense for them (as in the Catholic Church) either to forget the millennialist perspective completely or change it into a postmillennialist one. This happened in the USA and was taken over immediately in Latin America by the MANAGEMENT formation. The organizations mentioned above for Guatemala changed during the war not just their own discourse to a postmillennialist one. It was also a US-American person who sought through radio propaganda to supplant across the board the premillennialist convictions of Evangelicals and Pentecostals as well as the residual premillennialism of some Neopentecostals through a postmillennialism suited to the war. An analysis of the religious dispositions of the Neopentecostal movement of the time will easily uncover internal contradictions. Today, postmillennialism has won through with Neopentecostals of the upper middle class. These actors speak in recent times more and more about making God's Kingdom on Earth come true. This makes them poachers, so to speak, in the discursive terrain of Social Gospel Protestantism and Liberation Theology.

The concept of the Kingdom of God in present religious vocabulary is a multivalent one, in the USA as well as in Latin America.

In the USA it was at first loosely associated with the vision of national perfection, but without becoming a central discursive operator. That happened later in the program of Social Gospel. Social Gospel describes both a religious social theory and a current in Mainline Protestantism. At the beginning of the 20th century and under the impression of the social damages caused by the industrialization in the North of the USA, the theory of a belief-based and hermeneutically reflected social responsibility was developed in Mainline Protestantism (for example by Walter Rauschenbusch) and practiced in various social projects. The dominant understanding of the concept of the "Kingdom of God" was, however, not that the Kingdom of God would come true in the world through human effort. Rather, the prevailing assumption was that an orientation towards values associated with the Kingdom of God – above all social justice and peaceableness – would lead to an approach to the Kingdom, and thus to the experience, again and again, at least to a certain extent, of situations similar to what was expected from the Kingdom of God. This understanding, framed by Pan-American ideas, was predominant in the mission of the Historical Churches as discussed at the Panama Congress. Today, the influence of Social Gospel is found mainly in the churches of Mainline Protestantism organized in the National Council of Churches. In its work abroad it combines with interchurch partnerships and the promotion of development projects. In this tradition the idea of a mission for conversion has completely given way to the concept of common ecumenical learning based on partnership and solidarity. In the Latin American understanding, however, the concept of the Kingdom of God plays the role of an ethical framework for activities.[35]

While the Social Gospel in the USA is still associated with churches of the (upper) middle class, in Latin America it has undergone a different development. Historical Protestantism in Latin America tends to be anchored in today's downwardly mobile lower middle class and – through the earlier mission activities in the countryside – in the lower class. Not infrequently it is continued by social-reformist or even revolutionary groups among students – Iglesia y Sociedad en América Latina (ISAL) in Brazil and the Cono Sur as

35 A very special approach to a theology of liberation and justice, which operates with the motif of exodus, can be found in black Protestantism in the USA. As it has developed practically no entanglements with Latin America, it is not treated in the present study.

well as the Movimiento Estudiantil Cristiano – Comisión Evangélica Latinoamericana de Educación Cristiana (MEC-CELADEC). The historical-Protestant praxis "from below" places the socio-ethical conscience in a context of action in which the capacity to shape the future must in the first place be won in a fight against economic marginalization and political repression. This results in a similar position to the one that the actors of the Catholic Liberation Theology hold, which leads to ecumenical cooperation and theological exchange. Debates on theological questions in the narrower sense contribute less to an understanding and a common further development of the theological concepts than common work on social problems in institutes like the Departamento Ecuménico de Investigaciones (Costa Rica), the Centro Antonio Valdivieso (Nicaragua), the Koinonia (Brazil) or the Centro de Estudios Ecuménicos (Mexico). Similar developments are taking place in Latin American theological formation at institutes such as the Universidad Bíblica Latinoamericana (Costa Rica),[36] the Comunidad Teológica (Mexico), the Instituto Superior Evangélico de Estudios Teológicos (Argentina), the Instituto Superior Ecuménico Andino de Teología (Bolivia) and various others. The term "Kingdom of God" here usually does not connotate the perfect realization of an ideal state (as in the theocratic Dominion doctrine), but nevertheless a radical social change, certainly effected also with the means of armed resistance and revolution, as was the case in Nicaragua in the 1980s. The Kingdom of God thus acquires the function of a utopia which – strictly speaking and using a concept from Kant's philosophy – is nothing other than a regulative idea for social-revolutionary ethics. Here is a content element also found in the Liberation Theology of the Black churches in the USA, which incidentally also manifests itself in the fact that Protestant initiatives of this type in Latin America occasionally also choose Martin Luther King as leading figure (e.g. the Centro Martin Luther King in Cuba).

36 For more detail see Kirkpatrick 2019.

Perfectionism, Sanctification, Prosperity

Among the religious and cultural dispositions of US-American Protestantism, perfectionism plays a central role. The Methodist idea of sanctification – linked to emotionalism and piety of spirit – sees the faithful individuals after their conversion in a movement of an ever farther advancing religious and moral perfection. Some schools think absolute perfectionism possible already during one's lifetime while others focus only on the development to that goal. In the first half of the 19th century perfectionism was considered possible even for the entire nation. Tocqueville had already perceived that this motif of redemption through perfectionism could, in homology to religion, also be found in the prevalent, achievement-oriented economic thinking that was marked by a belief in individual property. After the societal split in the second half of the 19th century, the idea of perfectionism is carried on in the Holiness churches of the lower class as a form of religious discipline. Closer to the upper class, other religious experts, like Henry Ward Beecher, transformed the idea of perfection, adding a shot of evolutionism, into a fairly brutal social Darwinism. Beecher sent a written answer to the railroad workers on strike in 1877 pointing out that they would not be able to survive if bread and water was not enough for them. Already in the 19th century, the perfection scheme linked up with the vulgar-Calvinist motif of blessing for the promise of riches and health. The focus on riches in the so-called Prosperity Gospel became stronger and stronger in the course of the 20th century to reach its provisional peak in neo-liberal financial capitalism, with which its representatives find themselves in wholehearted agreement.

A similar split of the perfectionism motif occurs in Latin America. The salvation tradition is represented in the emotionalism of the Pentecostal churches and the duty to lead a "sanctified life" serves primarily to discipline the faithful. The transfer to national projects of moral perfectionism does not take place because the Protestant actors are either of too little importance or because they are too interested in their own access to political power, using morals if at all via such topics as "abortion" or "family" in a populist attempt of the right to mobilize voters. The deputies of the Brazilian Bancada Evangélica, in any case, are not particularly strict where morals are concerned; their corruption index is higher than that of the average deputy. Since the 1980s the Prosperity Doctrine has been introduced to the upper middle class by the actors of the MANAGEMENT formation. In a climate of stark social contrasts it serves initially a legitimizing function as a "theodicy of good fortune" (Weber) and removal of the marginalized from sight; then it orients the religious and social consciousness of its members to the accumulation of economic capital in the frame of neo-liberal economies; and, lastly, it offers the leaders of its movement a table richly laid with financial donations in full sight of its enemies. During fund raising the donations are often claimed to be paid back a hundredfold by God. In reality, this story has filled the pockets of the movement's leaders with millions and millions of dollars – which is hardly credible from a European perspective given the stubborn refusal of charitable religious gifts here. A more recent development is the transfer of the Prosperity ideology to Neopentecostal churches of the lower class, where the doctrine can connect to rife financial failure and put it down to the demoniac possession of its clientele. To be successful in life, you have to have your demons exorcised by the appointed officers. If success does not come despite everything, this is due to the small faith of the clientele. Under conditions of continuous axing of social services in many societies, there are no viable collective ways to improve matters, and individual success being the first and last option, all churches are full. Admittedly, the effort at perfectionism in the eternal cycle of trial and error invariably comes to nothing, and guilt rests of course with the victim of this mechanism.

Communitarianism/Individualism

In US-American culture, a tension between communitarianism and individualism has often been observed. In Biblicism, covenant theology and the piety of congregations one can see forerunners and counterparts of a communitarian conception of society and ultimately also of a republican concept of nation. At the same time, together with the Protestant individualist view of salvation (each individual is directly responsible to God) and a disposition to perfectionism, Biblicism is a precursor and counterpart of individualist conceptions of society as well as liberal views of politics and nation. A lot is to be said in favor of communitarian religious praxis being framed by the countryside, the lower classes or ethnicity; and as many reasons can be advanced for the assumption that individualist praxis operates more likely with the (sub)urban middle class, and is conveyed over time rather with agnostic than religious means. This distinction is mirrored in the social demography of Republican voters relative to Democratic ones – the former tend to live in the country, the latter in cities.

The same contrast between communitarianism and individualism is also found in Latin America. As far as religion is concerned, it can be attached to the tension between a culturally anchored communitarianism, not least due to Catholic corporatism and left-wing political movements on the one hand and, on the other, a conversion mission aiming at individual conversion. Accordingly, individualism is often found in Latin America in the rejection of collectively oriented policies of social justice with the argument that the individual conversion of the heart will likely have the desired social effects. As long as the seemingly harmless argument of individual conversion is directed towards eternal salvation, it also remains relatively harmless politically – except that it usually results in a system-stabilizing depoliticization. But if the goal of the many individual conversions is a completely converted society with correspondingly controlled political institutions, the concept loses its innocence and becomes recognizable as a covertly theocratic view – that is, as the very opposite of individualism.

Laicity

For the entanglement of US-American Protestantism with Latin American society, its different view of laicity is also of importance. The famous "wall of separation" between state and church is an interpretation of the First Amendment taken from a letter by Jefferson to a Baptist congregation. To be sure, it has been confirmed by later judgments, but strictly speaking the First Amendment establishes freedom of religion, prohibits the foundation of a state church, and says nothing about interference by religious actors in politics. Jefferson's interpretation in the laicist direction stands therefore also in strong tension with the political reality of the USA, marked as it is by religious acts at the inauguration of presidents, spiritual advisors and even veritable "court Evangelicals," religious lobbying institutions on Capitol Hill, and a huge National Prayer Breakfast, at which the president is forced every year to say a prayer. Contrary to Jefferson's formula, *God talk* is influential and present everywhere in the political public.

The laicity problem in Latin America is more complicated and at the same time simpler. As in the USA, the praxis of religious actors with an interest in politics moves between pushing the boundaries of religious freedom, which is now guaranteed by all constitutions, on the one hand, and secular or state-church restrictions on the other. Countries with a strictly laicist constitution, such as Uruguay and Mexico in particular, though in principle guaranteeing freedom of religion, have nevertheless severely curtailed it through restrictive legislation for religious organizations. No real estate except for ritual buildings, no access to the media, strict financial conditions, no political statements by clerics, etc. Even after the 1992 reform, religious freedom in Mexico does not mean freedom of political activity. Relative to the Catholic Church, freedom of religion for Protestants is also cut back in Costa Rica, where the former enjoys privileges as the state church which the latter do not have. In Colombia, freedom of religion was established with the 1991 constitution, without far-reaching secular restrictions having been imposed. On the contrary, the direct interference of the Catholic Church in public affairs over the centuries has deeply habitualized the view that the right of religious actors to political statements is a matter of course. This, finally, also contributed to the fact that the referendum on the peace treaty of 2016 resulted in a (narrow) 'no' because of religious propaganda. With regard to Brazil, one can speak of a "laicity *com jeito*" – so-so laicity. Freedom of religion and laicity of the state are indeed established, but for laicity neither an adequate juridical nor a practical framework has been created (Montero 2006), so that in the end everyone behaves as they please – which can be recognized very clearly from election propaganda and the Bancada Evangélica.

We have pointed out above that Samuel Huntington diagnosed a tension in US foreign policy between a readiness for crusades and isolationism (Huntington 1982, 241f.). A similar ambivalence can be observed with regard to central religious beliefs. If the self-image of chosenness and uniqueness as well as the millennialist project (especially in premillennialist understanding) is combined with the quest for moral and religious perfection, the result is greater plausibility on the part of isolation. If, however, puritanical dispositions are combined with the interest in territorial or resource-related expansion, then the mission motif and the readiness to demonize turn into symbolic operators of a crusade. In the past two hundred years the latter has had the upper hand (cf. Williams 1980).

With regard to Latin America it is safe to say that there are no strong linkages to the US tension between isolationism and crusade as a foreign policy pattern. International attacks and corresponding efforts are the exception in Latin America. Religious crusades by Latin American Protestantism have – until the recent past – only been carried out nationally. However, this has changed with the Neopentecostal megachurches. The Igreja Universal do Reino de Deus is active in well over 100 countries; many other megachurches from the most diverse countries also have enterprises in various other Latin American countries, the USA or – mostly very small branches – in Europe. Furthermore, in 1987 various Latin American organizations founded the Cooperación Misionera Iberoamericana (COMIBAM) and in 1995 the organization AD2000 and beyond (which carry out the mission through the 10/40 Window) as attempts to exert transnational influence (with support from the USA; cf. Schäfer 2013). The signs begin to turn in the direction of crusades.

The fact that US-American Protestantism can only be linked to Latin American society to a limited extent, and that the entanglement has thus provoked a whole series of changes, can also be traced back to a fundamental difference. Following the categories proposed by Vamik Volkan (2018, 17ff.), a Turkish-American psychoanalyst, for the identity formation of large groups (such as peoples), one could speak of a "chosen triumph" for the white Protestant population in the USA. That is, of an identity that goes back to the utopia of the New Jerusalem, the Light of the Peoples, and proved victorious with the War of Independence. Appropriate objects of externalization are – depending on the degree of exclusivity of the perceived triumph – immigrants (such as the Catholic Irish in the 19th century or Hispanos today), foreign powers such as communism or Islam, or simply all non-whites. What corresponding category could be established for Latin American Protestants? One cannot speak of "chosen triumph," that goes without saying. But when one takes account of the way the political active among them see themselves, one can perhaps speak instead of "chosen conquest."

The "chosen triumph" connects also to yet another observation. The revolution, the act of the birth of modernity, is perceived as having been achieved with independence or even earlier with the Puritan colonies. The nation and the religious community represent the successful revolution, the embodied utopia, the Light of the Peoples, the ideal shape of modernity. In its self-perception, society is therefore already revolutionary thanks to its religion, i.e. to Evangelical Protestantism. Another revolution would have no point and thus be meaningless. Society can at most fall away from the true Protestant orientation. Then it must be taken back to its origins. Revolution is therefore restoration. This view of things provokes in white Evangelicals a negative attitude to the developments of the 20th century, especially its second half (cf. Jones et al. 2016, 8, 17). If one does not share this tradition or only to a small extent (like the Black churches or the Hispano Catholics and -Evangelicals), the future looks rather positive (cf. Jones et al. 2016, 8). Revolutions – if necessary – and reforms are not understood as part of a restoration, but lie in the future and still have to be realized. Against this background, the otherwise rather problematic distinction between progressive and conservative makes sense; however, "conservative" should in that case be understood as synonymous with "restorative."

In Latin America, independence has not yet set the seal on the liberal revolution. The neo-liberal revolution of the last few decades may have fulfilled the dream of the economic liberals of the 19th century. For the majority of the population, however, and the majority of Protestants it has become a social nightmare. In Latin America, the revolutions are still in the future. The question is whether you want them, and if so, what kind of revolution you prefer.

4. The Social Question "from Below"

The Protestant movement in Latin America has indeed developed very different ideas about what the future society might look like. The Committee on Cooperation in Latin America (CCLA) consistently continued the work of the Panama Congress and after several regional conferences in 1925 convened another mission congress in Montevideo (Prien 1978, 916ff.). This congress was already much more strongly marked by Latin Americans. Of approx. 250 delegates only 50 were from the USA. In the meantime the CCLA had advanced interchurch networking, and several Historical churches had joined the transnational world federations of their respective confessions. Instead of this work aimed at religious reproduction and consolidation, the Chilean National Committee demanded that the relationship between capital and labor be thematized, while others put greater emphasis on peace work in the League of Nations or cooperation with governments in the fields of education and health. The follow-up congress for nations on the Caribbean, Havana 1929, is an important date for the history of entanglement, calling as it did for Latin American control over Protestant work in Latin America (Prien 1978, 919ff.). The congress was organized by Latin Americans. The US missionaries were told that they could no longer demand blind obedience and that they should study intensively Latin American history, culture and language before being sent to the conference. In Havana there was a break, and the beginning of a reorganization of the work of Historical Protestantism in Latin America under its own steam, produced especially through the youth and student work in the organizations Unión Latinoamericana de Juventud Evangélica (ULAJE), the YMCA and the Movimiento Estudiantil Cristiano (MEC). Many Evangelical and Pentecostal missions continued to work for several decades under missionary hegemony and later experienced their independence shock.

4.1 Brazil: Society and Church

This change in entanglement relations developed especially quickly in Brazil. It was assisted by two circumstances in particular, which allow to draw systematic conclusions about the interplay between international missions and national politics. First, the national independence of Protestant actors in Brazil and the Cono Sur is exemplified and strengthened by immigrant churches (such as the Lutherans), in which missionaries naturally played no role. Second, hardly any missionaries from the USA have been active in Brazil in Pentecostal churches (and only a few from Sweden). At the same time, national religious actors engaged very early on in politics at various levels, first at the local level. Our thesis is that missionaries prevent political engagement because their primary interest is quantitative success in church membership, this is after all what they are measured by at home. Accordingly, Pentecostal churches in other Latin American countries have also experienced from the 1960s onwards an increase in social and political commitment along with the increasing independence of churches from missionaries.

Christian Socialism

Historical Protestantism is associated with the conference in Panama by the Presbyterian churchman Erasmo Braga.[37] In addition, impulses from the ecumenical movement (from the working groups "Mission and Evangelism" and "Life and Work" in fact long before the foundation of the World Council of Churches [WCC]) contribute to the organization of a church youth movement and the umbrella organization Confederação Evangélica do Brasil (CEB; since 1934) with its managing director Waldo César. Influences from the student and trade union movements caused more and more articles

---

37 For what follows cf.: Prien 1978; Schilling 2016, 69ff., outstanding on the connection with the World Council of Churches; Sinner 2012, 58f.; Ferreira Vilela n.d.; Conrado 2008; Calvani 2015; Cesar 2007; Silva 2017; Barreto Jr. 2010; Lienemann-Perrin und Lienemann 2006.

critical of capitalism to appear in the magazine *Mocidade* (Youth) in the early 1950s. There are also theological publications from the pen of the Presbyterian missionary and Professor Richard Shaull, who was identified with the movement and propagated the European theology of Karl Barth and Dietrich Bonhoeffer. In 1953 César, Shaull and others organized an ecumenical working group on the social responsibility of the churches – at the very moment that the World Council of Churches in Geneva, founded in 1949, created the working unit "Church and Society." The General Assembly of the WCC in Evanston in 1954 and subsequent meetings in Latin America lent impetus to the founding of the Comissão Igreja e Sociedade (Church and Society Commission) in 1955 with three areas of activity: politics, rural problems, industry and labor force. Close cooperation was also arranged with the WCC.[38] Several consultations and meetings on social issues aroused the interest of many other church people in questions of the public responsibility of churches. The actors exercised self-criticism against the Protestant flight from social responsibility to hide behind pure moralism and work on socio-structural problems from an ethical angle. This dynamic – at the same time incidentally as the conversion campaigns of In-Depth-Evangelism were running in Central America – led to the foundation of the Latin America-wide association Iglesia y Sociedad en América Latina (ISAL) in 1962 in São Paulo (Schilling 2016, 100). The journal *Cristianismo y Sociedad*, published from 1963 onwards, was to be central through 2000 to the ecumenical movement in Latin America, which was engaged in the social question. The magazine's discontinuation shows a window on the current financial difficulties of socially engaged Christianity in Latin America and of the ecumenical movement worldwide.

38 As numerous members of the working unit were Methodists (Julio de Santa Ana, José Míguez Bonino, Oscar Bolioli et al.), study programs were developed from 1960 with the *Instituto Metodista* in São Paulo, while its activities were put on a broader academic basis.

Dictatorship and Resistance

In the early 1960s, the socially engaged Protestants worked in synergy with João Goulart's politics, which tended to meet the legal demands of disadvantaged classes and liberalized society culturally – Bossa Nova, Niemeyer's architecture, etc. Thus, like Goulart, they met with stronger rejection from conservative circles. In 1964, the military staged a coup, and General Castello Branco also took action against church activists with a hard hand and accusations of communism. Conservative Protestants, on the other hand, participated in the hunt for "communists" by denouncing "suspects" from among their own churches. The incriminated activists went into exile, into the underground or into open resistance. A special achievement in 1973 by the resistance together with the Catholic Bishops' Conference was the founding of the development organization Coordenadoria Ecumênica de Serviço (CESE), which still works successfully today.[39] Between 1979 and 1985 CESE secretly compiled a documentation of torture and other human rights violations: *Brasil Nunca Mais* (Brazil Never Again). Through its achievements in the resistance, ecumenically-oriented Protestantism has been able to hold its ground in Brazil beyond the dictatorship and today plays a clearly stronger role than for instance in Central America, Colombia, Peru or Chile. ISAL works as the central organ in socially engaged Latin American Protestantism, develops similar positions as Liberation Theology and has a close dialogue with it. In 1975 ISAL had to stop its work under increasing repression after an attack on the residence of its General Secretary Julio de Santa Ana in Uruguay. At the end of the 1970s the ecumenically oriented Consejo Latino Americano de Iglesias (CLAI) emerged from this line of ecumenical work in Latin American Protestantism. Most of the actors who today continue to work in this line maintain close relations with the World Council of Churches and with partner (not: missionary) organizations in the USA. The latter, in their turn, are the for-

39 https://www.cese.org.br/ (accessed 3 May 2019).

mer missionary societies generally transformed by experiences in Latin America and the Third World.

If one looks at the religious discourses as well as the goals and strategies of these actors, one still moves in the field of Protestantism, but in a completely different world from that of all its other religio-political formations. We are now not dealing with a transforming adaptation of US-American convictions to Latin American reality. Rather, the pedagogy of the oppressed that Paulo Freire developed in Brazil has been used here as a starting point to focus on social problems. Emotionality, miracles or the Ten Commandments have given way to topics like "problems in the countryside" and "industry and labor force" as objects of sociological analysis and theological reflection on ethical recommendations. Later in Protestant and Catholic Liberation Theology this way of working was called the "hermeneutic circle" of seeing, judging and acting. An important feature that distinguishes it from the other formations of Protestantism is theological self-criticism. This promotes open-mindedness for dialogue with all conceivable actors instead of a discourse of conversion.

Dynamics of Entanglements

As concerns the dynamics of entanglement, a multi-stage process can be discerned here. First, the impulse of the Social Gospel (Braga and the Panama Conference) was reformulated from the perspective of the radical problems of Latin American social inequality and structural violence. Second, the theological look was diversified by also receiving European Protestant thinking. Third, to obtain support for the new approach new international contacts were established with organizations with a similar focus (the WCC). Fourth, Latin American cooperative networks were built. Fifth, joint ecumenical learning also provoked changes in the worldview of the US-American partners so that the relations could be given a new definition. To these processes a biographical approach could also be applied.

The Presbyterian missionary Richard Shaull began in Brazil to develop his "Theology of Revolution," remained identified throughout his life with Brazil also through his exile and documented this attitude with diverse social engagements also in the USA in later years. Gloria and Ross Kinsler, another Presbyterian missionary couple, began working in the conservative Presbyterian seminary in Guatemala, came to identify with Liberation Theology both through their political experiences there and many years of cooperation in the program for contextual theological education of the World Council of Churches, and in their last years went to the ecumenical Universidad Bíblica Latinoamericana in Costa Rica. There they encountered the married couple Irene and Robert Foulkes, who in 1955 had been sent by the Latin America Mission to the ultraconservative Seminario Bíblico Latinoamericano (forerunner of the Universidad, Costa Rica). The Foulkes experienced a student "coup" in the early 1970s that put the school on the course to Liberation Theology and caused some missionaries to resign. The Foulkes decided to stay and change over to the Latinos. In 1957 Doris and John Stam were also sent to the Seminario Bíblico; they made the same decision as the Foulkes, but then also took on teaching appointments in Nicaragua and Cuba, and from Latin America they also became strongly involved in the USA to propagate a Liberation Theology of a Protestant mold.

Sometime later the Evangelical movement was also to experience similar developments, though in this case breaks were harder.

4.2 Cochabamba: Church and Society

The congresses in Montevideo and Havana and the experiences in Brazil indicated a new development, which admittedly did not spread to the whole of the missionary Protestantism in Latin America. The conservative Evangelical missionaries who were organized in the Interdenominational Foreign Missions Association (IFMA, 1917) and later, since 1945, under the Evangelical Foreign Missions Association (EFMA), as well as non-organized large Pentecostal churches have simply continued to missionize following the old model of leadership by missionaries. From the 1960s onwards, the Pentecostal churches have seen the emergence of new, now national, second-generation leadership strata, which development led to an increasing number of secessions from the US-American mission churches as well as new foundations. Thus, as already indicated, socio-ethical topics and undertakings were increasingly put on the agenda. The conservative missions – which did not yet form an organized religious right – reacted with accusations of communism and the insinuation that the reforming actors wanted to eradicate true Christianity in order to cooperate with the "communist" World Council of Churches.

CONELA

Along this line the foundation of the ecumenical Latin American Council of Churches (CLAI, officially decided in 1978 at an important Protestant conference in Mexico and founded in 1982 in Peru) was already answered in 1982 with the foundation of a counter-organization.[40] The idea for the Confraternidad Evangélica Latinoamericana (CONELA) originated with an activist group at a Billy Graham congress in Pattaya, Thailand, under the leadership of two coworkers of the US-American-Argentinian mass-evangelist Luis Palau. Palau financed the founding of CONELA in Panama in 1982 and provided the first Secretary General. CONELA did not succeed in recruiting a significant number of important members of the prevailing, liberal-conservative Fraternidad Teológica Latinoamericana. But CONELA denounced CLAI on the grounds of communism, radicalism and everything else that was usually marshalled, and the resulting polarization was made a theme or was at least noticeable in almost all talks with Latin American Protestants in the 1980s and 1990s. As an organization, however, CONELA is much less well known. The interlocutors who belonged to this organization

40 For a good treatment of CONELA see Stoll 1990, 132ff.

were characterized by tough fundamentalist positions and their orientation to Donald McGavran's Church-Growth strategy as well as US-American mission Protestantism. This corresponds to the fact that – as Stoll notes – CONELA is supported by the right-wing missionary establishment of the USA, including Billy Graham, Campus Crusade for Christ, Overseas Crusades and Luis Palau. In addition, many of their leaders and media personalities are stationed in the US. So here we have a cooptation and control model of transnational entanglement: a Latin American organization created and controlled from the USA represents positions of the conservative US-American mission movements and the religious right as "Latin American".

FTL

C. Peter Wagner, the US-American missionary and agitator, had something similar in mind a little earlier with the Latin American Mission Congress (CLADE I) and with the Fraternidad Teológica Latinoamericana (FTL).[41] Wagner was a missionary in Bolivia, later Church Growth guru for the quantitatively oriented US-American mission and finally Neopentecostal inventor of demonological subtleties like the territorial spirits. Wagner knows how to attribute the role of the protagonist to himself. The antagonists are, *pars pro toto,* three very well trained young Evangelical leaders: René Padilla from Ecuador, Samuel Escobar from Peru, and Orlando Costas from Puerto Rico.

As a continuation of the World Mission Congress of Billy Graham Industries in Berlin in 1966, Latin American Evangelicals organized the *Congreso Latinoamericano de Evangelización I* (CLADE I) in Bogotá in 1969. Moreover, one cannot help feeling that the Congress was to present an Evangelical response to the *Tercera Conferencia Evangélica Latinoamericana* (CELA III), which was organized by the World Council of Churches in the same year. The

41 Salinas 2009; Swartz 2012; Clawson 2012; Gutiérrez 2015b.

answer was in almost every respect US-American – except for the fact that very many delegates from Latin American churches were present who were locked in a daily struggle with need, violence and repression. Wagner arranged for his treatise on *Latin American Theology: Radical or Evangelical?* to be distributed free of charge to all participants. In it he distinguished three types of Christians in Latin America: conservative Protestants, the conservative Catholic hierarchy, and left-wing radicals with a secularized theology. Since nothing reasonable, he explained, could be heard about the relationship between church and world from Latin American Protestantism, the left-wing flood could only be stemmed with his model of church growth. While the Americans were all enthusiastic, the Latinos were indignant. Escobar, who according to the plans was to talk about the benefits of the free US economy in Latin America, gave a speech about the social responsibility of the church, about the sale of the gospel to a middle class ideology, the imposition of a US-American agenda, the necessary renunciation of foreign aid and the confrontation with "Anglo" theologies.

Already one year later, in December 1970, a group of Evangelical Latin American theologians founded the Fraternidad Evangélica Latinoamericana (FTL) in Cochabamba, Bolivia. Wagner failed on this occasion in his role as tormentor. He appeared at the founding meeting with a self-authored, finished draft of the FTL statutes and demanded that this paper be officially accepted. Wagner not only wanted to push through the inerrancy of Scripture, but also to tie the financial viability of the FTL to compliance with theological conditions. Of course, Wagner did not get away with it. Two years later the Evangelical Foreign Missions Association (EFMA, since 1945) threatened to withdraw a financial pledge if the FTL was to invite the liberal theologian José Míguez Bonino to a meeting. The reply states that "you are not going to tell us who to invite and who not to invite. This is the FTL [emphasis on the L]" (Swartz 2012, 120). The FTL represents Evangelical positions in many respects, but it takes seriously the hermeneutic procedure of Liberation Theology, appreciates its exegesis, criticizes US imperialism and the identification of faith with capitalism, and attaches great importance to the social responsibility of the churches. The attempt to reconcile Liberation Theology and Evangelical identity is hermeneutic, through the determination of the contextualism of all knowledge – a realization diametrically opposed to the naive positivism of conservative Evangelical theology in the USA. The FTL sees itself as steering a middle course between Marxism and militaristic anti-communism.

Effects in the USA

A special effect of these activities is their repercussions on Evangelicalism in the USA. Important representatives of the FTL have studied in the USA, maintain good relations with it and are invited to lectures and seminars. The bulletin of the FTL also appears in English and can thus make an impact on the USA. Escobar's appearance at the Congress of World Evangelization in Lausanne in 1974, which was organized by Billy Graham's organization, was particularly effective: about a dozen members of the FTL criticized the US-American narrowing of the Gospel to a head count and its attachment to North American culture, hit out at the war enthusiasm among the Evangelical elites, raised the issue of the rights of the Palestinians vis-à-vis Israel, and demanded holistic evangelization (*misión integral*). Above all, with the help of a pressure group they inserted a long article on the social responsibility of the church into the final communiqué of the conference and thus into the overall program of the Lausanne movement (World Evangelical Fellowship 1974, Section 5). Wagner and other fighters of his stripe would in no way agree with it, but the large number of delegates from the Third World did. In addition, the action increased the FTL's influence among the Evangelical left that was forming at the time in the USA around Jim Wallis and his Sojourners and Ron Sider's Evangelicals for Social Action as well as other organizations. To the present day, according to Clawson, the after-effects are still noticeable, for example when it comes to movements for integral mission according to Padilla's ideas.

Through the strategists of the FTL, who are more interested in social questions, Latin America has also been brought into sharper focus with the Evangelical left in the USA, which thus has reversed, if one can say so, the objective direction of entanglement, In this it is similar to the ecumenical Protestantism of Latin America, which has been supplying the discourses and practices of Mainline Protestantism with theological ideas for a long time – with the only difference that FTL knows how to address the Evangelicals in a language appropriate to them. This reversal of the entanglement direction can perhaps be understood as a Pan-Americanism from the south. It must not be forgotten that Bolívar and San Martín are also responsible for the Pan-American idea. In any case, the reversal was to play an important role in the conflicts over the wars in Central America.

5. Wars: Military and Spiritual

During the Central American Wars in the 1980s entanglements of a particularly intensive kind occurred between interested actors in the north and south, which went far beyond religious praxis into the political and military fields. Military support and the weapons of Spiritual Warfare were supplied by the USA. And the spark of the Central American fights fired political confrontations in the USA.

5.1 Spiritual Warfare

During the Cold War, its logic made itself felt also in the way religious actors in general and mission agencies in particular saw themselves. According to this view, the world wanted to be understood in a dualistic and antagonistic way. An increasing number of agencies perceived their mission as a war against demons.

Classic Pentecostalism makes a space for the exorcism of demons in the treatment of (psychic) illnesses when a physician would be too expensive. The shock of the civil rights movement, the protests against the Vietnam War and the student movement as well as the (upper) middle class perspective of the Neopentecostal movement brought about authoritarian forms of community leadership in the 1970s in the Shepherding or Discipleship Movements.[42] In this and similar environments, a hard dualistic interpretation of world events proved to be practical for internal discipline paired with aggressive external expansion. The motif of the struggle against demons is extended to the most diverse social fields, naturally also to politics. The logic is simple: the world is full of demons, which puts pressure on Christians and above all everyone else, which is why Christians have to enter into the anti-demon war. From the 1970s, this type of literature has been growing, not only in religious treatis-

42 Relevant names are Bob Mumford, Ern Baxter, Derek Prince. See Schäfer 1992c, 76ff.

es, but also in fiction.[43] This logic is followed also in the field of external mission by more and more agencies. In 1985 the Association of International Mission Services (AIMS, later Accelerating International Mission Strategies) was founded as an umbrella organization of 50 mission societies with about 1,000 missionaries, and was supported in every respect by EFMA and IFMA. AIMS has the objective "[to] generate the spiritual power to overcome Satan's rule among the nations" (Roberts and Siewert 1989, 38f.). Other mission organizations, such as the well-staffed Youth with a Mission (YWAM), also follow the line of the theocratic Dominion doctrine in external mission and are associated with the religious right (Diamond 1989, 206). This tendency has not passed by the mission specialist C. Peter Wagner. With its almost Fordist strategy of the production of numerically recorded conversion products, the Church Growth movement, now led by Wagner, was directed primarily to Latin America out of old feelings of solidarity. But the Latinos had snubbed him and his strategy. Escobar had publicly attacked it for its "cold pragmatism," and the FTL had signaled to him it could well do without him. The program of a war against demons together with the authoritarian turn of the Neopentecostals were offering a new chance. Wagner used his privileged position to proclaim, first, the "Third Wave" of Pentecostalism, the Pentecostalization of the Evangelicals – which also effected not least the legitimation of his own turn to Neopentecostal strategies. Towards the end of the millennium (at the beginning of the "Second Apostolic Age, roughly in 2001")[44] he proclaimed himself an apostle and member of an international apostle council; naturally with the ability to receive direct and authoritative revelations from God and with the mandate from God to represent the hardest 7-Mountain Dominionism. The Domin-

43 Bubeck 1975; 1984; Dawson 1989; Dickason 1987. See also for example the novels of Frank Peretti.

44 International Coalition of Apostolic Leaders: https://www.icaleaders.com/about-ical/definition-of-apostle (accessed 02.10.2019). Cf. also Eagles Vision Apostolic Team and New Apostolic Reformation (NAR).

ion doctrine, however, needs opponents. Wagner had therefore earlier established the ideology of Spiritual Warfare, respectively, in the missionary movement and the international communication of Neopentecostal actors in the USA and Latin America. The focus is on the political effects of the doctrine, interpreted as a struggle against territorial spirits that dominate entire countries. In military parlance, Wagner distinguishes the ground level for interpersonal exorcism from the occult level against witchcraft, astrology and Satanism, and finally from the strategic or cosmic level on which exorcism is practiced on demonically possessed governments. For the latter, one must – as carried out in praxis in Guatemala – undertake a spiritual mapping of regions which allows the war aims to be precisely determined. It is manifest that Wagner and his mission friends did not get to first base with this ideology with the socially responsible Evangelicals of the FTL. To make up for this, he gained financially more potent allies in the Neopentecostal upper class, who – like Harold Caballeros from Guatemala – are occasionally mentioned in the Panama Papers. The Spiritual Warfare ideology, however, was no longer imposed mainly as a doctrine of missionaries on the native Protestants; many of the classic missions remained with Church Growth. After all, what were starved and militarily oppressed small farmers to do with Spiritual Warfare – unless use it as an artful deterrent against "communism"? The arsenal of Spiritual Warfare was instead much more acknowledged, actively received and used by the Neopentecostal groups in the upper and upper middle classes, especially in Guatemala, as a religio-symbolic weapon in the counter-insurgency war in Central America.

5.2 Guatemala: City upon a Hill

Hotel Panamericano

On entering the restaurant of the prestigious *Hotel Panamericano*, you see in the small foyer on your left in a glass case the hotel's open visitors' book from the 1950s. The number of US American military officers among the guests is astonishing. It is somewhat less surprising if you remind yourself that a coup d'état was staged against the Social Democrat President Jacobo Arbenz because of his "communism." The putsch took place in 1954 at the request of the United Fruit Company (Chiquita), the putschists being helped by the first secret operation of the CIA. From this time on through the late 1980s, military dictatorships and the resistance of guerilla units determined one of the bloodiest histories of Latin America. In an interview with the present author, Julia Esquivel, a Presbyterian human rights activist who died recently and was a member of the Iglesia Guatemalteca en el Exilio, shared a reminiscence when she heard as a little girl bombs being dropped by US American airplanes that scared the city's inhabitants. She also recollected how she discovered in her youth, under the impression of the dictatorship, a simple gospel, that of Jesus of Nazareth, who was poor himself and always prepared to help the poor and outcast. In the late 1970s, at the start of the period of the worst repression, she was brutally tortured but managed to make her escape into exile with the help of *indigenas*. If you talk – as I did on the very day of the interview – with one of the leading Neopentecostals about that time today, you will find that what counts for him above all is that his organization saw a dramatic upturn in those days. He had nothing but praise for the Neopentecostal dictator Efrain Ríos Montt, who transformed what before were random killings into a systematic operation thanks to his military training in the USA. The general, he asserted, had to order the public execution of only nine bandits, after which things calmed down. The problem was the European human rights organizations, he continued, who beleaguered Guatemala. The picture is, however, completely different if you talked to people in the war zone: a boy in Nebaj told us he had to watch how his entire village, including his parents and brothers and sisters, was slaughtered.

Figures

The figures of the Truth Commission established by the UN (CEH 1999) also are a little higher than the pastor claimed. The total number of victims is about 200,000 people, in their majority indigenous civilians massacred by the army and paramilitary forces; there were also hundreds of villages burnt down, in part using napalm; countless cases of torture and "disappearances" of people; about 1 million war refugees and serious ecological damage in consequence. The army was responsible for more than 90% of the dead. The Reagan administration was involved with material and personal military assistance, ending an embargo in 1983 which had been imposed for human rights violations. Reagan was pleased with Montt's Christian attitude. The violence used was, however, of such drastic nature that Bill Clinton felt impelled to make an official apology to the Guatemalan people. Ríos Montt was sentenced to 80 years in prison in 2013 for genocide and crimes against humanity. But what is that to do with religious entanglement?

US Politics and Religion

A general answer to this question can be obtained from the document "The Road to Damascus. Kairos and Conversion" (Catholic Institute for International Relations 1989), produced by a commission of theologians from Guatemala, Nicaragua, El Salvador, South Africa, Namibia, South Korea and the Philippines. The document states that in order to preserve the idolatry of money in the North Atlantic interest, the strategy of low intensity conflict is applied in the Third World – a strong form of entanglement, so to speak. This strategy is directed against the new phenomenon of guerrilla warfare, combining military violence with social projects as well as ideological and religious propaganda. Very specifically, the US Army's Field Manuals FM 31-16 and FM 31-176 (Fort Bragg) recommend that religious conditions be observed in military and psychological operating areas. In 1976, the Senate's investigating committee on secret service activities under Senator Frank Church found a direct operational use of 21 US American religious individuals – not counting foreigners (United States Senate 1976). Journalist Sara Diamond (1989, 207) cites the Evangelical magazine *Christianity Today* (CT), which asserted that employees of preacher Luis Palau were regularly debriefed by the CIA in the 1970s. According to CT, between 10% and 25% of US missionaries passed on information to the CIA.

Since the 1960s, religion has also become the political focus to a greater extent in public studies of Latin America. Thus, in the larger context of the Alliance for Progress and in cooperation with the Rockefeller Foundation, a research project of the University of Notre Dame examined the Catholic Church in Latin America.[45] Soon after, Nelson Rockefeller, the Governor of New York, set out on a fact-finding trip to Latin America at the request of President Nixon. In his 1969 report the young military officers and the Catholic Church are portrayed as forces of possible revolutionary change. The church is "more responsive to the popular will," "vulnerable to subversive penetration" and – with the legendary Bishops' Conference of Medellín in 1968 in mind – "dedicated ... to revolutionary change if necessary" (United States 1969). The Santa Fe papers, prepared for the Reagan administration by a planning group from 1980 onwards, present the situation in an even more dramatic light and give the advice to proactively attack Liberation Theology instead of only reacting after the event. Consequently, it goes on to say, it is necessary to analyze and fight the Christian grassroots movement,[46] and to use religion for psychological warfare.

45 D'Antonio and Pike 1964, containing only one contribution on Protestantism by Emilio Willems.

46 This was proposed also in the documents of the XVIIth Conference of American Armies, 1987. Cf. Duchrow, Eisenbürger and Hippler 1989.

War: Verbo and FUNDAPI

The situation in Central America around 1980 was indeed worrying for the strategists in Washington and the local oligarchies. With the help of US embassies, these oligarchies had for the best part of the 20th century exploited people and kept them under the thumb of political violence, torture, kidnappings, murders and massacres. The dynasty of the Somoza's in Nicaragua was particularly prominent in this respect. To give just one example of the horror of which I was informed by a credible eyewitness well known to my wife and me, who was a resident of the village of Masaya: after the liberation of the country, the Sandinistas opened the dungeons of the Coyotepe fortress and found people some of whom had had to lie in their own excrement without light for decades, pale, debilitated, disfigured. Many of the inmates died of light and air after their release. The spirits of these and other atrocities began to persecute the oligarchies of El Salvador, Honduras and Guatemala in the late 1970s, and the spirit of communism represented by the guerrilla troops caused alarm in the US military.

In Guatemala,[47] the oppression under General Romeo Lucas García in the late 1970s also became rampant in the capital with massacres and random murders, and since the victory of the Sandinistas in Nicaragua in 1979 the guerrilla movements and the people's uprising gained new momentum. The Panamericana – the most important highway in the Americas – was no longer safe to drive on, the guerrillas were advancing to the capital, and General Lucas disposed of no viable military strategy. But General Ríos Montt, a modern military man trained at Fort Gulick and the School of the Americas, came up with a couple of ideas. He was also a member of the Neopentecostal group El Verbo/Gospel Outreach, which had

47 There are several very competent histories of the war as well as of the general. This is why I can restrict myself here to a few notes. Melander 1999 is highly recommended; also important is Garrard-Burnett 2010, as well as other work by this historian; Stoll 1990; on military violence from an ethnological perspective cf. Montejo 2008.

been missionizing in Guatemala among the upper middle class since the mid-1970s, like many other organizations that came to the country after the 1976 earthquake. Now, whether Ríos Montt had a part in the planning of the coup that brought him to power in March 1982 or whether it was an invitation to join the military junta, issued by God himself following a prophecy, as El Verbo claims, who can say? In any case, Ríos Montt fundamentally changed military strategy: keep the capital as quiet as possible but scorched earth in the countryside, where the press has less easy access.

The selective repression against the catechists and activists of the Catholic Church in indigenous areas was continued. The bishop of the Quiché diocese was forced into exile. And lastly, many rural Catholics called themselves Protestants in order to enjoy at least a comparative security. Above all, however, the new military strategy operated, according to the counter-insurgency doctrine, with a combination of military cruelty and social projects, bringing conservative Protestant aid organizations into play. After Ríos Montt took power, the leaders of the Verbo Church seized the opportunity to assist the government of the new "King David" by substituting funds for the social part of the counter-insurgency. In the hottest conflict zone, the Ixil Triangle in the north of the country, they took part in an extensive program that offered various services.

El Verbo was partner of the US Gospel Outreach mission, which founded the organization International Lovelift for fundraising and infrastructure purposes. In Guatemala, El Verbo, the medical Carol Berhorst Foundation and the Summer Institute of Linguistics jointly set up the Fundación para Ayuda a los Pueblos Indígenas (FUNDAPI, Foundation for Indigenous Peoples). Harris Whitbeck, an ex-marine, coordinated the work with the government. The foundation supported the military counter-insurgency campaign "Plan Victoria 82" in a variety of ways, by providing aid and organizing civil activities such as food for work programs. The fact that Lovelift's work consisted not only in collecting donations and transporting relief goods is important for the nature of the entanglement between religious actors in Latin America and the USA. It was also linked to a broad public campaign, for the support of which important actors of the religious right in the USA were mobilized, such as the Neopentecostal TV preacher Pat Robertson, Bill Bright from the Campus Crusade for Christ, and Jerry Falwell, the dyed-in-the-wool fundamentalist representative of the Moral Majority. In addition there were semiofficial government contacts, as when Francisco Bianchi, the Verbo elder, met with government members on the issue of help for Guatemala in the USA in June 1982 (Diamond 1989, 165). The organization's information policy towards donors and visitors to Guatemala also helped. Interestingly, the arguments used were often in line with imperialist strategies on raw materials in the context of the East-West conflict. The advertisers simply assumed that this was a plausible religious argument – and probably were not too far wrong if you look at the addressees of their advertisements. Carlos Ramirez and Bob Means, both members of the Verbo board, addressed donors in a circular on 1 September 1982 and let them know that by helping Ríos Montt they would weaken the Marxists' position and reduce their ability to derive benefit from Guatemala's rich oil, titanium and other resources (Schäfer 1992b, 223).

On site in Guatemala, the Verbo employees advertised counterinsurgency measures to visitors and attributed proven massacres of the military to the guerrillas. Such "alternative facts" then generated "specialists" who, after returning to the USA, claimed in the main that the atrocities committed by the army were actually carried out by infiltrated Cuban agents scattered throughout the country (Stoll 1990, 192, 206). It is in this sense that Lovelift describes itself as US-America's most effective contribution to the cause of freedom in the Latin world. Maranatha Campus Ministries, similarly, was going to exterminate communism in this Central American country (Schäfer 1992b, 229). It really seems as if social work – like the charitable work of the early conversion missions – was not entirely focused on the social, but on some third objective. And this third goal was now no longer the conversion to Christ in the narrower sense, but the conversion to a God with a specific political position.

In an interview with the journalist Viola Schmid on 27 October 1987, Ríos Montt summarized his position in this way. When asked whether Verbo maintained something like medical aid programs he answered:

> That means humanistic religiosity. We have, due to present circumstances, hospitals and all that sort of thing. But that's not what concerns us or even interests us. (Schäfer 1992b, 229)

It is fairly clear that the decisive contribution of El Verbo and the whole network was the cooperation with the counterinsurgency. This also applies to psychological warfare. Field Manual 31-16[48] thematizes the traumatic consequences in counterinsurgency soldiers of operations against suspicious children and women. In the late 1980s, Ríos Montt used the "Project Whole Armor" to bring in 70,000 Bibles for military personnel from the USA to Guatemala. An advertising leaflet from Bible Literature International described how a caregiver used the Bible to release a soldier from his guilty feelings about burning children and women. A preacher from Paralife Ministries, Texas, expressed this in somewhat different terms in front of soldiers in El Salvador:

> Killing for the joy of it was wrong, but killing because it was necessary to fight against an anti-Christ system, communism, was not only right but a duty of every Christian. (Diamond 1989, 177)

Religious Demand and Supply

This conflict of low intensity had psychological consequences of high intensity primarily for civilians, and was far from hitting only those soldiers directly involved in counter-insurgency operations. Different civilians were affected in different ways, depending on their social class and (consequently) their residential area. The indigenous rural poor were thus most directly affected while the urban

48 Department of the Army Headquarters 1971, 222; cf. also Schäfer 1992b, 233.

middle and upper classes suffered least. Above all, however, the different actors of these social classes managed the various hardships of the war in different religious ways. They brought with them religious dispositions which depended on their positions in society: indigenous religion and popular Catholicism versus Orthodox Catholicism or Evangelicalism. They were exposed to different new offers from religious production: classic Pentecostalism and Evangelicalism versus Neopentecostalism. In the end, they had different chances to act and survive. Out of these factors arose a specific religious demand for experts (national religious leaders or missionaries from abroad, for example), who had to put together as best they could a topical religious offering tailored to the respective situation and social position of specific actors, and which was also able to mobilize as many people as possible in their respective religious organizations.[49] For a specific society, all this adds up to a complex picture of religious actors (cf. Schäfer 2015, 204, 215). Here we will have to confine ourselves to the simplest of all simple differentiations that between above and below – which is by the way quite well suited for the observation of a society polarized by two warring parties locked in class conflict.

This simplest of all possible differentiations manifests itself, incidentally, in homologous terms in the political perception of the social conflict by right-wing religious actors.

49 If you now think this concept of religious praxis is neo-Marxist or crudely materialist etc., I would like to refer you to Donald McGavran's and C. Peter Wagner's Church Growth Movement, whose missionary activities were carried out exactly according to these strategies in class-specific (!) terms. To be sure, this was rather more from a market-economic instinct for how religious praxis works in conditions of freedom of religion (i.e. under market conditions). For a scholarly approach you may want to refer to the classic treatments by Weber 1978, 468ff. Durkheim 1995; and also Bourdieu 1991. Lastly also to Schäfer et al. 2015a; 2015b, or to Schäfer 2020.

Left-Wingers and Right-Wingers

From a sociological point of view, the difference between the polarized US American missionary actors was that the ecumenical organizations identified with the interests of the lower social classes, that is those who suffered from the production and power conditions; the religious right, on the other hand, acted in the interest of those who wanted to maintain the existing power relations in a modernized form. Pat Robertson transformed this situation into a political mapping of the landscape and an adroit self-positioning of the religious right at the "center". He saw himself and people of his own kind *between* the "oppression of corrupt oligarchies" and the "tyranny of Russian-backed communist totalitarianism" (Stoll 1990, 182). In plain sociological language this means: on the position of the ascending, technocratic and neo-liberal wing of the upper and upper middle classes. For him, the ecumenists thus were on the "Marxist" side. Both groups of US-American actors clearly took up opposite positions in the conflict and so their association with power was also different: the party on the right was positively associated with the rulers, the ecumenists positively with the powerless.[50] This influenced the objective conditions for action in the entanglements. The right had substantially more freedom of movement and physical security; the ecumenists found themselves threatened with persecution, which manifested itself for example in the torture and exile of their church members and the departure of missionaries from Guatemala. The objective positioning was also reflected in the dispositions of the actors. The religious right showed a kratocentric, power-oriented religious habitus and identified with the very promising positions of the technocratic upper class. Their discourse revolved around the power of God and the exorcism of "demons". The ecumenists, by contrast, designed their strategies on the basis of identi-

50 This is the case in Nicaragua too. Power relations were turned on their head under the government of the Sandinistas, it is true, and the ecumenists were closely associated with power. But in external relations power rests with the USA, which becomes apparent in the embargo, the war against the Contras and the consequences of both in the country.

fication with a powerless Jesus *compañero* as an action of solidarity in the interest of a complete reorganization of the power relations, for example through reforms or revolution.

Mobilization from Above

The religious people among the well-to-do can safely be assumed to be religious because they get something out of religion and religious praxis has a personal meaning for them, and not because they want to cast a web of priestly deceit on society or lust after the role of a Rasputin. For religious actors to turn politician and then maybe come to like the role of whisperer, politician or even dictator, certain social conditions must be met which make that possible or likely. Much depends on the perception of their own position in the specific social situation – in our case on the perception of the war. The turn to politics is of course simpler and more probable for religious experts than for lay people. We have already briefly thrown some light on the dynamic for El Verbo, so now we can turn to the question of what was the situation of the lay people of the bourgeois middle and upper classes.

Even these people are not immune to the military, political and economic situation. The social psychologist Ignacio Martín-Baró – one of the Jesuits massacred by the military in El Salvador at the Universidad Centroamericana in 1989 – diagnosed for these social classes serious psychological consequences of war, such as persistent bulimia, alcoholism and other losses of control (Martín-Baró 1984). The analysis of my interviews with Neopentecostals of the upper middle and upper classes of Guatemala shows a whole range of statements that indicate futile search for meaning and addictive consumption behavior, which confirm Martín Baró's analyses: general pleasure-seeking, heavy consumption of drugs, stimulants and other consumer goods, bulimia, alcohol abuse, frequent visits to discos and parties as well as frequent changes of sexual partner. Martín-Baró speaks of the "amusement bulimia" of the Central American upper class when facing a crisis of hegemony (Martín-Baró

1984, 509). This amusement bulimia, he claims, was an expression of a negation of reality and a loss of reality. The incorporated upscale consumer goods are symbols of endangered or desired social positions. However, the strategy was counterproductive since it greatly reduced their ability to react to the crisis. The bulimic and at the same time compensatory incorporation of harmful consumer goods he takes to mean a somatization of the crisis and thus a subjection to it. The Neopentecostals, for their part, with their logic of Spiritual Warfare, exorcisms on believers and demonization of their social opponents, preferred to externalize the problems: devils and demons. The already internalized evil, the harmful substances and actions, were identified with demons and could thus be symbolically cast out by exorcism. On the other hand, the power of God and a joyful mood were incorporated during the services, through which affective problems were treated. As one of my interviewees said:

> I have now attained a joy and an inner peace that I did not have before. You always live with fear. Especially in a country like ours, which has so many problems, I lived in fear. And this fear in me is now gone. (Interview 88, with a Guatemalan peasant, 1986)

The social position of the upper middle class was, by the way, also objectively precarious. They found themselves between the extremes of the reactionary old oligarchy and the militarily active left. Under Lucas García, the upper middle class, former upwardly and then downwardly mobile, had no effective political representation in times of war. With Ríos Montt, such an alternative came into play because he was the Christian Democrats' candidate for the presidency in 1974. At the same time, Ríos Montt also offered a religious alternative. This was not unimportant because the rising middle class had a problem with religious belonging and therefore lacked the chance of a religious handling of psychological problems. Since Archbishop Penados del Barrio (1983 to 2001) at the latest, the Catholic bishops took a positive attitude towards human rights, while the religious orders had long been on the side of the insurgent rural population, and the indigenous catechists were anyway not the people to turn to and the charismatic movement's focus was still on the countryside. In the first half of the 1980s, the period of the most violent conflict, more and more alternatives established themselves in Guatemala. These were Neopentecostal groups, similar to El Verbo, from the USA and increasingly national ones. They included Fraternidad Christiana (1979, national), the Full Gospel Business Men's Fellowship International (FGBMFI [FIHNEC] 1979), El Shaddai (1983, national), and also at that time Elim Zona 10 (national), Hombres Cristianos (national) and Shekina. The positioning of all these groups is clear in terms of social class. A member of the Hombres Cristianos assured the present author that this group had "something special," "which is out of reach of the superstitious normal Pentecostal churches." There was, first, the social exclusivity of the meetings which took place in luxury hotels and "better" neighborhoods. It was also a change in the usual Pentecostal and Evangelical discourse, in Guatemala already well established (approx. 20% of the population was Protestant). While up to then premillennialism was invariably dominant and Protestants usually waited for their rapture into heaven, now the power of the Holy Spirit was moving into the center of their discourse and the time perspective was opening up in the direction of social change. This corresponded to a demand for meaning on the part of a social class that suffered from a loss of control but still had political and economic resources for action. The impulse was clearly strengthened by the dictatorship of Ríos Montt for the short time of his administration, and he also succeeded in anchoring the Neopentecostal option more firmly in the upper class. Members of oligarchic families such as the Verbo elder Francisco Bianchi built corresponding alliances (cf. Casaús Arzú 2007, 169f., 257).

Resistance to this approach was, nevertheless, considerable in the majority of Guatemalan Protestantism. This was not only the case among the marginalized population, for whom such a discourse made no sense, but also among the leaders of the important Pentecostal and Evangelical mass churches like the Asambleas de Dios, the Iglesia Centroamericana or Príncipe de Paz. These churches were firmly committed to premillennialism, made it obligatory in their creeds and were thus difficult or even impossible to mobilize for the struggle for a theocratic Guatemala. Even national Neopentecostal groups whose leaders were recruited from Evangelical and Pentecostal churches and who grew up with premillennialism were affected by the premillennialist inheritance. A habitus analysis of the Neopentecostals of 1985 clearly shows that in the movement itself there were contradictory positions on matters of millennialism. The mobilization of the population for a theocratic state under Ríos Montt or – after Ríos Montt – for a struggle for a radical transformation of society according to the US-American model was difficult to achieve if people were waiting for the rapture of the faithful within the next few weeks.

"But where there is danger, rescue grows stronger as well" (Hölderlin). John Carrette served as a Green Beret in the Vietnam War, went later to Guatemala and since the early 1970s had been running a hotel – however financed – in the tourist town of Antigua as well as the Hotel Panamericano in the capital.[51] Carrette recounted that he came to faith in the Vietnam War through a vision in his heart that told him that Jesus was Lord. In Guatemala he was, after the outbreak of the serious phase of the war and especially after the takeover of Ríos Montt, one of the central activists able to solve the millennialism problem. As a committed member of the FGBMFI and the Shekinah organization, Carrette spent much of his time on religious activities of political relevance: he organized Shekinah mission campaigns against communism in EI Salvador, founded the group of Intercesores de Guatemala (Intercessors for Guatemala; with participants from higher social classes), organized events for the nation of the FGBMFI, published religious-political treatises, spoke on radio and in 1979 financed in part the foundation of a new Protestant organization of Indian pastors, the Asociación Indigenista

51 Cf. Stoll 1990, 215ff.; Melander 1999, 175f. Interview with Carrette, Jan van Bilsen and Dirk van der Sypen, Belgian Television, 1986; Hotel Panamericano; based on the present author's research together with a profiler.

de Evangelización (ASIDE). In ASIDE, he propagated that Protestant indigenous people were not allowed to nominate or support their own candidates for political office. For counter-insurgency purposes, it was not the least important thing to exclude subaltern people from political participation opportunities – as long anyway as it could not be safely ruled out that they would organize in their own interest, and this was difficult to guarantee in the case of the Guatemalan Maya. The urban upper middle and upper classes, on the other hand, must be mobilized and indoctrinated with religious class struggle ideology. In March 1980, one and a half months before the coup of Ríos Montt in March 1980, Carrette drummed up for this purpose a group of pastors to join in a prayer for national salvation. What was special about the prayer was:

> They bound the devil in the name of Jesus and ordered him to leave the nation, and then having removed this hindrance to the blessing of God, they asked Jesus: now, heal our nation.[52]

His success, he said, was due to the fact that God through divine intervention had appointed Ríos Montt to take care of national affairs. Why was it necessary to bind the devil? Because, according to what Carrette explained in the same interview, he dominated Guatemala. Through a vision God made it clear to him why Central America was spiritually alive, but still at war. This vision sounds as if God had either looked into the handbook of the Puritan colony or dictated the handbook himself. The sickness of Central America, he continued, was therefore due to the fact that during the indigenous past the devil had dominated everything and that later the Catholic Church could not really do anything about it. When finally the gospel – the Neopentecostal one? – came to Central America, "the light began to spread" and the region came more and more "under the dominion of Jesus", the devil was not prepared to give up just like that his possession of a thousand years but started "to rob, kill and destroy" – which could be seen especially clearly in the persecution of Christians in Nicaragua. Carrette rendered outstanding services to

52 Interview with Carrette, Jan van Bilsen and Dirk van der Sypen, 1986.

the imposition of the Spiritual Warfare motif on Guatemalan Protestantism. He kept infecting politics with religion. When Jorge Serrano Elias, the "Prophet" of the Elim Church, came forward in 1985 as presidential candidate, Carrette belonged to the committed advocates of a presidency of this candidate of God. No sooner had this candidate of God entered the presidency in 1991 than he had to flee to the USA in 1993 because of serious accusations of corruption and a coup against his own administration. As far as I know Carrette has never commented on this. In answer he would presumably offer a feint of the devil. Anyway, a profiler who has close knowledge of such cases assumes that he was sent to Guatemala by his professionally anonymous clients in order to always have down pat the "right" religious answers for political questions.

In any case, the Spiritual Warfare doctrine in combination with the theocratic Dominion ideology has retained its significance for Central America beyond the time of the war. A prominent example is the former Guatemalan Foreign Minister Harold Caballeros (1999), who carried out a national crusade of Spiritual Warfare with his El Shaddai Church in 1990 to support Serrano, in parallel with Serrano's own election campaign. Caballeros represented the doctrine in its purest form, according to C. P. Wagner, and with his campaigns of "spiritual mapping" made a strong contribution to the discrimination of the indigenous population, and strove for an Anglo-Protestant culture with a neo-liberal economy in Guatemala. Incidentally, Caballeros also had a hand in carrying to extremes the authoritarian claims to truth of Charismatic Protestantism. This he did through the foundation of a Council of "Apostles" (Consejo Apostólico de Guatemala, 2000), to which currently belong about 20 self-appointed "apostles," whose apostolate consists in their direct access to divine revelations. A collective of individualistic know-it-alls.

As regards the logic of entanglement, the balance of power and interests has been changing from the 1980s to the present day. The organizations of the MANAGEMENT formation – in part today megachurches worth millions – are in every respect independent and autonomous actors, some of them with missions in the USA or on other continents. These actors exert themselves influence in the USA, but are also interested in more recent developments and better developed competencies in the USA. That is the reason why they take the initiative and invite specialists from the USA, such as distinguished motivational speakers, with the aim to make their organizations interesting for business people.

Mobilization from Below

Mobilization from above has, however, put considerable pressure on the Protestants in the lower social strata. Reactions vary. One follows the line that we call the HOPE FOR AN AFTERLIFE formation, while another follows the VALUES formation.

The former were mostly Evangelicals or from congregations of classical Pentecostal churches like the Asambleas de Dios in the countryside or in lower-class quarters. It was the rural churches in particular that experienced the full force of military actions, expulsions and massacres. It is possible that many had sympathy with the justice agenda of Liberation Theology or the indigenous Historical Protestants, but their objective situation of extreme need and repression threw them back upon the expectation of the Kingdom of God in the life hereafter. The US-American ethnologist and expert in the Ixil Triangle Benjamin Colby put it in a conversation in 1986 as follows. If indigenous people in a remote settlement are used to celebrating the morning and evening ceremony with the "holy fire," and one morning several Bell helicopters come flying over the mountain range and throw napalm, and soldiers come to burn down the huts, then the ceremony can no longer respond with anything meaningful. Instead, the descriptions of apocalyptic threats by the Pentecostal preachers become plausible.

In 1985, an indigenous farmer from a residential area near a barracks told us how his brother-in-law was taken from his house by the military at night and found the next morning with his throat cut. Later in the interview we turned to religious issues:

> [I like] above all what is being preached at the moment: that Christ is coming, and that one has to prepare for it. That is the entire certainty that you have: to prepare yourself to be able to be present at the encounter with the Lord. You must not do things that are not pleasant before God, because – I'll say it again – you don't know whether death will surprise you or the rapture will take you away. We cannot decide what happens tomorrow or the day after tomorrow, because we do not know the future. In two hours from now, death can come or rapture… What is of great interest to me is the return of Christ, so you can prepare yourself and because you have such hope, don't you. (Interview 9, with an Indigenous peasant, 1985)

This praxis evaded military violence by withdrawing from all social, political and, above all, military activities. In return, the military tends (but gives no guarantee) to leave the respective congregations and individuals in peace. In this way, the premillennialist expectation functions as a ruse of reason. Anyone who prepares for Rapture with pious exercises within the framework of his congregation and keeps apart from society at large can form solidary relationships in the congregation that help to alleviate the worst need, and survive without losing his self-respect.

This praxis is, however, also ambivalent. On the one hand, the respective congregations can be politically indoctrinated by their preachers, usually against "communism" and for obedience to the state authorities. On the other, they can be used – taking into account the restrictions of social control – to support the tactical withdrawal of or to provide camouflage for the activists of the popular uprising. In an interview of 1986, collaboration and manipulation as well as camouflage become clear in the assessment of the situation by such an activist, a member of the Asambleas de Dios. Among other things, he described how already under Lucas García *evangélicos* collaborated with the military, set fire to houses and raped women and children. The pastors, he claimed, had turned a blind eye to this because the murderers were working together with "the authorities." He continued:

> The Evangelicals behaved badly. If they did not take part in the fighting on the side of the military, they cooperated with them through theology. That is, if they merely happened to hear the word "communism," their hair would stand on end, they became alarmed and very afraid. ... [This pastor and the deacons] said in their sermons: "Brothers, ... subversion, that is the beast [of the Apocalypse, HWS] which does not want us to believe in God. Let us thank God that we live in a democratic country where the word of God can be preached."

This discourse speaks for itself. It takes just one element to extend it beyond the war situation. Democracy is equated with the possibility of "preaching the gospel," i.e. with freedom of religion. This figure of thought is found in all Latin America again and again and can be put more pointedly like this: as long as we can work for the enlargement of our organization, we could not care less about everything else.

Things looked completely different in the VALUES formation, where in times of war the issues were social justice, an end to racial discrimination and an early peace. In Guatemalan Protestantism, resistance to the oppression of the military and – to a certain extent – the cooperation in the uprising go back to the work of the Historical churches with the indigenous population. As a consequence of the earthquake and on an indigenous Presbyterian initiative the NGO Consejo Cristiano de Agencias de Desarrollo (CONCAD) was founded. On the occasion of the disaster relief, CONCAD developed relationships with ecumenically oriented relief organizations in the USA, with a focus on the Church World Service of the National Council of Churches, the Lutheran World Relief, the Mennonite Central Committee and the Presbyterian Church USA. During the hot phase of the war, many Guatemalan activists became the targets of the military and had to go into hiding or exile. In this situation, relations of solidary support were developed between the US and Guatemalan partners. In 1987, CONCAD was merged with the Conferencia de Iglesias Evangélicas de Guatemala (CIEDEG), which continued the tradition of resistance and, in addition to social work, carried out theological education work that was very similar to the consciousness raising of Liberation Theology. The organization now also worked transnationally by joining the Ecumenical Latin American Council of Churches (CLAI) and the World Council of Churches (WCC) in Geneva. Similarly networked was the education and aid organization CEDEPCA (Centro Evangélico para Estudios Pastorales en Centroamérica), which was formed in 1985. The entanglements just mentioned were able to protect the activists of this formation to some extent against violent attacks from the military. CIEDEG remained active after the war, not least in supporting the peace process until 1996 as well as the referendum for a multi-ethnic Guatemala in 1999. Actors of the MANAGEMENT formation were not involved in the peace process, and from the LAW formation the Alianza Evangélica de Guatemala was so only marginally. These formations even mobilized against a multi-ethnic Guatemala.

Who also mobilized when he was no longer dictator was Brother Efraín. Ríos Montt traveled to the USA in 1984 for a tour of Evangelical talk shows, supported by Luis Palau and *Christianity Today*. In events organized by FGBMFI, Religious Broadcasters and the National Association of Evangelicals he presented himself as a victim of religious persecution. Was there not communism in all those places, he asked, where you are not allowed to freely mix religious opinions with politics? Ríos Montt came to the USA at a time when many others also put in an appearance there.

5.3 USA: Ideological Battlefield

With the conflict in Central America, conservatives and imperialists in the USA felt that the East-West conflict had come uncomfortably close to home.[53] The cooperation between missionary societies such

53 In this chapter I have drawn primarily on Blanke 2003; Diamond 1989; Melander 1999; Stoll 1990; Garrard-Burnett 2010; Ezcurra 1982; Fuerstenberg 1984; and my own research of the 1980s.

as World Medical Relief and government agencies, which had already proven its value in Southeast Asia, also promised some advantages for Central America.

Guatemala

In Guatemala we have already seen the coordination between the Guatemalan government, El Verbo and Lovelift. There were coalitions, collusions, synergies and so on between the International Christian Embassy Jerusalem (Jorge López, Fraternidad Cristiana), the Gospel Crusade of Gerald Derstine (who cooperated with Col. Oliver North) and the Friends of the Americas (with Jorge Serrano on the Guatemalan board), who in turn worked closely together with US ambassador Alberto Piedra. The strength of complex networks lies in their complexity, through which actors can unite in attack. In this case against Nicaragua.

Nicaragua

After the victory of the Sandinistas against Somoza's dictatorship in Nicaragua in 1979 and unsuccessful attempts to win the USA for cooperation with a social democratic partner, the mixed bourgeois-socialist transitional government in the country had to come to terms with the unfavorable fact that Ronald Reagan had become President of the USA from January 1981. Thus it became clear what was clear already before to the representatives of the religious right: Nicaragua was from now on classified as a Marxist-Leninist submarine in the region and treated as such. This included not only an economic embargo – a popular means to bring insubordinate societies and governments to their knees even today – but also the organization of a large and powerful terror force, the so-called "Contras."

In the uprising against Somoza, a great many Protestants – among them Pentecostals – had also taken part; some of them armed, but more often with actions of civil disobedience and subversion. A Pentecostal pastor told me in an interview in 2013 that the youth group of his church had organized martial arts training sessions. While some were the lookouts, others did exercises in their church. As soon as Somoza's national guardsmen appeared, the youth began to sing and pray. At night they built barricades. After the victory of the Sandinistas, 500 pastors gathered for a solidarity meeting with the revolutionaries. Conversely, the Sandinistas took an open position on cooperation with religious organizations. No less a person than Tomás Borge, commander and Home Secretary, attended FGBMFI meetings in Managua for some time – as David Stoll reports – and asked for 800,000 New Testaments to be sent, but this went on only until the FGBMFI headquarters in the USA banned any contact with the Sandinistas. Despite all the openness to religious actors, which I saw for myself in the early years of the revolution, the labeling of the Sandinistas as Marxist by conservative organizations led to tensions and people keeping their distance. In 1980 I was riding on horseback with a priest in a very remote highland area wanting to visit local communities. In one village, churchgoers told me that there were problems with the polio vaccination campaign. The local pastor of the Asambleas de Dios preached against it because it was meant "to inoculate people with communism." The Asambleas de Dios and other large, classical Pentecostal churches claim to be politically impartial and interested only in preaching the gospel; so too did the then head of the central department for world mission of the Assemblies in Springfield, MI, Loren Triplett, in an interview in 1986. Triplett said that the Asambleas in Nicaragua were interested only in evangelization. The problem, he said, was that they were labeled "right-wing." I have the very strong impression that the "Marxism" label preceded the other. It is interesting in this context to look at two interviews with representatives of the Asambleas, which I conducted in Guatemala and Nicaragua in 1986. Under the right-wing dictatorship in Guatemala, it was officially a sin for the Asambleas not to do military service because Paul had decreed obedience to the powers that be in the Letter to the Romans, chapter 13. While in Nicaragua, at the same time, under the leftist revolutionary government it was a sin for the same Asambleas de Dios to do military service in the Sandinista army because it says in the Acts of the Apostles, chapter 2 that one should obey God more than man. And it is through the Church that God is represented.

In August 1986 the "Only Life" operation of the publishing house "Editorial Vida" of the Assemblies of God undertook a fund-raising campaign so as to be able to "smuggle Bibles into Nicaragua." Now, whereas you could no longer get spare parts for buses, and food was getting scarce you could get Bibles wherever you wanted and nobody would hinder you. But insinuating that Christians were being persecuted in Nicaragua (and generally under Communism) was a cheap propaganda argument of the religious right in the USA and was used by Only Life as such. A little later, Pastor Triplett stated that the advertisement was a serious mistake. The responsible editors of the mission department, he claimed, were not available to check the ad, which was submitted shortly before the deadline. For the Asambleas in Nicaragua, he continued, the whole affair was compromising.

Although this kind of propaganda was maybe not representative of the work of the Asambleas de Dios, it was thought small fry by other actors in Nicaragua and the United States. The US embassy in Nicaragua, for example, worked together with pastors of the Consejo Nacional de Pastores Evangélicos de Nicaragua (CNPEN), founded in 1981 as a conservative roof organization, and organized tours for pastors to the USA.[54] The primary activities of the organizations of the religious right in the USA are to be found in this religio-political entanglement project.

USA, Ríos Montt and the Contras: the Religious Right

A few months after Ríos Montt's coup d'état, his adviser and brother in faith Francisco Bianchi – as already mentioned – traveled to

54 Religious News Service (rns), 25 August1986. This information was confirmed by the State Department.

Washington on the initiative of the US ambassador to the OAS, William Middendorf. The purpose of the meeting was to tap private sources for funds for Montt's counter insurgency (see Diamond 1989, 164ff.; Melander 1999, 171f., where further sources are listed). Pat Robertson, who was also present, had promised Montt in the *New York Times* in May 1982 a contribution of billions of dollars. Perhaps this was made possible through a semi-official coalition between religious organizations and governmental agencies. On the part of the government, the meeting was attended by presidential advisor Edwin Meese, the Secretary of the Interior James Watt and the then Ambassador to Guatemala Frederick Chapin – all devout Evangelicals. In addition to Pat Robertson, there were present also two other heavyweights of the religious right: Jerry Falwell, the leader of the then still important Moral Majority, and Loren Cunningham, the leader of the powerful[55] Youth With a Mission (YWAM). According to information from Maranatha Campus Ministries, another meeting for policy coordination with representatives of the religious right was held at the State Department in October 1982 to coordinate the Guatemala operation. It can be assumed that a considerable number of other such meetings took place in the 1980s (and vastly more under the George W. Bush administration). On the basis of a copy of the official letter of invitation, Melander reports about a meeting in March 1984, also arranged on the initiative of Middendorf, of Evangelical and Jewish executives at the State Department for the coordination of Central America policy. Interestingly, no Catholics were invited, who were not exactly lacking in the religious right. Melander suspects that this might have to do with the fact that at that time the Catholic Bishops' Conference no longer approved of the policy of the government in Central America.

---

55 At the time it had ca. 4,000 permanent staff in active service and 14,000 short-termers in ca. 80 countries. Naturally, its income is not listed. Cf. Roberts and Siewert 1989, 248.

A further obstacle as regards Nicaragua – the hotspot of the conservative *angst* – was the Boland Amendment of 1982, which forbids the government to support activities that could contribute to the overthrow of the Nicaraguan government. The fact that a private organization lent a helping hand became publicly known on 1 September 1984, when the Sandinistas shot down a Contra helicopter carrying members of the paramilitary Civil Military Assistance Group from Alabama, who all died in the firing. In October 1984 the Boland Amendment was tightened by a general ban on support of the Contras, making private assistance to circumvent the regulation even more important. The Denton Amendment, also of 1984, equally made a small contribution by allowing the US Army to transport private aid. Moreover, the resourceful Neopentecostal Col. Oliver North, as everyone knew, concluded an arms deal with Iran, a highly creative move the monetary profits of which could be put to the support of the Contras. This deal was exposed in 1986 in the so-called Iran-Contra affair and legal proceedings followed. The other religio-military support networks, however, remained largely unaffected.

Private aid was mainly provided in three areas. First, there were the well-known political lobbying groups of the right: American Security Council, Citizens for America, International Business Communications etc. Second, paramilitary groups were also active, such as Refugee Relief International or Civil Military Assistance mentioned above. Third, the religious right took part in the activities fielding organizations like the Christian Broadcasting Network, but also a religious pariah organization with a lot of money and good intelligence connections: the CAUSA of the Korean messiah Sun Myung Moon, who had a firm base in Honduras (see Fuerstenberg 1984). It is not clear whether there was ever a joint prayer association between one representative of the "Christian" right and one of the Unification Church. In any case, acting in synergy was no problem.

The list of organizations serving the Contras and in direct contact with them is long (The Interhemispheric Education Resource

Center 1988). World Medical Relief channeled aid worth about 300,000 USD to them. Gospel Crusade Inc. of Philipp Derstine, Gerald's son, took food aid to the Contra camps and cooperated with Enrique Bermúdez, a former officer of Somoza's National Guard. At a conference of the National Religious Broadcasters, Derstine said that Oliver North introduced him personally to the Contra leaders Adolfo Calero and Enrique Bermúdez. Friends of the Americas – not religious itself, but coordinated with the religious right – transported large quantities of relief supplies via US military bases, from the Kelly Base in Texas to Honduras for example. In addition to medicine and food, the Christian Emergency Relief Team (CERT) also transported high-tech combat boots. The America Freedom Coalition acted in cooperation with the Moon Organization and the Contras. Other participants were the organizations of Pat Robertson,[56] the Knights of Malta, and so on.

What struck me time and again in conversation with missionaries of this stripe was the naive directness with which they legitimized political and military actions simply by associating a religious meaning with them – a rhetorical pattern that was never used by interview partners from Liberation Theology. For the friends of the Contras and military dictatorships, the correct US Evangelical religiosity would seem to justify everything. Nothing else comes to mind when you look at the Derstines' websites today:[57] visions, "supernatural events," "family and business matters: order & profit," "purpose for life"... Clearly, you cannot put a foot wrong there! In any case, Diamond (1989, 173) quotes an enthusiastic report by Phil Derstine on one of his visits to the Contras, among other places to their "secret map room," in the company of the ex-national guardsmen Bermúdez and Calero. Derstine: "I have been preaching

56 700 Club, Operation Blessing and Christian Broadcasting Network.

57 Christian Retreat (https://www.christianretreat.org/our-history/, accessed 8 October 2019) and Phil Derstine (http://philderstine.com/, accessed the same day).

to the Contras. They're so open to the gospel." From another source one gets a more precise assessment of Derstine:

> We are not really taking a political stance. The freedom fighters are deeply committed to God, 100 percent as far as we can see. The Contras know that the Gospel is the answer. (The Interhemispheric Education Resource Center 1988, 44)

Probably he did not even notice that the Contras were mainly interested in answers from Nicaraguan farmers and used "la cucharita," among other things, to motivate them to talk. In 1986, I was told about the "little spoon" by farmers on the Honduran border, who had made their escape from the pious Contras to a refugee camp: an egg spoon is almost exactly the right size for a human eye socket.

Of course, one can assume the activities of these religious organizations from the USA to be coordinated with the CIA. This conclusion is already indicated by the fact that the Honduran-Nicaraguan border area on the northern side was controlled by US forces so that no organization could work there without their consent. In addition, Derstine kindly informed Sara Diamond that when he returned from a trip, he was always debriefed, either by CIA officers from Langley or the State Department. The good relationship was documented in an even more official manner when President Reagan congratulated the Christian Emergency Relief Team in May 1986 on their successful work (Diamond 1989, 175).

The International Court of Justice in The Hague did not send congratulations, but an invoice. On 27 June 1986, the USA was sentenced to cease all activities and pay reparations amounting to ca. 14 billion dollars for supporting the Contra War. The sentence and a subsequent dictum of the UN Security Council were ignored or blocked by the USA exercising its veto. The Contra activities continued even after the signing of the peace treaty in 1988. Worn down by the war and the economic embargo, the Sandinistas lost the 1989 election. The next president, Violeta Chamorro, relinquished all claims to reparations and "waived" payment from the USA. The Nicaraguans took the repairs into their own hands, but had to suffer large-scale robberies in their work from subsequent neo-liberal administrations, especially that of Arnoldo Alemán. In 2006, the Sandinista Daniel Ortega won the election with an overwhelming majority, turning Nicaragua into his patrimony – but that's another story.

National Council of Churches and left-wing Evangelicals

In the fight against Somoza and the attempt to rebuild Nicaraguan society in the 1980s in particular, churches and NGOs received support from religious actors from the USA, as did the religious organizations in the resistance in El Salvador and Guatemala.

A prominent organization of this in the USA is the National Council of Churches (NCC), an umbrella organization of Mainline churches such as Methodists, Presbyterians, Lutherans and Episcopalians. This organization goes back to the Federal Council of Churches (FCC), founded in 1908 in the spirit of the Social Gospel which at the time adopted a creed with commitment to social justice as the basis of its work, and took a stand against fundamentalism. After the founding of the World Council of Churches (Geneva) in Amsterdam in 1948, the FCC was transformed into the NCC in the USA in 1950, which has maintained close contacts with Geneva ever since. The NCC adopted the social creed, modernizing it in 2007.

Different from the missions of the religious right, which saw it as their vocation to bring their absolute truths to bear against communism in Latin America, the missions organized in the NCC underwent a deliberate process of "ecumenical learning" (Blanke 2003). This development was similar to that in Catholic orders, especially that of Maryknoll, whose members had gone with an anti-Communist concept to Latin America, but gained the experience of the oppression of the peasants, and reflected it in the USA in their theological views. The Brothers Daniel and Philipp Berrigan, the Catholic Peace Fellowship as well as Clergy and Laity Concerned about Vietnam (CALC) made known participatory approaches to cooperation in the USA as early as the late 1960s. Similar processes were taking place in parallel in the missions of the NCC. In 1972, missionary William (Bill) Wipfler, in an article entitled "Latin America: US Colony" questioned the previous missionary praxis because it ultimately only served the interests of the USA. What was important, in contrast, he claimed, was to act in the interest of the "legitimate aspirations of the Latin American people" (Blanke 2003, 40f.). Very much along these lines were the activities of many missionaries who contributed to a change of praxis in several ways. Firstly, from this point on, staff from the USA was to be integrated into the structure of the partner organization with specific functions and would no longer be directly subordinate to the sending organization. That explains the strong reduction of the number of "real" missionaries of the Mainline churches in the 1970s by half (from about 8,000 to about 4,000; see Roberts and Siewert 1989, 36f.). The numbers of "fraternal workers," on the other hand, as well as support for the employment of national forces by partner churches and exchange were increasing. Secondly, the importance of development work without intention to convert was going up; the Church World Service gained in importance. Thirdly, attention was focused on advocacy, advocacy that is for persecuted, oppressed, deprived people or grassroots movements in Latin America. This required scientific or at least thoroughly researched journalistic data. For this reason, religious and student initiatives founded the National Council on Latin America (NACLA) in 1966 and asked Presbyterian Liberation theologian Richard Shaull, who had been exiled from Brazil, to join the board. With a similar but more religiously oriented aim, Phil Wheaton and Bill Wipfler founded the Ecumenical Program for Inter-American Communication and Action (EPICA) in 1968. And advocacy was indeed soon to be sorely needed, for there were to be many persecuted and oppressed people under the dictatorships of the 1970s in Brazil, Chile, Argentina, Uruguay, Bolivia, Nicaragua, Guatemala, El Salvador and so on. After the coup in Chile, the NCC, together with the Catholic Bishops' Conference in 1974, founded the Washington Office on Latin America (WOLA), a fully-fledged research and lobbying organization with a focus on human rights issues. Today WOLA is supported by European actors with strong human rights policies such as the Norwegian and Swiss states, as well as liberal foundations in the USA such as George Soros' Open Society Foundation. The factual clarification of the many reports of torture and other human rights violations is the prerequisite they take for case-related actions and for general human rights lobbying in Congress.

Along with a developing Latin America movement with a church background, it was only natural that relatively independent grassroots initiatives were also formed. One of them was the National Nicaragua Network (today NicaNet), founded in February 1979 – five months before the victory of the Sandinistas – which supported the Sandinista revolution and stood up for a Latin America policy for which the self-determination of peoples, social justice, human rights and international law were a matter of course. Another grassroots organization for solidarity was the Committee in Solidarity with the People of El Salvador (CISPES), founded in 1980. Just a few months after the organization started its work it was infiltrated by the FBI because of its connections to the FMLN guerrillas in El Salvador, which is the reason it has brought several lawsuits against the FBI since the mid-1980s.

In Latin America, the already mentioned activities of EPICA gave rise in 1974 to the Servicio para Paz y Justicia (SERPAJ), whose first director was the later Nobel Peace Prize winner Adolfo Perez Esquivel. This line of religious work naturally established working contacts with ecumenical initiatives in Latin America, such as the Latin American Council of Churches (CLAI). For the NCC-related missions and organizations the years of sharing the grassroots activities of the churches as well as human rights and advocacy work in Latin America resulted in the fact that they were already compromised in the Central American conflicts by their partnerships. The consequences of accompanying the Presbyterian fraternal workers in Guatemala showed up in the fact that the Presbyterian indigenous people in general as well as their organizations CONCAD and CIEDEG had of course to be supported against the persecution by the military. This also established solidarity with the

Comité pro Justicia y Paz, founded in 1977, although Catholic in its majority, and the Iglesia Guatemalteca en el Exilio. In addition, it went without saying that the exiled persecuted Presbyterian poet Julia Esquivel was helped. In Nicaragua the result of the cooperation with the Baptist-based umbrella organisation CEPAD was that the churches of the NCC became partners in reconstruction or entered into close cooperation with the ecumenical Centro Antonio Valdivieso. In Guatemala they were clearly positioned against the military dictatorship, and in Nicaragua they sided with the Sandinista reconstruction and counter-activities.

All these activities established a scenario for a culture war in the USA about the role of religious actors in the Central American conflict.

Institute on Religion and Democracy

The saying goes that it never rains but it pours. So, in addition to the conflicts that raged in El Salvador and Guatemala, Ronald Reagan was elected president in the USA – a man of dyed-in-the-wool political ideas, content with half-truths, averse to facts and possessed by confused Apocalypticism: "I swear I believe Armageddon is near."[58] At the 1983 annual conference of the National Association of Evangelicals,[59] he coined the formula of the "evil empire" for the Soviet Union, probably created by apocalyptic Hal Lindsay, one of his spiritual advisors. In short, the framework for the religio-political offensive of the religious right was in place, and the hunt was on for the National Council of Churches and other ecumenically oriented Christian actors.

The Institute on Religion and Democracy was to be developed into one of the most potent hunters, but this plan was only moderately successful. The Institute was founded right at the beginning of the Reagan administration (see Howell 2003; Diamond 1989,

58 An entry in his diary, see Brinkley 2007.

59 … who were far from being as peaceful then as they are today.

148ff.; Ezcurra 1982). The foundation was preceded by a controversy in the Methodist Church. One of its members, an employee of the conservative trade union AFL-CIO and chairman of the Social Democrats USA for a time, presented a report to the General Conference of the Methodist Church in 1980 on support for organizations in the USA and the Third World which he considered communist and terrorist, including NACLA and WOLA. The NCC also came under fire. The initiative was supported above all by a biblicist group in the Methodist Church linked to the magazine *Good News*. This controversy is usually seen as an impulse for the foundation of the Institute on Religion and Democracy, which however took place already one year later in 1981. It was founded on the initiative of a group of Catholic and Protestant neo-Conservatives: above all Michael Novak, Richard John Neuhaus, Penn Kemble and David Jessup. Naturally, the organization described itself as an institution of the political center. In view of Kemble's history as anti-Vietnam protestor and the party affiliation with the Social Democrats of two IRD founding members, this may even seem plausible at first glance. That this would be mistaken becomes clear however when one considers that it was the harsh anti-communism of the Social Democrats that above all contributed to the legitimation of anti-communist attitudes, and that (ex-)members such as Paul Wolfowitz even were appointed Secretary of Defense under G.W. Bush, and that, finally, the IRD supported Bush's war against Iraq. Mark Tooley, the current chairman, worked for the CIA for eight years before joining the IRD in 1994. In our view it is much more reasonable to interpret the IRD's placing itself at the political center as the creation of a false balance,[60] the camouflage of choice for radical positions. However that may be, in the course of its history the IRD was financed by foundations whose "center" was very far to the right, such as Scaife, Smith Richardson, Castle Rock/Coors, Bradley and Fieldstead. The IRD had good connections and did successful

60 In classical rhetoric also called *argumentum ad temperantiam* or "golden mean".

journalistic work – which does not mean that it carried out thorough research. The popular magazine *Reader's Digest* (14 million readers) published an article with the title "The Gospel According to Marx" already in 1982, in which ecumenical organizations like the NCC, the World Council of Churches in Geneva (WCC) and even the South African Council of Churches, which was engaged in a fight against apartheid and accordingly endangered, were sharply attacked for "communism" and the support of terror.[61] The matter was taken up in 1983 by the television show *60 Minutes*. The WCC was attacked there – as Diamond writes – because of its support for the communist literacy campaign in Nicaragua, although the program makers failed to realize that this literacy campaign was also supported by US-AID. In the 1980s, Central America was the main front for the IRD's work. Alan Wisdom – who as IRD vice-chairman later supported G.W. Bush's war in Iraq (Wisdom n.d.) – explained to me in a conversation in October 1986 that the IRD had no knowledge of its own of the situation in Nicaragua; that none of its employees at the time had been there, and that information was processed from external sources.[62] I was able to see one such source: a message from "White House, Robert Reilly, Assistant to the President on Public Liaison, to Penn Kemble, 12.12.1984 ... Dear Penn... Bob." The letter offers the IRD information on Gustavo Parajón, the director of the Baptist-led ecumenical aid fund Consejo de Iglesias Pro-Alianza Denominacional (CEPAD) in Nicaragua. CEPAD was alleged to have embezzled money, Wisdom said. But that was not the main point. The real problem, he went on, was that CEPAD cooperated with the Sandinista district commit-

61 Austin, Charles. 1982. "National Council of Churches Faces New Type of Critic," New York Times, 3 November 1982, Section A (https://www.nytimes.com/1982/11/03/us/national-council-of-churches-faces-new-type-of-critic.html, accessed 10 October 2019).

62 In stark contrast to the report by Loren Triplett of the Assemblies of God quoted above, Wisdom said that the Assemblies worked in secret and had invited the IRD to a meeting with a pastor from Nicaragua – presumably the same person from whom Triplett distanced himself.

tees.[63] When CEPAD's medical aid and literacy work in the countryside was publicly praised by the Nicaraguan government, this was the reason for IRD staff member Diane Knippers – well positioned as she was also in the National Association of Evangelicals – to swing into action. She started a disinformation campaign against CEPAD as a "communist" organization. This in turn got the CEPAD staff in the rural clinics into trouble from the Contras. As a result, the IRD could not maintain this piece of false information and in the end suffered a journalistic defeat – probably also because lying had not yet been imposed as a general mode of communication. More successful was a scientific coup.

Social Science

The religious struggle for the interpretive sovereignty of the conflicts in Central America, and the role of different actors in particular, which was fueled by the clear attack of the Santa Fe I paper on Liberation Theology and the IRD's journalism, was making itself felt in the field of science too. The ecumenical actors were the first to open the match because they had been interested since the end of the 1960s in an appropriate, scientifically supported information basis for their praxis in Latin America, and regarded it their duty to criticize foreign policy through information of the public, for which purpose they had founded WOLA and NACLA (Goff 1966).

NACLA sent a two-member sociological team for 8 months to Central America with a specific focus on political practices. Deborah Huntington and Enrique Domínguez – both experienced scholars on Latin America with a good command of Spanish – published a 36-page report "Salvation Brokers" in the *NACLA Report on the Americas*, in January 1984. In it they clearly stated one reason for their work: the furious (and endangering) attacks on committed liberal Protestants in Central America like Julia Esquivel at the hands

63 … which was absolutely normal so as to be able to organize actions in an effective way.

of the IRD. In complete contrast to the uninformed propaganda of the IRD, a fact-finding mission for the report was carried out. In accordance with their concentration on politics, the authors link religious attitudes with political commitment, differentiate between actors according to their political praxis, and investigate with some historical depth the implication of US-American missions in politics. One chapter thematizes the counter insurgency of Rios Montt, another the cooperation between churches (including the Asambleas) in development activities in the context of the Nicaraguan revolution. All in all the publication, though journalistic in appearance, offers a differentiated picture, which due to its focus on political-scientific matters did however not fulfill all expectations of theological readers. In any case, the slim publication contradicted everything that was spread by the religious right. And it had a very strong impact on the debate in the mid-1970s. The IRD itself could not respond to this challenge. It simply did not have the scientific resources for it.

But there was Peter L. Berger, conservative sociologist of religion at the University of Boston (and Director of the Institute for the Study of Economic Culture) and a member of the IRD's Advisory Board. It cannot be said with certainty that the subsequent action was coordinated with the IRD; but in the hour of need his institute launched a research project on Protestantism in Latin America. The sociologist David Martin of the London School of Economics was awarded a contract to carry out the project, although (or because?) he had been concerned with secularization up to that point and not with the Pentecostal movement or even with Latin America, and spoke neither Spanish nor Portuguese then or in later years. In only three years a book of 350 pages was finished (Martin 1990), thanks to the help he got with reading and translations as well as a couple of trips to Latin America undertaken mainly to interview people who could speak English. The book was well placed (with Oxford University Press) and put the seal on the victory of the neo-conservative view of things for the US public. It has not been translated into Spanish. Latin American readers of the English-language version that I spoke to explained this by saying that they found the book very superficial on the one hand, and that it reproduced too much US-American ideological and hegemonic knowledge on the other.

As I have mentioned at the beginning, the argument of the entire book boils down to the fact that the Protestantism which emerged in England and the USA brought progress and "betterment" to the poor in Latin America. The strong power imbalance between the USA and Latin America is made to disappear by simply giving it no role to play or at most – in a proven rhetorical strategy – by being hidden behind metaphors taken from nature: "... social earthquake which follows as the tectonic plates of two world civilizations pass one under the other" (292). Incidentally – as Martin remarks with regard to other authors – observers draw again and again connections to the "Electronic Church" in the USA and to conservative foundations.[64] The debate, he writes, is "fraught with propaganda," so that a researcher is virtually caught in a crossfire (291). Instead of taking seriously the fact that Protestants were apolitical and only concerned with "salvation," the debate, he claims, often revolved around their position on "liberation" and their presumed role as bearers of a foreign culture (233). Martin is also willing to explicitly refrain from framing the worlds of the Latin American poor (of whom he had no knowledge since he did not do any field research) "in a language of covert political hostility" and to judge the actors in a "secular version of the 'last judgment'" (1). He is surely right that the debate on "sects" in Latin America was often quite prejudiced. But he deceives himself and his readers in two ways. First, he implicitly insinuates that all his colleagues hold prejudices. Second, he pretends that theoretical assumptions do not have a framing effect. This is precisely what is not true, as I have just mentioned. A positive prejudice is also a prejudice; and Martin's

64 Martin does not quote at this place the article by Huntington and Domínguez, whose work is listed in his bibliography, but whose argument he does nowhere engage with. Instead, he has a reference to Ezcurra 1982.

readers look in vain for verifiable or falsifiable criteria for the critical production and examination of research results. This is also due to the fact that the book's content consists to a large extent of summaries of the secondary literature.[65] Furthermore, descriptive passages are often not given an interpretation. In connection with earthquake relief in Guatemala, we only learn the commonplace that Protestant groups liberated people from alcohol, small crime and corruption (92). Ríos Montt appears as a good ruler who combined a "drive against violence and corruption" with a "ferocious and effective attack on the guerillas who offer beans – and death." Some Protestants, he says, may have sided with the guerrillas and fled the country with the Catholic left, but most of them supported Ríos Montt (92). As regards Protestant resistance (254), the US-American distinction of "radicals" versus "liberals" (which does not work at all for Latin America) is used and we learn that indigenous Protestants are "deeply affected by radicals" and even formed a "fiercely anti-American" group. Many "radicals" fled, he continues, and the other Protestants offered "spiritual refuge," while the Christian general distributed beans or bullets. FUNDAPI receives a mere 7 lines from Martin, containing the information that the organization was taking care of the beans and using money from fundamentalist sources. Finally, the good general was driven out of office by right-wing political forces because of his actions against corruption. In Martin's book, then, Montt is positioned – just like the IRD – between the right and the left, firmly at the political center and has certainly not organized a genocide. Well, the Guatemalan courts see it differently. If you now wonder where this knowledge comes from, you will find the answer, but no consolation, on page xii. Martin's source in Guatemala is Virgilio Zapata Arceyuz, a speaker of English and an extremely conservative Evangelical who supported the

65 To the mass of secondary literature must be added (unlisted) conversations to obtain information with ca. 12 partners and ca. 60 unpublished papers. How the literature is presented depends on the various perspectives of the authors so that one can hardly find uniform criteria of assessment.

regime of Ríos Montt to the best of his ability. When I met Zapata in Guatemala shortly after the coup against Ríos Montt, his greatest concern was to make good the all too close ties between him and other Evangelicals and Ríos Montt, and to be accepted as a useful conversation partner by the new dictatorship.[66]

In Martin's case study on Nicaragua we are told that to achieve "balanced" reporting he preferred to rely solely on the Evangelical *Christianity Today* (248). Admittedly, what he says about CEPAD is balanced and not a rehash of the IRD's propaganda. But his case study on Protestantism and politics in Brazil leaves the dictatorship largely out of the picture, unless it happens to be about internal church effects (255); in the case of Mexico, what goes completely by the board is its laicity, so constitutive of the country (261). Finally, as regards the field of social and economic relations we learn that Protestant networks not only guarantee stable relations: "Beyond that they inculcate American norms of behavior and educate members in such matters as household budgeting, social comportment and table manners" (218); and further, they also bring the gift of marriages, "sexual discipline" and a break with "endemic corruption." Just talk about this with members of the Bancada Evangélica in Brazil. They will have a lot of fun for an entire evening. In short, Martin – supposedly without "framing" and without field experience – looks at Latin America from the perspective of the North Atlantic, mildly neoconservative secularization theorist, highlights what he feels are positive observations, does not see many things at all (like the genocide under Ríos Montt) and finally wraps the presence of Protestants in Latin America in a mildly neoconservative "spirit of capitalism."

66 In his follow-up book, *Pentecostalism: the world their congregation* (Martin 2001, XII), you learn of a conversation with Arturo Piedra, Costa Rica, who is introduced as one of the leading representatives of the "Pentecostal intelligentsia" in Latin America. Arturo was my colleague at work for almost 10 years, an expert in Latin American Protestantism, a reformed Christian to his fingertips, and a distinguished critic, if not enemy, of Pentecostals.

British restraint was not the style of the IRD. Nevertheless, IRD activists will have been delighted with the publication.

While the IRD and its friends continued to promote dictatorships, terrorist organizations and wars, in Guatemala it was the indigenous Protestants (Martin's "radicals") and not the friends of Ríos Montt who were working with international organizations to achieve a successful peace treaty; while in the USA the NCC and its partners in the Sanctuary Movement were looking after the victims of the Central American wars. The wars were ended by peace treaties and gave way to a precarious peace in which social injustice was continued. But if you think that the end of the fighting caused the pious offensives from the USA to decrease, you are in for a disappointment.

Governmental Fundamentalists

Donald Trump's decree of 3 May 2018 (Trump 2018) on religious initiatives is a rider to George W. Bush's earlier decrees. Bush's initiative was already heavily criticized for undermining the separation of state and church and for giving too much funding to the religious right. The new regulation was likely to attract growing criticism. The small change in the name from "White House Faith and Opportunity Initiative" to "White House Office of Faith-Based and Community Initiatives" might have been taken to indicate that now it was not so much the activity of the White House itself that was of interest but rather that of the initiatives that came together there. Many indicators suggest that the office has become a romping ground and an instrument of legitimation for the "Court Evangelicals" (Fea). The initial reactions were correspondingly positive, emphasizing the extension of the scope and the greater closeness between churches and the state. Paula White was quoted in the *National Catholic Reporter*: "This order is a historic action, strengthening the relationship between faith and government in the United States and the product will be countless, transformed lives" (Banks

2018). Whose lives were to be changed was the subject of a journalistic investigation[67] that brought to light the following.

The failure of their own search for a website for the office of the Initiative was confirmed by the journalists who found that Trump and the religious actors involved kept a low profile, probably to avoid the above-mentioned criticisms. In any case, requests for interviews and information from the journalists were rejected. According to the research collective, the action platform was used by actors from the LAW and MANAGEMENT formations, who had gained a more or less official advisory status as a result of their assistance at the time of the election and who are referred to by John Fea as *Court Evangelicals*. In his book *Believe Me*, John Fea deals with the question of how Evangelical support for Donald Trump came about. He establishes the category of Court Evangelicals for Trump supporters and divides them into three very instructive subgroups: the old religious right, part of the legalist wing; the Prosperity Gospel; and the Independent Network Christians (INC), closer to the charismatic wing.[68]

The office serves a double purpose. It gives religious actors the opportunity to strengthen their symbolic capital by linking their identity closely to the White House, which opens doors for them through which to advance their own ministries. At the same time, Trump's advantage is that religious people support his policies 100% (perhaps a slightly lower support percentage as regards Hispanics where migration is concerned), promote them politically, and give them added religious significance. In consequence, the Evan-

---

67 The remarks that follow are based on Segnini and Cordero 2019. The report is the result of a cooperation of 16 Latin American media companies under the direction of the Columbia Journalism Investigations of the School of Journalism at Columbia University, New York. The study is part of a larger investigative project *Transnacionales de la fe* (https://www.elclip.org/category/investigaciones/transnacionales-de-la-fe/, accessed 11 October 2019).

68 See the paragraph on "Formations" in the Introduction. On what follows see Fea 2020, 115ff.

gelicals were able to arrange briefings with Trump or Vice President Pence for guests that were favorably disposed to the cause. The Cuban Mario Bramnick, founder of the group "Latinos for Trump" and the "Latino Coalition for Israel," saw himself as a member of the office, and agitated for the transfer of the embassies of as many countries as possible from Tel Aviv to Jerusalem. To this end, he established, primarily in Latin America, right-wing religious-political networks with politicians such as Bolsonaro and Jimmy Morales, and with Netanyahu in Israel. According to the journalists' research, Bramnick and other members of the office achieved an interesting arrangement to support Trump's embassy initiative. President Jimmy Morales in Guatemala was having problems with the Commission for the Prosecution of Corruption (CICIG), set up by the UN a few years before in coordination with a previous government. His brother was then being prosecuted for this charge, and he felt the matter was getting uncomfortably close to home. So far, however, the USA had always supported CICIG. Morales allowed Bramnick to explain to him that Trump was very interested in as many countries as possible moving their embassy in Israel to Jerusalem. So Morales made his embassy move, and thus was free to move against CICIG, which had to stop its work. Michelle Bachmann from the then defunct Tea Party and Evangelical member of the office advised her "friends" in Brazil by video message (and unlawfully) to choose the candidate who wanted to have the embassy moved. Bolsonaro wanted to, but could not oblige because the Brazilian military was against it. Clearly, "Faith and Opportunity" pretty well describes the activities of this government agency.

In addition to the more or less official office, Pastor Ralph Drollinger manages to place his "Capitol Ministries" as epiphytes, so to speak, at the government offices in Washington. Here is again what the research collective found out: Drollinger had a bad reputation among clergymen. He was expelled from his former organization by an overwhelming majority of his colleagues on the grounds of unsuitability for the spiritual office, autocracy and financial irregularities – the usual things, then. But Drollinger was introduced to Trump by Jeff Sessions – the future Secretary of Defense – in 2016 and supported his election campaign. He even did religious campaign advertising in which he mentioned Trump by name, thus committing an offense for Trump's sake. This loyalty was rewarded with a special position for Drollinger's "Capitol Ministries" in political prayer lobbying. He and his people now have hegemony over the (semi-official) prayer circles in the White House, the Senate and the House of Representatives. Drollinger sets about his work with an ultra-rightist doctrine of faith, which can also be easily found on his website. Ecology, it says there, is a false religion; illegal migrants must be imprisoned and deported; the wrath of God falls on same-sex marriages; sins are punished; and the death penalty is a biblical blessing. "Capitol" turns into capital for Drollinger when he uses his position as a White House Bible teacher to expand his ministries. In Latin America he is in the process of establishing international branches of his ministries in presidential palaces and parliaments.[69] His initial agenda consisted of these countries: Mexico, Honduras, Brazil, Perú, Uruguay, Ecuador, Paraguay, Costa Rica and Panama. It is particularly interesting to note that Nicaragua was not part of Drollinger's program, but that President Ortega himself came forward. The president invited him to speak at the 40th anniversary of the Sandinista revolution in July 2019. Ortega, who is under heavy pressure because of human rights violations, wrote in the letter of invitation[70] that he knew that "born again" governments would rule according to the Bible. Drollinger thanked him for this by talking only of peace, love and patience in his speech (Drollinger 2019) – exactly what Ortega needed at the moment to demobilize the population, and what he was already able to make many Prot-

69 On Capitol Ministries alias "Parlamento y Fe" in Argentinia see Carbonelli 2014.

70 "Nicaragua President to CM: Come Establish Bible Studies to National Leaders!" 2019. Capitol Ministries. 13 July 2019. https://capmin.org/nicaragua-president-to-cm-come-establish-bible-studies-to-national-leaders/ (accessed 12 November 2019).

estant leaders swear to by co-optation. With Honduran President Juan Hernández – currently under suspicion of drug trafficking – Drollinger is already in business. Two members of the US government contributed to this.

Vice President Mike Pence and the Secretary of State and ex-CIA Director Mike Pompeo are both devout Evangelicals and probably also Drollinger's Bible students. Together with members of Trumps *Court*, they urged Hernández already in 2018 to install Capitol Ministries for the spiritual aspects in his institutions. Ever since John Winthrop, this mingling of politics and religion has obviously been in the tradition of political thinkers "confusing metaphor with reality" and who were attached to the heretical belief that the "City on the Hill has the right (…) to control the world" (Williams 1980, 208). It could also be the other way around. Then the city upon a hill would not be a metaphor, but a metonymy: it would stand, pars pro toto, for all the rest of the ruling system. And US politicians would use the Pilgrims' religion in an attempt to give their claim to power some plausibility in the first place. Which would make the program of Capitol Ministries even more attractive to these politicians: "Making Disciples of Jesus Christ in the Political Arena throughout the World" ("Capitol Ministries" n.d.).

Some of the Latin American migrants are doing something similar, only the other way around in the USA.

6. New Millennium: Prosperity and Migration

The new Millennium has come, but quite differently than many of the faithful had expected: quite unspectacularly, as a simple turn of the year. Admittedly, between the 1980s and the present day things have changed, also with regard to the ways and kinds of entanglement. For religious praxis the enforcement of the neo-liberal hegemony in economy and society will likely be of great importance, insofar as it creates broad plausibility for the Prosperity doctrine and religious self-optimization strategies. In addition, the South is becoming an increasing, dynamic force for religious entanglement. In this chapter we will concentrate on Mexico and California, but let us first take a look at the connection between neo-liberalism and the Prosperity doctrine.

6.1 Neo-Liberalism and Prosperity

After the end of the conflict between East and West and the end of many dictatorships in Latin America, a development set in toward an ever stronger hegemony of a neo-liberal economic and social organization.[71] The political and military polarization within Latin American societies and the cold war between the USA and the Soviet Union gave way to a less visible economic polarization between, respectively, increasingly rich or dependent social sectors under the umbrella of neo-liberal hegemony. New economic winners emerged in finance and technocracy. A new middle class formed in the service sector, although under precarious conditions. The old middle class of civil servants and local small and medium-sized industry were coming under increasing competitive pressure. The already marginalized lower classes were pushed more and more into the informal sector, the youth into gang crime. And in almost all classes, drug-related crime gained increasing economic significance. Similar processes were taking place in the USA even if on a much higher overall economic level. In macro-sociological terms, a change

71 On Central America cf. Schäfer, Reu and Tovar Simoncic 2013.

could be observed from a strong political and military polarization between more or less well-organized social blocks to a blurred situation with very different future perspectives for the various social groups. Above all, the potential of social organization from below in Latin America – trade unions, socialist parties, farmers' organizations – was brushed aside by the neo-liberal logic of individual advancement. In the USA, individualism had long been established anyway and only needed to be adapted to neo-liberalism. In micro-sociological terms, the individual struggle for advancement, seen as the only alternative, can be said to have changed greatly the perception of the social structure, and the individuals' chances of survival. The Mexican theologian Elsa Támez speaks of a logic of "Every man for himself!" (*sálvese quien pueda*). In confusing processes of disintegration the goal is the integration of one's own life, especially of one's economic activity and the stability of family structures.

For religious praxis, the transition from political polarization to dominant neo-liberalism has had profound consequences, especially for the rising middle and the technocratic upper class (less so for the landed oligarchy as well as the money aristocracy of New England). The dualistic theories of God's struggle against the devil tended to lose ground. In the USA, where a more or less paranoid view of the foreign had been common since the time of the Pilgrims (Williams 1980, 221, 224), Satan and his territorial demons were requartered in the territories of Islam to the south very soon after the end of the Soviet Union. In this way, the desirable external enemy was preserved. Moreover, mainly in the MANAGEMENT formation, overtones of demonology are found in the Dominion doctrine, which is about the conquest of different social fields out of the hands of the godless (and thus also of demons, depending on how it pleased the respective actors). At the same time, the Prosperity Gospel came to the fore. In Latin America the disposition to fight demons moved away from the center of the web of the actors' religious dispositions, although remaining active in the context of the Dominion Doctrine. Religious actors were thus primarily concerned with self-optimization and "positive thinking" in order to conform to the system and move close to the magic horn of neo-liberal capitalism. "Smile or die!" (Ehrenreich 2010) is the motto of the management-religiosity of modern Neopentecostals in the USA and Latin America. The promise of salvation is "this-worldly," as Max Weber would have put it. Ultimately, it is all about economic success. While the current economic development is calling traditional social structures into question, the conversion of religious interest into material success allows habitūs to be redirected towards the new form of reproduction. Weber already saw this:

> The capitalist success of a guild member undermined the spirit of the guild – as happened in England and France – and hence capitalist success was shunned. But the capitalist success of a sect brother, if legally attained, was proof of his worth and of his state of grace, and it raised the prestige and the propaganda chances of the sect. Such success was therefore welcome. (Weber 1946a, 322)

Compared with Weber's impressions, the parameters of success among the "sect brothers" today have changed a little. While Weber saw the interplay between probation through "moral discipline" (316) in the congregation on the one hand and a confirmation of one's own "self-feeling" (309) by admission to a capitalist club on the other as a decisive factor in the overall success of the religious strategy, today it is simply the economic success of the individual and the quantitative success of the preacher as evident from membership numbers. Today's megachurches do not function through the exclusive admission of "the qualified" (316), but through the sheer mass of donors and through the investment of monetary capital in business enterprises – preferably in the area of the media, but also in real estate and many other things that can be hidden in Panama. And this development has taken leave also of the old Christian criterion of economic success: having your needs satisfied is no longer seen as an indicator of "enough" but has given way to the envious comparison with your neighbor. There can be no "enough" if there is someone who has more. The religious praxis in the MANAGEMENT formation has itself become a business with the accumulation and centralization of capital projected into infinity.

The Dominion doctrine transfers this logic of the functional connection of religiosity and economy to the field of politics.[72] By asserting that Christianity – or more precisely: your own religious opinion – has the competence and the right to conduct state business, a re-sacralization of politics is pursued. This can be observed in the USA in the times of Presidents Ronald Reagan, George W. Bush and – in the form of the *Court Evangelicals* – also Donald Trump. There are corresponding attempts in Latin America, above all in Brazil and Guatemala, but also in other countries. Religious strategies and discourses postulate universal validity in a genuinely fundamentalist way; and attempts are made to impose religious logic on political institutions.

Desperate individualism and self-accusation on account of lack of economic success are widespread in the middle and lower classes. All this notwithstanding, at the center of religious praxis is what is feasible: the stabilization of the family and the demand for law and order. The bourgeois nuclear family, regarded as "natural" and "God's will," functions socially as a last refuge and is understood in religious terms as divine duty and grace. (This explains in part the harsh rejection of the LGBT movement). The faithful closely link their desire for family stability with the talk of "God." "God" legitimizes their own longing. "God" created the family. "God" has a law that says exactly what you wish for. "God" is – from a semiotic perspective – an "empty signifier" (Levi-Strauss, Laclau), which ultimately only says: "What I have just said is irrefutable." That is a lot, if you consider that in the disintegrating life worlds of most people in the lower and lower middle classes in the USA and Latin America there are hardly any certainties left.

The change in the overall conditions also includes an enormous improvement in the means of communication, if not in the freedom to travel. All the factors mentioned so far have contributed in part to a change in the conditions for religious entanglements between Latin America and the USA.

---

72 On the connection between religion and politics cf. Schäfer 2019.

6.2 Everyday Border Crossings

Even if missions from the USA in Latin America are still an ongoing process, the praxis of Latin American actors in the USA is becoming more important for today's entanglement dynamic. This has a history dating back to 1848, when the USA annexed large parts of Mexico's territory. In the course of the next 150 years, waves of immigration alternated with waves of deportation.

Catholics

Most of the Spanish speaking inhabitants of the USA are Catholic. Many of them import a ritualistic Catholicism that revolves around the veneration of saints and the Virgin Mary. The number of holy shrines in the residential areas of these people is increasing, and conflicts occur with bishops of the Vatican II Orthodox line. However, it is possible to distinguish between different types of Catholic immigrants. The sociologist Olga Odgers of the Colegio de la Frontera Norte (COLEF) in Tijuana sets up three different types of Catholic immigrants in Los Angeles, according to the degree of organization of the Church in the region of origin.[73] The state of Zacatecas is firmly integrated into the Catholic hierarchy in Mexico. The majority of immigrants from there attend regular Catholic congregations in the USA. In Veracruz, Catholicism is poorly integrated and religious diversity, including Protestants and magical cults, is very advanced. Migrants from there tend to convert to various offers on the religious market, whether Hispanic or Korean Pentecostals or even Mormons. Catholicism in Oaxaca, for its part, is of a strongly indigenous stamp. Among immigrants from this region, there is still strong regional cohesion, manifest in collective celebrations and the establishment of places of worship for native saints in the USA. In these varieties, religious praxis also serves to maintain cross-border relations with the home countries. An example is the veneration of a

73 Alarcon, Escala and Odgers 2016, 151ff. and Olga Odgers in conversation in Bielefeld, 6 December 2016.

Virgin Mary from San Juan de los Lagos (Jalisco), whose cult was continued in San Juan (Texas) (cf. Vasquez and Marquardt 2003, 145ff.). Another instance is reported by the migration researcher Liliana Rivera of the Colegio de México, who spoke in an interview[74] about a regionally bound community in New Jersey which had a duplicate of their local saint made and blessed in order to have him flown in his own seat on an airplane to the USA. In the course of time and due to the ever-increasing presence of Latin American Catholics, the demographic focus of Catholicism in the USA has shifted from Rhode Island to the southwest.[75] Hispanic Catholicism is slowly gaining recognition, too. Architectural proof of this is the "Cathedral of Our Lady of the Angels" in Los Angeles, built in 2002. This building can be read architecturally as a "compensatory gesture by the American church toward ethnic and national Catholics" and as an "emblem of a pluralist vision of American Catholicism" (Lint 2009, 69). The cultural universality of the mother figure here creates a symbolic unity while allowing the cultural diversity to remain: on the portal, 15 different representations of the Virgin Mary from across the world have been gathered by a Mexican artist. With its universalist habitus and organization Catholicism overtakes regionalist tendencies on both sides of the border. Spontaneous entanglement with its frictions and contradictions is regulated and enclosed by a supranational hierarchical institution.

For all the universality of the Pentecostal movement, the actions of each individual church are – different from the transnational religious enterprises! – more often oriented to the everyday border crossings.

---

74 Mexico, 26 October 2016.

75 Between 1970 and 2016 the Latino population grew from 9.6 to 57.5m people (Flores 2017b, 1).

Pentecostals

The Borderlands between the USA and Mexico are a microcosm of entanglement not only for Catholics. There is, indeed, a specific form of entanglement of religious praxis of the Pentecostal movement at the social grassroots. It is brought about by migrants who become missionaries and church founders; and thus – in the sense of Clara Buitrago – turn from *migrants* into *expatriates*. The central example of this development is furnished by the history of the Iglesia Apostólica de la Fe en Cristo Jesús (IAFCJ).[76] The church originated from the direct impact of the famous Azusa Street Revival of 1906 on Mexican immigrants in Sonoratown, north-central Los Angeles and other areas on the southern border of the United States. The experience of speaking in angel-like language (glossolalia) and receiving revelation caused some of the subaltern Mexican workers to see their vocation as planters of new congregations with this form of piety, in the USA as well as in Mexico. Among a number of about 10 people who in the early days moved the Mexican mission from US-American to Mexican soil, one woman is considered a special icon: Romana Carbajal de Valenzuela. She greatly contributed to the dynamics and religious orientation of the movement. The work of the Pentecostal missionaries in "El Norte" – the northern border area of Mexico – found favorable conditions during the Mexican revolution. American Methodist missionaries, for example, were leaving the country, while Mexican evangelists, such as Antonio Nava, oriented themselves towards the authority and authenticity of revolutionary leaders like Pancho Villa, and offered a Pentecostal alternative to the Methodist congregations in revolutionary times. The first activities outside the USA were directed towards

76 In what follows I rely on historical work by members of the church, in particular the excellent monograph by Daniel Ramirez (2015) as well as various contributions in Torres Alvarado (2014): Castillo Hernández 2014; Chiquete Beltrán 2014; Bustillos Almendáriz 2014; López Torres 2014; 1999; lastly also on an interview with Samuel López Torres of 1 November 2016.

Villa Aldama (Chihuahua) Torreón (Coahuila) and Gómez Palacio (Durango); the first permanent congregations were established in Mexicali / Calexico (Baja California Norte) and Santa Rosalía (BC Sur) (with about 30 congregations in the USA). For the mobilization and organization of a religious movement, identity-forming differences are inevitable. Glossolalia is sufficient for competitors like the Historical Protestant churches, but not for large (white) ones like the Assemblies of God. Thus, at the meetings of the leading heads – not least through the insistence of Romana Carbajal – the idea arose to adopt the theological theory of God's unicity (oneness) instead of His Trinity (as taught everywhere else); this is basically a strict adoption of Jewish monotheism into Christianity with the subtle difference that Jesus is the only divine person. Since this was expressed in the non-Trinitarian baptismal formula, it furnished a practical religious detail that strengthens the stability of the group membership of baptized members still today. In the 1920s, the first international meetings of church activists took place, which should be imagined less as business meetings than as religious service events emphasizing spiritual unity and Pentecostal identity. In addition, the Mexican missionaries were closely connected with the African-American Pentecostal Assemblies of the World, a oneness church, and took over material without, however, formally joining this church.

This last point is of interest for the mode of entanglement in as much as the Afro-American churches in the USA as a rule did not pursue missionary activities, which made this contact the result of solidarity between actors who both held a marginalized social position in the USA. In the long run, however, the Mexicans preferred to found their own organization in the USA, the Apostolic Assembly of the Faith in Christ Jesus (AAFCJ, 1930).

As migrants, however, they were largely without any defense against the social dynamics of their destination country. In the aftermath of the economic crisis of the 1920s and 30s, economically motivated hatred of Latino immigrants in the United States increased – as is often the case – leading to a repatriation program.

The number of more or less "voluntary" deportees varied, depending on the respective source, between a half and two million people. For the Church, the deported Pentecostals were a blessing. They increased both the potential of activists and their geographical distribution in Mexico. The Latino Pentecostals from the USA themselves, however, were getting out of the frying pan into the fire in so far as in Mexico the so-called Cristero conflict (1926-1929) between government and Catholic extremists had triggered a wave of violence against Protestants. The bottom line is that the development initiated by the deportation strengthened the Mexican side of the church and produced a partnership – through the increasing institutionalization of the churches on both sides of the border.

Where the social dynamics of the destination country required it, the flow of migrants went in the opposite direction. In 1942, due to the demand for labor caused by the entry into World War II, the USA and Mexico decided on the so-called *bracero* program which was to bring contract workers to the USA. But no sooner was the war over than the border police (from 1947) once again cracked down hard, and made aid for illegal immigrants (*wetbacks*) a punishable offense. Subsequently, a clearer distinction between legal and illegal immigrants was attempted through a quota system (Hart-Celler Act, 1965) and the Immigration Reform and Control Act (1986). Given this background, the congregations on both sides of the border assumed a strategic importance for the accompaniment of migration and the evangelization among migrants. Due to the great number of migrants, a second floor for migrant accommodation was to be constructed in the Apostolic church building in Tijuana in 1946, but this was not permitted for constructional reasons. A large kitchen – as is usual in all Apostolic churches (cf. Chiquete Beltrán 2014, 367) – and the use of various rooms as sleeping places nevertheless made it possible to supply migrants with what they needed. At the same time churches in the USA invited *braceros* from their camps to eat and to be evangelized. With this renewed pressure after the war the number of illegals in the Apostolic congregations increased, which usually tried to protect the newcomers to the best of their abilities. For communication and mutual recognition of church members – just as Weber described it for the early USA – letters of recommendation with additional notes from host congregations were used. For the support of all migrants, identity-creating symbols were also employed, such as the hymn “La Biblia es la Bandera” (The Bible is the national flag). In poetic analogy to the construction of the US flag, the song sings of the Pentecostals as citizens of the universal “eternal city”. It is a symbolic subversion – according to Ramírez’ interpretation – of the immigration policy of the USA (131 f.). Ramírez emphasizes that the Apostolic Pentecostals never understood their behavior as civil disobedience, but as the expression of a higher, religiously legitimized hospitality. This observation also applies to our studies (by Clara Buitrago and the author) in the Borderlands of today. It is religious dispositions that guide the perception, judgment and actions of these faithful.

The cross-border relations between the Apostolics in Mexico and those in the USA have been cultivated to this day through “international services,” conferences and mutual visits. Geographical proximity and kinship relationships have led to frequent everyday contacts, such as the visit of an Apostolic pastor from Los Angeles to Tijuana, who in a normal Sunday service performed a small show of new spiritual songs in the style of Frank Sinatra as a greeting to the congregation. However, the proximity between Apostolics on this and the other side of the border should not lead one to assume a proximity between Mexicans and Americans. A conversation with a leading personality of US citizenship revealed many experiences of humiliation in the USA, which contributed to a clear rejection of the American way of life, social inequality in the USA and the growing influence of US media.

Representatives of the IAFCJ count among negative influences from the USA in particular the Neopentecostalism since the 1980s in the upper middle class. Castillo Hernández (2014, 76ff.) criticizes its Prosperity, Dominion doctrine (*Kingdom now*) as well as management ideology. In addition, he parallelizes the Neopentecostals with the projection of the USA as a world power. Now, you could think that the IAFCI itself makes a fundamentalist claim to truth, since it describes itself as Apostolic. But this is not so because, first, there is a tendency to understand the development of the church and its doctrine as a process of change (Luque 2014, 168ff.). Second, there is no apostle. The term *apostolic* in this case refers to the assertion that the doctrine and practices of the Church correspond to *how* the apostles defined them at the time. The apostles of Neopentecostalism, by contrast, claim to *be* apostles themselves.

This is not to say that the IAFCJ has a liberal theological profile. Rather, doctrine and practices are conservative to the point where women wear headscarves in religious service. However, this conservative, typically Pentecostal doctrine is seen within its context. Castillo places the praxis of his church since the 1990s in the context of postmodernism, which spreads relativism, nihilism and consumerism, amongst other things. With recourse to the left-liberal German theologian Jürgen Moltmann, Castillo demands that the churches oppose postmodernism. To meet this goal, the Latin American culture is to serve as a model for church praxis, whereby Liberation Theology would become a theme to be critically examined, but could give impulses too. These would above all consist in the church's identification with the marginalized, in which process the church would have to stay non-political though it could of course point the government in the direction of meaningful action. And, finally, it would have to identify – despite certain criticisms – to a certain degree with Latin American popular culture.

Cults

In parallel with this selective identification with popular culture, the Apostolic Church in Tijuana also clearly distinguishes between two popular cults. While it views the cult of San Juan Soldado with a certain sympathy, it meets that of Santa Muerte (Holy Death) with rejection.

Saint Juan Soldado is modelled on a recruit of the 1940s who was sentenced to death though innocent, and is often revered as a miracle worker during migration. At the Panteón #1, the number one cemetery of Tijuana, his grave is found and the place where he was shot. The recruit was convicted of murder with rape, which was in fact committed by one of his superiors. On All Souls' Day, the *Dia de los Muertos*, the cemetery is full of visitors to the family tombs, who also make a visit and supplications to San Juan Soldado. Votive tablets speak of miracles, but graffiti also tell of pious enemies. In contrast, a rather robust man with tattoos all over his body told me that he brings flowers every week, because the saint keeps helping his family. Two apparently well-off ladies laid down a bouquet and crossed themselves. A taxi driver revealed what had already become clear from the conversations with the Apostolics: a Catholic person can go to San Juan Soldado without any problems because this man, like Jesus, was innocently murdered.

Completely different is *La Flaca* (the Skinny Lady), *La Santa Muerte* (Holy Death), the addressee of the eponymous cult. This cult is strictly rejected as satanic by Pentecostals and (official) Catholics. The cult originated in the 1960s in Catemaco, Veracruz. At its center is the worship of death as an archangel, represented by artfully dressed skeletons. The places of worship confuse not a few observers because of the frequent skeletons and a somewhat sinister atmosphere. The cult's representative in Tijuana was not available for interview, but the archbishop of the Church of Angels Mexico/USA – the official name of the cult – in Los Angeles was very friendly and obliging. A small building on Melrose Avenue houses a shop with merchandise and a tiny chapel. The Archbishop is a relaxed man who emphasized in an interview (10 November 2016) that Holy Death guides people into the light at the end of their days and helps them during their lives with all kinds of miracles. She does, however, not bring great prosperity, but helps instead relatively poor people in their everyday lives. People seek economic miracles and protection on the dangerous roads in the lower class districts. Besides the normal benevolence of saints, however, a special feature of La Santa is that she also helps criminals. Unlike other saints, she does not make a distinction between the underworld of the outlaws (*bajo mundo*) and the world of normal society (*alto mundo*). She protects thieves from the police and may under certain circumstances also help to kill someone who deserves it – in the same way as God helps the Israelites in the Old Testament against their enemies. She also helps to get rid of the fear of death. Without being able to undertake an in-depth analysis here, it seems to be the case that the cult gives a reverse mirror image of the living conditions of many people in the face of everyday criminality and illness by seeking to transform them into their opposite. Under some conditions of existence, death is always near; you have one foot in the grave and in the worNd of experience death always triumphs. If you experience the drama of life in this way, it may be more plausible to declare death itself the bringer of salvation instead of combating it, as does Christianity, through a religious projection of eternal life. In any case, it is evident that the cult of Santa Muerte – even if this was not intended by its inventors – has become the cult of choice of gangsters in the drug business (*narcos*).

Another very popular cult among narcos in the Borderlands is that of Jesús Malverde, whose central shrine is in Culiacán, the capital of the Sinaloa cartel. Jesús Malverde is a Robin Hood-like figure who emerged from the cult of a bandit and is in charge of similar tasks as the Flaca. In any case, shrines to Malverde and the Santa Muerte can be found along the roads near the border, and are said to follow the routes of drug trafficking and migration.[77]

These cults are indeed also associated with the drug trade by political actors. One of the propagandistic measures taken by President Calderón (2006-2012) in his "war on drug trafficking" was to have the shrines mentioned above destroyed by the military. The idea for this measure came most likely from his political advisors from the Neopentecostal milieu, the Orozco couple from Casa sobre la Roca.[78] In Tijuana, the action was supported by religious actors in

77 Interview with Liliana Rivera, COLMEX, 26 October 2016; Manuel Valenzuela, COLEF, 3 November 2016.

78 More details in Schäfer 2019.

the spirit of Spiritual Warfare as the conquest of the city from the clutches of evil. This violent action met with little understanding, at least among my conversational partners from apostolic circles. This was no way, they said, to deal with religious actors, even if you thought them illegitimate.

Drugs

Mexico's northern border cannot be imagined without the formative presence of drug trafficking. The cartels infiltrate the region's economy, politics and administration. They fight among themselves for *plazas*, border locations for trade connections with the USA, and often throttle civilian life for many months by covering them with powder, lead and blood. Not infrequently, they make use of migrants to transport drugs in backpacks or they forcibly recruit young men and condition them to become murderers, and compel women to work as prostitutes. They also make use of churches, whose various organizational levels have to handle the problem. Compared with the Catholic Church, it is the lower levels of Pentecostal churches that are involved: many aspects remain to be dealt with by the individual pastors as best they can.

In a seminar on ethical issues taught at the Centro Cultural Mexicano, the training center of the Apostolic Church in Tepito, a lower-class district of Mexico City, I was presented at the end of the 1990s with an ethical problem by participating pastors who saw it as relevant to their everyday lives. Quite a few pastors from congregations near the border received visits from representatives of some sort of cartel, who made an offer of *plata o plomo*, money or lead. The standing offer at the time was $1,000 a month – according to the pastors – if they allowed a drug depot to be set up underneath their church building. They were free to use the money for their church, family, or something else. But if the pastors did not agree, there would be lead. We could of course discuss the problem in terms of consequentialist ethics, but improve the precarious practical situation of the pastors we could not.

The usefulness of Pentecostal churches for the camouflage of criminal activities has long since been recognized by drug cartels and translated into their own strategies. There are by now whole denominations, networks of congregations that serve as an infrastructure for drug trafficking, the *narco-iglesias*. There is such a group for example in a village in the western highlands of Guatemala. It was the only church where the pastor received a salary and the members of the church choir a fee from the head office. A few years before, the pastor had had enough, but knew too much. His daughter studied at a provincial university. When he handed in his resignation, so to speak, it was rejected and the girl killed for good measure.

In a way, Neopentecostal megachurches are predestined for another form of entanglement in drug crimes. With the immense amount of donations, which in most cases – but not in Mexico – can be managed without any controls, these organizations are ideally suited to money laundering.[79] Investigations in this direction (most recently at the Casa de Dios in Guatemala, 2018) have been repeatedly carried out by government agencies.

The drug mafia is also in other respects a highly ambivalent presence for some Pentecostal churches. In cities where the families of higher officers of the cartels live, it is not uncommon for their wives and children to attend Pentecostal churches and incidentally provide strong financial support for the work of the congregations. What was he to do, a pastor of such a church asked me, throw them out or insult them by refusing their money?

And lastly, there are Protestant initiatives at congregational level for the "exit without *exitus*" of gang members, a widespread praxis throughout Latin America. Socially well-established churches or individual activists receive people willing to leave, convert them and turn them into church members. They give the gangs a guarantee that the converts will not defect to other gangs but will be active in the church from then on. These activities take place at various levels, even up to the higher echelons of the cartels.

---

79 De Sanctis 2015 offers a good survey.

Pastor Rivera of the Apostolic Church in Tijuana experienced a not very common case.[80] A few years before our interview, he was called for an appointment for a pastoral interview. In time for the appointment, an elegantly dressed man appeared in his simple office in the somewhat ramshackle church building. The man explained that psychological advice was no use for him: he could no longer sleep, was extremely nervous and had nothing but arguments with his family. All he wanted was peace at last. He offered the pastor a large sum of money for a successful course of treatment. The entire setting made the pastor feel that the man was involved in drug trafficking, so he confronted him with a conditional offer of a pastoral care process. One of the conditions was that he would not accept money, neither for himself nor as a donation to the church. The man was also not to come to church services. (Given the social position of the members, this would probably have led to confusion anyway). Instead, the pastor continued, he wanted to work with him at the man's home. A process of four years began, in which the pastor also got to know the man's wife and daughter. First he introduced the man to religious reflection and rudimentary religious practices: prayer and laying on of hands. Then he got the wife and daughter involved in their conversations. A first obstacle was the altar of Santa Muerte ("Leave out the 'Santa' when you talk about it! It is simply death") in the daughter's room. It had to be removed in the course of time. (The pastor did not speak about any resistance to this.) As time passed, it turned out that the man was a high-ranking functionary in the regional drug cartel and the owner, among other things, of a chain of companies set up from his mafia businesses. The pastor made it clear to him that he could only find peace if he repented, freed himself of all illegitimate possessions and resigned his activities in the cartel. That was the biggest obstacle, the pastor said, because that meant he had stood up against the cartel. After initial talks with the head of the cartel, the cartel had conducted intensive investigations into the man's life and that of the pastor for more

80 Interview with Pastor Rivera, IAFCJ, 4 November 2016, Tijuana.

than two years. Further talks with the boss followed. The functionary returned all his assets to the cartel and meticulously documented the transfer. He was left with nothing but a small apartment that had long belonged to his family. At present he works in a civilian profession, does not go to the pastor's Apostolic congregation and can sleep peacefully again. Conclusion of the pastor: finding a new member for his church was not the point. The point was to change your life with the help of God.

From a sociological perspective it becomes clear that there are more aspects to conversion than proselytism. For those who have become believers a whole new view opens up of themselves and their capabilities. In other words, it generates courage. "Everything is possible to him who believes" (Mark 9:23). This includes also the overcoming of the border fence that cuts through the borderlands. Whether this means that the Promised Land has been reached remains an open question, for the time being.

6.3 Promised Land?

While the USA was the Promised Land for the Pilgrims and remains so for some White Anglo-Saxon Protestants also today, immigrants and seasonal workers from Latin America can be expected to make more down-to-earth assessments. The USA is a place for migrant workers where they can find work and then, if they manage to legalize themselves, build a life in a Latino community in "Spanglish." Members of the Sanctuary movement in the USA offered refugees in the 1980s protection from the wars in Central America, which were largely fueled by the US government. Since then the Sanctuary movement has been closely associated with the ecumenically oriented churches of the National Council of Churches. The Riverside Church of Pastor Coffin in New York was an important Sanctuary congregation; it is located round the corner from the Interchurch Center – the so-called God Box – where the NCC and some of its member churches are based. These actors, and by now entire cities, are still active today in providing shelter for people fleeing from the consequences of the authoritarian neo-liberalism in Latin America. And again they are today still the object of attacks from the religious right. The religio-political struggle in the USA for inclusive or exclusive concepts of salvation has by no means been settled. The more white Evangelicals see their share of the population dwindle, the more they view strangers as a danger. And the stronger the objective entanglements, the more intense the fear of entanglement. For Franklin Graham, Sanctuary places are "just a little picture of Hell" (cf. Smith 2018). For people like Mr. Graham, who travel only by plane at home and abroad and whose imagination is just about sufficient to grasp their own religious symbolism, it will likely always remain inconceivable that illegal migrants experience the border fence, the deserts on this and the other side, and the reception camps of the border police as a very concrete hell.

Through the Desert to the Promised Land

For Francisco Quiacaín – an old acquaintance – this is true.[81] He was born in the 1950s, lived as a Maya in a highland village in Guatemala and survived the war as a deacon in a congregation of the Asambleas de Dios. He began by struggling through in the capital with various casual jobs. Back in his village, he worked at first as a farmhand and developed an unconventional business idea. Then, as a traveling ice cream vendor with a small handcart he just about made ends meet. After all, he was able to marry and have five children with Magdalena, to whom he is still faithful today. After the war he was committed to environmental protection in his village (ban on plastics), and worked as sports commentator and on the environment for a pirate radio station. He also changed from the Asambleas to an indigenous Pentecostal church. His engagement

81 He was one of our informants during our field research in the 1980s and again in Clara Buitrago's project (2014) as well for my own field research in Los Angeles in 2016. The sources for the present passage are interviews in Los Angeles, one by Clara Buitrago, 2 June 2014, and the other by me on 10 November 2016.

there as a singer, accordionist and organizer brought him prestige and deepened his ascetic habitus and belief that every step you take depends in some mysterious way on God. He built a house on a small plot of land which belonged to his family. His economic situation got worse and a bad debt threatened. So he considered going to the USA. He talked to his family about it and they decided to wait for a sign of God's will. The illegal trip to the USA was said to cost about 2,500 dollars. If this amount could be borrowed, it would be the will of God, if not, it was not to be. In the event, the money came and on 10 August 2004 Francisco set off to follow the will of God. The journey then was less dangerous than the same journey would be today, because the drug cartels – especially the Zetas – had not yet discovered the refugees as easy prey for robbery, blackmail and kidnapping. Most of the journey was organized by Mexican traffickers, popularly called *coyotes*. People traveled in freight cars of the infamous refugee train *La Bestia*, or cars, buses or walked as far as the Sonora desert near the border, from where they started on a laborious march to the border fence and into the Arizona desert. They ran out of water. Things got difficult. On the US side, they were picked up by *coyotes* at some distance from the border and transported further in a closed truck. The air ran out, they struggled for oxygen. At the last moment – "we would have had it in twenty minutes" – the truck reached its destination.

Francisco only survived because God walked with him. In his description of the way, the communal prayer in the group of migrants plays the decisive role. A detailed analysis of the praxis of Pentecostal migrants in Los Angeles confirms the importance of religious convictions for the entanglement of Pentecostal migrants with US society. But the USA itself is not given a religious connotation. It simply offers a good opportunity to earn money to help educate their children in Guatemala and build a house on the outskirts of their home town. Moreover, the USA is a country with many vices and libertinage, where you have to observe closely God's commandments in order not to get lost. You can really trust only religious people, or rather: religious Latinos. You are in the USA so as to be able to return to Guatemala one day.

To be sure, people like Francisco Quiacaín are not typical of all religious migrants and transnational religious actors. It is necessary to draw distinctions.

Types of Transnational Actors

The most elegant way to approach the transnational praxis of religious actors would surely be to use the methods of HabitusAnalysis.[82] For a general map of the relevant actors, however, the necessary data is lacking. We will, therefore, only present three types here. Nevertheless, it is possible to take a look at some micro-sociological depth. Clara Buitrago uses habitus analysis to examine two of these typical formations; her work furnishes a more precise insight into the religious identities and strategies of these actors (Buitrago 2021).

The three types mentioned above, as developed by the author of this study, are managers, church founders and migrants.[83] Each of these types of transnational religious actors is associated with their own social class position and their own form of transnational entanglement. Even if the social sciences have been threatened with suffocation from the dominance of culturalist approaches for some

82 This would mean proceeding in three steps. A transnational religious field would have to be established, in which to show the competition between religious providers. Furthermore, transnationally relevant formations of religious habitūs would be gathered for a differentiated view of the demand for salvation goods. Finally, one would have to construct a space of transnational allocation of the most relevant forms of capital, which relates religious praxis to other forms of social practice. Cf. Schäfer 2013, 2016 and 2020.

83 Cf. Schäfer 2016. Originally, Ms Buitrago's research project was designed to compare managers and migrants. It turned out to be not feasible because management organizations – i.e. megachurches and the like – were unwilling to grant Ms Buitrago interviews or access for observation.

time now, we should follow Anja Weiß (Weiß and Berger 2008) who has shown that there is no way we can avoid taking economic capital into account as a decisive factor in distinguishing between forms of transnational praxis. It is similarly evident that other forms of capital, such as social or cultural, play a role on a subordinate level. Managers, at any rate, have considerably more capital at their disposal than church founders, and the latter in turn more than migrants.

The category of managers refers to the functionaries or owners or gurus of religious event agencies working transnationally, in the church vocabulary also called *ministries*. The model of the mission agency free of ties to a denomination goes back to the so-called Faith Missions, which originated in the USA in the 19th century and influenced a fairly large part of the US mission in Latin America, particularly in the Neopentecostal phase. Enterprises such as those of Billy Graham, Donald McGavran, Jimmy Swaggart or Luis Palau determined for a long time the direction of entanglement from north to south. This is not quite over today but has weakened (in favor of media presence) and is counteracted above all by Latin American religious firms with considerable communicative clout. Probably the most successful is the Brazilian Igreja Universal do Reino de Deus (IURD), which is active in well over 100 countries – including the USA, that goes without saying – and not only fills stadiums with interested parties but also founds congregations. To these must be added in Brazil a whole string of transnationally engaged megachurches. In Colombia, for example the Misión Carismática Internacional swears by transnational dissemination. And even in small countries like Guatemala there are megachurches like the Casa de Dios that operate across America, and propagate Guatemala – more precisely: their own buildings – as the new Jerusalem to which peoples (should) now make a pilgrimage. A self-presentation that is in competition with that of the IURD, which in São Paulo allegedly built the Temple of Solomon according to old plans, thus making the same claim. Quite incidentally and without commenting explicitly, these self-dramatizations also question the claim of the US-

American religious right that the USA is the New Jerusalem. Of course, the Latin American actors mentioned also operate in the USA, primarily through mass events, to which a mainly Latino clientele comes, but which are in competition with similar events, for example by Benny Hinn. As for the history of entanglement, from a formal point of view the geographical direction of the initiative has changed; or at least a space of transnational operations has opened up in which not only northern but also southern actors operate. Much is to be said for the usefulness of a description of a transnational space or a transnational class, along very similar lines to those used by Sklair (2001) for the world of finance. Indeed, there is small difference either in the mode of action or even the contents conveyed. In general, the focus was on the successful management of your own life, positive thinking and prosperity. Without precise analysis, the only impression that suggests itself is that Latin Americans talk a little more about miracles and US Americans a little more about Dominion. It would seem then that a relatively uniform vocabulary is developing in the transnational religious management class, at least in the Americas. Entanglement here becomes a fusion due to increasing equality of global positioning.

Less economic capital, but a closer cultural integration into local religious praxis is instead established among the type of "church founders." By this category we primarily understand (besides smaller local initiatives of active pastors) relatively large churches that operate in the lower class, such as the Brazilian Deus é Amor, Ebenezer from Guatemala or Restauración Elim from El Salvador.[84] In addition to these relatively large companies, pastors from small churches also travel to the USA to found congregations of Latin American immigrants and visit them more or less regularly, as does Pastor Eladio Velázquez from the Samaria Church in Guatemala. These founding organizations function according to the traditional model of the missionary church, which establishes congregations

84 In as much as IURD also forms congregations it can also be counted among this type.

abroad while continuing to play the role of "mother church." The latter represents a religious identity shaped by national identity even abroad (for example, through a national flag in the church building). In the "daughter churches" there are often disproportionately many compatriots of the founder and local pastors, male and female. But an internationalization is also taking place, not so much according to national identity as to social class affiliation. An example is the mostly poor Bolivian migrants in Argentina who gather in the local congregations of the Brazilian underclass church Deus é Amor. Entanglement occurs in a culturally deepened but unilaterally dominant way due to the formation of congregations, the social position of the actors, the anchoring of the members in different cultures and the asymmetrical power relationship between founders and clientele. Pastors working at the economically "lower edge" of this formation are usually quite proactive. These are close to the religious migrants in many respects. The most important difference, however, is in the possession or not of a material basis for transnational religious expeditions.

Our category of "migrant" refers to people like Francisco Quiacaín who came to the USA under difficult conditions in order to work – not to missionize. In contrast to the managers, both the small church founders and the faithful migrants are rooted in a Latin American Pentecostalism that has undergone important, culturally determined changes in religious habitus, which we have already examined above. As for entanglement, a relatively strong dynamic is to be expected here too, which works in a dialectical fashion so to speak: a Protestant doctrine is transplanted to Latin America, is transformed there and then returns as a transformed doctrine to the USA, where it admittedly operates mainly among Latino believers, but nevertheless in a US-American cultural and social context.

A further difference between the marginal church founders and ordinary migrants is their respective religious position, i.e. the founders represent a Latin American institution that may already have branches in the USA; as religious professionals they have a visa; and they have the backing of their institution, no matter how small it is. Clara Buitrago's HabitusAnalysis shows a discursively mediated religious identity that revolves around the building of communities. The central problem has been specified as lack of ambition and fear of leadership positions. *God as restorer* – according to the discourse – forms a leader out of the fearful preacher, who stands up for prosperity (that of the church members). By means of various forms of proclamation (including coaching), this leader fights the lack of faith that leads to a despondent attitude. The founders seek to strengthen the members' engagement in the churches they have planted, which also always means propagation of their own faith in the US-American neighborhoods. With regard to entanglement, where these preachers and their congregations are concerned we can see a clear reversal of the direction of impact.

Migrants usually have none of the prerequisites that the founders bring with them. Many of them even live illegally in the USA without the slightest institutional support. At best they are reliable workers in churches – like Francisco Quiacaín – and thus acquire symbolic and social capital. Nevertheless, close analysis shows that religiosity works important transformations in them. Many Pentecostal migrants, according to Buitrago, deal with the harshness of their situation by using a logic of Spiritual Warfare. They meet the most widespread problems such as loneliness, sadness, economic hardship and alcohol by attributing them to the work of the devil and by counteracting it with the authority of God. By submitting themselves to God's authority, they find in the church, to quote their own statements, comradeship, "brotherhood" (Weber), health and happiness. If you look at Francisco Quiacaín's everyday life from this angle, it has happened in exactly this way for fifteen years: being obedient to God's authority means being a reliable worker; covering the 20 km every morning at 5:00 am to Santa Monica and waiting for casual work at the DIY superstore; sending home much of the money earned; housing and instructing his sons in Los Angeles; never working on Sundays, but playing the accordion in at least two services and perhaps preaching, and occasionally wearing a colorful jersey to a football match. Above all, however, as in the march through the desert, it means asking and thanking God at all times. Out of this praxis emerges a relatively stable position in the midst of the instability of an illegal life in a foreign country. Insofar as this country is also marked by libertinism and many other errors, the migrant himself participates in church activities, now also preaching occasionally, and has greater responsibility: he now proclaims the truth to an erring people in order to lead them back to the ways of the Lord. In other words, the new strategies have radically changed his identity. Buitrago summarizes this in her study as the difference between *migrants* and *expatriates*. *Migrants* are uprooted and needy people, in the perception of the public as well as often in their own. The term *expatriate*, on the other hand, refers to experts who are sent, for example, as development workers for a certain period of time. Francisco Quiacaín does something similar. He is an *expatriate* serving a double development aid task: spiritual aid in the USA and material aid for his family in Guatemala. His term of service will soon be over. He will probably return to his village next year.

Needy *migrants* turn into *expatriates* who offer spiritual help. By a change in the self-positioning of the actors and their objective position in the churches, a change in their strategies takes place and thus a change in the impact they have in the USA. Today, Latino Pentecostals fill large churches, and their preacher's entire stadiums; and Latino Catholics are transforming Catholicism in the USA. Entanglement in the USA means not least religious competition as well as social and political alternatives.

Changes in US Protestantism

Protestantism once went to Latin America with an individual message of salvation and an economically liberal social doctrine, and now returns to the USA with migrants and church founders who carry with them an option for the extended family and big government. The "return" of Protestantism from its trip south to the USA has consequently not only quantitative but also qualitative aspects. In addition, this return does not sever the connections to the South.

Due to the rapid development of the media over the last two decades, migrants remain in constant communication with their families and church groups – at home. Their ancestral social and religious identities persist more stubbornly.

To be sure, it is first of all the sheer increase of the Hispanic population that makes white Evangelicals fear the end of the "Christian nation" is approaching. After all, in 1991 they still made up half of the US population; this has shrunk today however to only one third (Jones and Cox 2017, 23). The development in the "New Southwest" must appear to them particularly drastic. Over 30% of the population are Hispanics in these states: Arizona, California, New Mexico and Texas. About 13% of the total US population speak Spanish at home. If you want to move around in Southern California, you can get by with Spanish very well – but you won't feel lonely in New York either (Flores 2017a). After all, it is not as if Catholics were the only factor causing angst in White Anglo Saxon Protestants. In the last decade if not earlier, a clear trend has become established among Hispanics from Catholicism to Protestantism – mostly to Pentecostal churches. Whereas 69% of those surveyed in 2006 still described themselves as Catholics, by 2013 this figure had fallen to only 59%. The increase in the number of Evangelical Pentecostal organizations was almost complementary (Pew Research Center 2014, 37f.).

If you wonder about the reasons for this trend, you will not find it in a "US-Americanization" of Catholicism or some such thing. What will strike you instead is that most converts are relatively recent Catholic migrants. 16% of foreign-born migrants in the USA changed their denomination.[85] There is a lot to suggest that they experience a more immediate integration (not just welfare) in Pentecostal churches, which goes hand in hand with a religious redefinition of their identity and role. This corresponds in Pentecostal His-

85 Pew Research Center 2014, 12. About 30% of foreign-born immigrants have left Catholicism through conversion, 16% after entering the USA and 13% in their countries of origin.

panic churches to the fact it is not charitable programs that are increasingly established, but enthusiastic liturgical forms, such as are also known in weaker form in the Catholic charismatic movement. In case they do not yet know them from Latin American Pentecostal and Neopentecostal churches, the converts learn about practices of spiritual empowerment from the perspective of subaltern migrants. Anyway, almost half of the members of enthusiastic Protestant groups claim to have experienced at least some of the following practices:[86] divine healing, direct divine revelation, exorcism of demons and glossolalia.

From the population development mentioned – and this is surely only one of the reasons – an important difference can be derived also between white Evangelicals on the one hand and Latino as well as black Protestants: expectations for the future. 75% of the Protestant Latinos surveyed expected the overall situation to improve in the next 10 years.[87] A similar survey found that 70% of the white Evangelicals were of the opinion that the situation in the USA since the 1950s had become worse, while only 38% of Latino Catholics shared this view.[88]

Many of the white Evangelicals, especially of the religious right, react to this development with jeremiads about the decay of the nation, the development of a circle-of-wagons mentality or apocalyptic expectations. This in turn provokes debates in the Evangelical scene with New Evangelicals who, like Gregory Boyd, roundly call the idea of the Christian nation a myth (Boyd 2005). In this way the increasing presence of Hispanic Christians among the white Evangelicals triggers a debate about their religious identity and the way they see their politics.

---

86 On average, 48% of Protestants as opposed to 22% of Catholics. See Pew Research Center 2014, 95f.

87 The Hispano average is 72% (Pew Research Center 2014, 131).

88 The Latino Protestants were not included (Jones et al. 2016, 8).

In their political views the average Latino Christians differ greatly from the white Evangelicals.[89] Of central importance for the US-American political discussion is the issue of the competences and responsibilities of government, of big or small Government. It is striking that easily the largest majority of Hispanics prefer further government competencies.[90] A strong state is perceived as normal throughout Latin America, especially in Mexico, with 62% of Protestants and 72% of Catholics being in favor of big government. This result is entirely consistent with the more corporatist and communitarian orientation of the Catholic Church, which reinforces the Hispanics' inclination toward the welfare state.

In terms of party politics, white Evangelicals are firmly aligned with Republicans (49% R, 14% D),[91] while Latinos are clearly sympathetic to Democrats. However, there is a small difference that offers food for thought: 40% of Catholic Latinos side with the Democrats (9% R), while only 30% of Protestants do so (with 17% R; see Jones and Cox 2017, 36). Why this is so, I am currently unable to answer conclusively. It probably has to do with the influence of the political tendencies of the leadership of the Catholic Church on the one hand and those of the Evangelical spokespersons on the other. There is likely also the fact that Catholicism among Hispanos is more a matter of habitual religiosity with low acute mobilization potential, while the awakened Protestantism among them represents a younger and strongly mobilizing form of religion. Thus, the generally observable connection between the intensity of Christian religious praxis and political conservatism in the USA would be relevant to the explanation of this difference: the more often individuals go to church and pray, and the more strongly they represent Bibli-

89 For the USA always including the classic Pentecostals!

90 On average 67% for big versus 21% for small government; see Pew Research Center 2014, 130.

91 The remaining respondents only lean towards one side or are completely undecided.

cism, the more they are anti-abortionists and inclined toward the Republicans.[92]

As for entanglement, we find in these political attitudes an interesting repercussion of the political system on the structuration of the Hispanic presence in the USA. This effect can be seen even more clearly for Protestantism. Two Hispano-Protestant umbrella organizations have emerged that replicate the sharp political polarization of the US in the Latino community.

Latino Organizations

At the beginning of the new millennium two large Protestant Latino organizations established themselves in the USA and directed the return of Protestantism to the north through political channels. Both were Evangelical-Pentecostal in religious style. In religio-political orientation, the larger tends more towards MANAGEMENT and is on the right, while the smaller leans toward VALUES and is left-wing liberal.

The left-liberal National Latino Evangelical Coalition[93] (NaLEC), founded in 2010 by the pastor of the multi-ethnic Lamb's Church in New York Gabriel Salguero, represents about 3,000 Evangelical Latino churches, NGOs and individuals. Besides lobbying for the reform of the immigration laws which is omnipresent among Hispanics, NaLEC seeks to raise its profile as an advocacy voice for social justice and the common good. This is achieved through long-term partnerships with aid organizations, programs for the further education of member organizations, and political advocacy. The organization maintains contacts with the New Evangelicals and corresponds to their combination of theologically conservative and socially progressive programs. Thus, the organization always "seeks God's guidance" and at the same time distinguishes itself through campaigns to facilitate social action and coalition building for the com-

92 Nota bene: 29% of the religiously non-affiliated say a daily prayer.

93 http://nalec.org/ (accessed 19 January 2019).

mon good and social justice. Measures are aimed at these areas, among others: poverty and hunger "among U.S. under-served communities"; reform of immigration legislation; educational justice; health reform; youth work; reform of the penal system; current emergency aid, especially on the border with Mexico. NaLEC also works together with NGOs such as International Urban Strategies, Evangelical Immigration Table, Evangelical Environmental Network and Evangelicals for Social Action.

The National Hispanic Christian Leadership Conference (NH CLC)[94] was founded in 2001 by Rev. Samuel Rodriguez to "unify, serve and represent the Hispanic Evangelical Community," as the website informs. The organization claims to represent 40,000 congregations. Very much in the style of the MANAGEMENT formation, Rodríguez wants to tailor the "divine (vertical)" and the "human (horizontal)" dimension of an imaginary space to the "Lamb's agenda" through the seven directives of the organization. This means roughly that as the supreme "leader" he wants to shape born-again people into "key influencers" in the "marketplace." He even claims that the NHCLC reconciles Billy Graham's program with that of Martin Luther King. The means with which to counteract the media image of the angry white Evangelical is a "…convicted yet compassionate multi-ethnic kingdom-culture community committed to sharing truth with love".[95] Besides, he adds, a multi-ethnic firewall is to be erected of biblical marriage, rejection of abortion and freedom of religion against moral relativism, cultural decadence and half-hearted support of the church. "Influence" must be brought to bear on education, the media, business, art, government and church. An interesting difference to NaLEC is his concept of justice. While NaLEC understands by social justice a non-guaranteed condition of humanity, NHCLC places justice in the context of compassion on the one hand, and understands it on the other as retributive restoration of an abstract balance through wages and punishment. Freedom

94 http://nhclc.org/ (accessed 19 January 2019).

95 https://nhclc.org/mission-vision-statement (accessed 25 October 2019).

of religion is conceived as the freedom of political representatives to admit religious influence on politics. Given this program and its strong co-optation performance (40,000 congregations), it is small wonder that Rodríguez is a member of the religious advisory circle round President Donald Trump, the so-called *Court Evangelicals* (Fea).

Samuel Rodríguez of the NHCLC was born the son of Puerto Rican parents – that is, with US citizenship – in the USA. He has both feet firmly planted on US American ground. His unique political selling point, however, without which he certainly would not have made it into the White House, is to mediate between Republican politics and the interests of those Latinos who are still affected by the laws on immigration and deportation. He serves Republican standards with a recurrent emphasis on legality and occasional minor defamations, such as the reference to the "birthing industry" to obtain citizenship for babies by giving birth in the USA. On the other hand, he modifies Trump's proposals and advises against a constitutional amendment, for example to abolish the birthright.[96] He used an advertisement in the New York Times to spread the message that "immigrants and immigration strengthen these United States."[97] In connection with the "caravan" of migrants from Central America he affirms the duty of Christians to help those in need. But he entrusts this task to the churches in Mexico and Central America,

96 'We Could Do Better' – Trump Faith Advisor Says President Should Talk About More than Immigration (http://nhclc.org/we-could-do-better-trump-faith-advisor-says-president-should-talk-about-more-than-immi gration/ and https://www1.cbn.com/cbnnews/us/2018/november/we-could-do-better-ndash-trump-faith-advisor-says-president-should-talk-about-more-than-immigration (accessed 21 January 2019).

97 'How We Treat Immigrants Reflects Our Values': Christian Leaders Publish Pro-Immigration NYT Ad http://nhclc.org/how-we-treat-immigrants-reflects-our-values-christian-leaders-publish-pro-immi gration-nyt-ad/ from: https://www1.cbn.com/cbnnews/us/2018/july/how-we-treat-immigrants-reflects-our-values-nbsp-christian-leaders-publish-pro-immigration-nyt-ad (accessed 5 July 2018).

quite in Trump's spirit, arguing that states must protect their borders and that illegal crossing – by the 70% of young men in the caravan – is a violation of the law. Rodriguez has so far solved such migration problems in a legalistic way. In doing so, he relies quite clearly on the established Latinos in the USA, the *pochos*,[98] because although illegal immigrants are indispensable as agricultural workers, they have no lobby. This, too, is probably entirely to Trump's, but less so to Francisco Quiacaín's liking.

Trump in the Perception of Illegal Pentecostals

On election night in November 2016 I was in church. In a small Pentecostal storefront church, not far south of McArthur Park in Los Angeles, where a congregation meets that is largely made up of illegal immigrants. The sober room with the everlasting grandstand on one side and a few tables with coffee machines on the other was decorated with a long row of flags representing all Latin American nations.

The atmosphere around 6 o'clock in the evening before the prayer service began was tense. Trump's racist and xenophobic election campaign had not left the politically less interested members of the congregation untouched; even less so the threats against migrants. For the thirty or so people present, the question now was what God was likely to do about it. The conversations showed that they had a clear political opinion: no Trump! The pastor also shared this view. She also knew very well that they should have no illusions about Trump, especially when you were an illegal immigrant. The meeting this evening took place under a special sign.

The pastor routinely began the service with the usual entry rituals, prayers and the usual unspecific greeting of the congregation. Then she decided to leave the usual format and asked all present to

98 The term *pochos* is used to refer to US citizens of Latin American descent who have lived in the USA for a long time, can even be second or third generation citizens, and whose identity is often predicated on their demarcation from Latin America.

line up in a circle in front of the platform. She began her address with a gloomy description of the situation. It is an important day, she said, for all Latinos and especially for the illegal migrants to whom Trump represents a very real danger. If Trump is elected, she continued, you can expect a lot of despair. The country is in great danger and in a serious crisis. Following this analysis of the situation, she did not, however, call for protest or political action. She even said in so many words that protest with placards in front of the White House was not the means to counter Trump, but rather "the knee," i.e. prayer.

That was why a "defensive wall" against the influence of the devil was now to be formed from within the circle, with everyone reaching out and linking their hands in prayer. In this way, she assured her congregation, the devil could not carry through his interests. In prayer, they should ask for God's intention to be fulfilled and his will to be done. In prayer itself, where the pastor's voice was occasionally buried under the swelling hubbub of the faithful saying their prayers quite loudly, she first of all invoked the blood of Christ in the usual way. Then the prayer's content was not developed in the direction of exorcism, which could have been expected if the believers had had sufficient opportunities for action. No, the implicit identification of Trump with the devil was relativized instead in a number of different ways, but all with the same vanishing point: religious action and God's unfathomable advice as the last word. God has a plan, she said, even if we cannot know it. God can also transform the heart of a person like Trump. And finally, she "declared" – completely in the style of the Dominion doctrine, but without political consequences – "God's rule over this nation;" and this rule was to make itself felt as religious "awakening," so that "people recognize that there is hope only in you [God]." *Gloria a Dios*!

At that time, the people who attended the service had no idea which way the projections were going and the same went for statisticians. The performative unity – created by the "protective wall" with an implicit demonization of Trump on the one hand and the prayer text offering only religious compensation on the other – left the outcome of things undecided. If Trump lost, this was a success of spiritual containment of the machinations of the devil. If he won, then God surely knew the reason and would reserve a field of action for himself – the transformation of the heart. And finally, the politically completely powerless illegals were not overtaxed with demands for political action, but were shown a way out in the form of danger-free religious action (prayer) with a religious outcome (revival).

In a similar way the pastor continued her discourse after the prayer with a – quite well informed – explanation of the political context. Even if Trump became president, he would not be able to do what he wanted because there was still the Supreme Court. Besides, a president was dependent on advisors and officials. So they should pray for the ministers, the heads of the various departments. So far, so good; at least a relevant political issue had found its way into the religious consciousness of the faithful.

This was, however, followed by the systematic confusion of spheres, which makes so many believers of the lower classes to be taken in by the religious right: if only believers and "God-fearing" people came into government offices, they would pass correspondingly good laws and pursue good policies. In another free prayer, the main topic of the migrants was first the economic stability in the form of jobs and a modest livelihood. Then the pastor inserted into her sermon the permanent topic of "Israel," popular with Evangelicals the world over. She did not, however, talk about a transfer of the US embassy to Jerusalem, a goal that the religious right had been pursuing for a long time, but stayed firmly in the religious field. More precisely, she got stuck on the perpetual paradox of conservative Evangelical and Pentecostal enthusiasm for Israel: the Israelis were to be converted to Christianity and to Jesus as the true Messiah.

Time passed with a long speech by a guest preacher and a Bible lesson, neither referring to the elections. Toward the end of the service at 10 p.m. (Pacific Time), reasonably reliable projections were available, and the mood hit rock-bottom. The pastor said that although Trump was a dangerous man for the immigrants, it was God's will that he should rule. God was able to use his power to change the heart of the president and therefore they should pray that God would turn Trump into a pious man or at least one that obeyed the law, and that he would find him the right counselors. But the church members should know – no matter what happened – that God would carry out his plan for the benefit of "his people".

The bottom line is that the pastor's message is maybe the only thing that can be told a group of illegal migrants that find themselves without any political or social means of action in this situation. The fact that emphatic prayers for economic stability were said in a situation of great political tension indicates the urgent concerns of the congregation. Even three years after this service, Francisco said in a Skype conversation that because of God's plans, Trump was not really important to him; what was much more important was that he could find work regularly and send money home. That is obvious. Highly vulnerable to clever political manipulation is, however, the widespread belief that people with a religious facade are the more acceptable politicians. But the effects of this belief are likely to be minimal among people who are not allowed to vote or cannot afford to get nabbed at political events. And finally, because of the Israel topic, people attending church services also easily get into the bad company of those who would like to deport them immediately – who make great journalistic efforts, of course, in order to score points with their electorate among the white Evangelicals and the *pochos*.

The day after Trump's election, I listened to a Latino religious radio station in Los Angeles. The commentator was impressed by God's decision to put Trump into office. Of course, migrants had problems, he gave his listeners to understand. But to a large extent, he said, it was their own fault if they crossed the border illegally. In short, the commentator played down the difficulties that migrants were now expected to face and, in addition, he also blamed the victims themselves for their hardships. More important, the speaker continued, Trump would now put an end to homosexuality and drugs. This showed him to be on the side of God. Besides, this great country also had a great democracy. "God bless America." End of show.

7 Panama 2016 and the Social Context

After 100 years of US mission against the background of the 1916 Congress of Panama, Panama opened its doors again to a congress and meeting in 2016 – this time without threats of excommunication by the Archbishop. Both gatherings recalled the earlier missionary congress, although from very different perspectives. The conference of Latin American Pentecostals put on the table a counter proposal for church praxis. The World Evangelical Alliance Congress seemed to open up new horizons under the motto of polycentric mission; but on closer inspection it continued the old model. Before we take a look at these events, we will briefly list some sources of confusion between Latin American and US Protestants.

7.1 Misunderstanding

In our reflections on the Promised Land we have focused on confusions caused by the emergence of more and more religious Latinos among Protestants in the USA, and especially among white Evangelicals. By far the greater source of confusion in Latin America is caused by the Protestant mission, in particular that of the conservative Evangelicals. Entanglement occurs here not as intended, but as systemically inevitable misunderstanding.

Christian Nation

A large part of the mission activities is carried out by the LAW and MANAGEMENT formations. Many of these actors consider the USA to be a Christian nation with the obligation to spread "the Gospel" all over the globe – or to be more precise: their rather particular version of it. I have met many missionaries who do this with deeply held conviction and the cheerful certainty that they are doing something really good for their addressees. (Others have given up this idea and become theologians alongside their Latin American colleagues, without claiming a special assignment from the USA). If they are convinced that the USA is a Christian nation or even *the* exemplary Christian nation, they are suffering from a dangerous delusion. Gregory Boyd describes this error from the perspective of the New Evangelicals (Boyd 2005). He poses the question of the role of the idea of the Christian nation in the context of mission and US foreign policy. As an example he takes the Iraq war under President G.W. Bush, who waged this unjust war as a practicing Evangelical combined with the rhetoric of spreading "freedom" around the world. But what "some people around the globe" heard, Boyd says, was "that American imperialism is alive and well" and that the US was aggressively and selfishly trying to bring other governments under its control. But the crux of the mission is not this connection. It is

> that this disdain gets associated with Christ when America is identified as a Christian nation. The tragic irony is that those who should be most vehemently denying the association for the purpose of preserving the beautiful holiness of the kingdom of God ... are the primary ones insisting on the identification! The result is that it has become humanly impossible for many around the globe to hear the good news as good. Instead ... they hear the gospel as bad news, as American news, explosive capitalistic news, greedy news, violent news, and morally decadent news. They can't see the beauty of the cross because everything the American flag represents to them is in the way. (Boyd 2005, chapter 6.2, paragraph 1)

It is precisely because Boyd does not doubt that the US mission is meaningful, and does himself some work in foreign countries for his church (this however more in the area of social services), and advocates for Evangelical convictions himself – it is for these reasons that his criticism is in effect particularly trenchant. The white Evangelicals – above all those on the religious right – conceive of the USA as a Christian nation and through this belief do harm to the reputation of the Gospel, i.e. the only authoritative message there is, by using it to give the state and its practices a higher religious standing in the eyes of their addresses. To make a theological point: in doing so they practice blasphemy.

So much for Boyd. But even from a faithful Christian perspective you are entirely within your rights to question whether mission is necessary at all.

Pentecostal Encounter

Well, if mission is out, at least partnership meetings are surely conceivable for the promotion of mutual understanding and cooperation for good purposes. Such meetings would appear to be particularly promising among followers of the same confessional tradition. But even on these paths of understanding, pilgrims can get lost in the quicksand of systematic misunderstanding.

This is exemplified by the experience that the Mexican-American historian Daniel Ramírez (Ramirez 2015, XIff.), a member of the Iglesia Apostólica de la Fe en Cristo Jesús (IAFCJ), had at a conference of the Society of Pentecostal Studies (SPS) in Guadalajara in 1993. It has been the only annual conference of the SPS outside the USA from 1971 through today. His report explains why the 1993 attempt at direct communication will not lead to a repetition of international meetings at foreign venues. This is what Ramírez reports: the English-language sessions were held at the conference hotel, while the Spanish-speaking ones took place in a church. A roundtable at the end was to bring the two groups of theologians into conversation with each other. In the course of the discussions the moderator Manuel Gaxiola asked the US-American representatives:

> What is your opinion of the dangers that neo-liberalism poses for the well-being of our church members in Latin America, and what can the North American churches do to slow its expansion?

The answer was:

> We should be wary of all currents of liberalism that can sway the church. Perhaps we in North America can do a better job of publishing materials to help the church in Latin America mature theologically and be on its guard.

Ramírez' first comment is that the Latin American conference participants were not just a little surprised and that yet another opportunity for dialogue between the global South and North had been wasted. Behind Gaxiola's question was concern about the neoliberal NAFTA agreement[99] and its devastating effects on Mexican small farmers and medium-sized industry, as well as the incipient Zapatista uprising in the South. What did the Americans have to say to that? They understood nothing. By the socio-economic term "neoliberalism," however, they understood theological liberalism that threatened the Church. This danger was to be fought by theological tracts for whose production the Americans thought themselves particularly qualified since the Latin American church was not yet mature enough to mount an adequate theological guard. While the Latin American Pentecostals were busy thinking about the socio-economic problems, according to Ramírez, it was characteristic of the comfortable life of the Americans to see a theological threat – perhaps a new Liberation Theology. The incommensurability between Pentecostals on this and the other side of the Rio Grande was deeper than theological opinions: it rather concerned "epistemic-experiential prisms:"

> The Pentecostal South, whose theological reflection and religious practice, like that of the liberationists, were shaped by economic exigencies, was decrying inequitable arrangements in the production and consumption of food. In earnest response, the Pentecostal North pledged to produce better food for thought.

The reference to "epistemic prisms," the fundamental conditions of the perception of reality, must be taken even more seriously than does Ramírez. When Latin American Christians adopt US positivism as "food for thought," this entanglement amounts to nothing less than the colonization of thought. An even more far-reaching problem is presented by the refeudalization of thought through the programs of the MANAGEMENT organizations.

99 As usual, it was only the goods traffic that was "liberalized," not that of people.

7.2 Colonization and Refeudalization

When you talk to progressive Pentecostals and other Protestants from Latin America, many practices of the religious right and conservatives are attributed to US influence. Missionaries, it is said, mostly come from the South of the USA and represent the most conservative currents of Protestantism. They cover the impatience of apocalyptic thinking with a layer of everyday Pentecostal religiosity and promote anti-socialist and anti-ecumenical attitudes. They are responsible for intolerance when you meet them, show dogmatic insistence and use harsh sanctions against progressive pastors and church members, even when it is only a case of the wrong use of vocabulary by the latter. They restrict the spectrum of church work to issues such as abortion, sexual practices, family and gender. In addition, they also impose the topic of Israel, which is rather far removed from the concerns of Latin Americans for the time being. A newly emerging, young and fairly progressive ruling class is suppressed in this way. Above all, however, important issues such as social justice and the environment are suppressed by this eternal proselytizing. Instead of the issues arising from church praxis, the measure of all things is the number of conversions. Numbers, numbers, numbers.

But counting as such is not the problem. The fixation with numbers and the doctrinaire conception of truth is based more on a colonization of the spirit by a tradition of Evangelical-fundamentalist epistemology. An attempt is made to meet today's challenges with the means of an empiricism from the 16th and 17th centuries.

Colonization

As we have seen throughout this book, there is a profound difference between two theological styles of thought in Latin America. The one emerged in Latin America from a transformation and amalgamation of three different traditions: European Catholic theology, and European as well as US Mainline Protestantism. It is cultivated by the VALUES formation. The other goes back to a transmission of conservative, biblicist or charismatic Protestantism from the USA, which was broken by cultural dispositions. It is represented above all by the LAW and MANAGEMENT formations.

In the first style of thinking you always find a more or less strong trace of hermeneutic relativism. Theological knowledge and consequently religious truth are programmatically (!) always developed relative to the body of knowledge already learned and the social situations of the interpreters and is further developed in constant dialogue. That has been the case anyway since the Second Vatican Council also in official Catholic theology. Hermeneutic reflexivity is also explicitly represented by ecumenically oriented Protestantism and parts of the Pentecostal movement. And it is also implicitly found in the discursive praxis of many small Pentecostal churches or congregations, in which lay persons discuss as quasi-experts the truth valid for certain situations in a continuous dialogue, and sometimes also in heated argument.

In the orthodox Evangelicalism and "Charismatism" of the USA, in particular in the religious right, however, there is a positivist understanding of truth, which was developed in the 19th century from the scientifically oriented empiricism of Francis Bacon, and has shaped biblicist fundamentalism in the form of Princeton theology. Here the Scriptures are understood "literally" as representing scientific facts from which unambiguous conclusions can be drawn about eternal divine facts; a reading which – in theory – restricts a given scriptural passage to only one meaning. Divergent interpretations are thus categorically excluded. In actual praxis, this simply means that the most powerful person imposes his or her interpretation. And finally, since verses from the Bible express an irrefutable, timeless and thus superior truth, mundane problems like food production under neo-liberal conditions cannot even come within sight as theological problems. Instead, theological and social liberalism that overcomes the positivist understanding of the Scriptures is regarded as dangerous.

In order to spread such fundamentalist doctrine, relevant actors take astonishing measures. The Brazilian Pentecostal pastor and professor of theology David Mesquiati from Vitória reports for example that one day a truck full of books arrived at his university, neatly addressed to the library but without a sender's address. They were Portuguese translations of fundamentalist literature from the USA. A lot of thought was given to the question of what to do with them. The sender was impossible to find. The library refused to have that kind of books under any circumstances. But the burning of books had a bad tradition. A long discussion followed on whether to take them to a dump. Again, respect for the written word made people give up that idea. It was decided instead – in all ecumenical openness, I think – to distribute the books to houses for the rehabilitation of drug addicts and homeless people, institutions that were maintained by conservative Pentecostal churches for one reason only: the books corresponded to their world view. Quite apart from the question whether the books' use was beneficial, there was also the further question of who had provided the money for such unwelcome "book gifts."

Refeudalization

This question brings up the connection between the refeudalization[100] of today's societies and the religio-political interests already mentioned in the introduction. The theory of refeudalization analyses and interprets the economic, social and cultural dynamics associated with the growing concentration of capital in large fortunes. It is evidence, among other things, of a strengthening of family background and its associated assets that is reminiscent of the estates model of society; a work and risk-free income for a few people; and the transformation of social policy into the giving of alms. There are, moreover, other characteristics of this development that

100 Cf. Kaltmeier 2019 and Neckel 2010, the latter building on Habermas' ideas.

seem important to us for our question about the role of religion in this scenario.

The first is the bid for political power by money oligarchs. In the United States, whether or not you consider the presidency of a multi-billionaire a fluke or coincidence, the plutocratic features of the political system ensure anyway that it is only very rich people or people with rich donors that are able to enter the race for the presidency. In Latin America, as in other parts of the world, more and more new millionaires and billionaires enter politics through the back door, right at the top as presidents or presidential candidates.[101] Or else praetorians of billionaires like Jair Bolsonaro come into office, with the support of the national oligarchies and the religious right.

What does this have to do with religion? On his trip to the USA, Max Weber also observed the relationship of multimillionaires to religion and reached this astute conclusion:

> As is well known, not a few (…) of the multi-millionaires and trust magnates belonged formally to sects (…). However, in the nature of the case, these persons were often affiliated for merely conventional reasons, as in Germany, and only in order to legitimate themselves in personal and social life – not in order to legitimate themselves as businessmen; during the age of the Puritans, such 'economic supermen' did not require such a crutch, and *their* 'religiosity' was, of course, often of a more than dubious sincerity. (Weber 1946a, 308)

Weber is right in seeing that billionaires do not need religion. What we see perhaps more clearly today – but what was evident even then from John D. Rockefeller's patronage of the mission to promote trade – is this: billionaires do not need religion, but they make use of it. Other people's religiosity comes in very useful for them in many ways. That is why they support acceptable religious groups in

101 As presidents: Sebastián Piñera in Chile, Mauricio Macri in Argentina, Donald Trump in the USA, Petro Poroshenko in Ukraine, Bidsina Ivanishvili in Georgia, Thaksin Shinawatra in Thailand, Saad Hariri in Lebanon, and Silvio Berlusconi in Italy.

a variety of ways. A president can appoint religious actors to a "court" and thus reap mutual gains in symbolic capital. But in most cases, religious actors are supported directly by the magnates or through foundations, as we have seen with the IRD. One only needs to think of such names as Rockefeller, J.P. Grace, Richard de Vos, Arthur de Moss, Adolph Coors, the John Birch Society, the American Enterprise Institute, the American Heritage Foundation and many others. The religious right, financed by these sources – and also from sources of its own, such as the millions of donations – functions as a religio-political brigade for private intervention in political affairs, as can be seen clearly from the infrastructure aid for the Nicaraguan Contras. And finally, our third characteristic is the action of religious experts, who are millionaires and billionaires themselves. Where the laicity is weak, religious freedom receives a broad interpretation and religious actors have free access to the media, it is above all organizations of the MANAGEMENT formation that develop into economic empires of tremendous influence on public opinion. In this way, the religious oligarchs themselves become political kingmakers, and that through their religious propaganda – although in their own view it is actually "God who appoints kings." But this is only what the clientele is supposed to believe in meetings, in front of the television and in the (a-)social media. What the religious oligarchs really seek to advance is the appointment of those with whom they can achieve the best synergies. And religious experts promote neo-liberalism in exchange for the liberalization of religious legislation in their favor. In concrete terms, they gain, for example, the free use as well as ownership of the media, coupled with the tax exemption of "religious" broadcasters. Supported by them, the authoritarian actions by the state against left-wing opposition groups are of similar use to right-wing rulers and religious oligarchs since there are very often also ecumenical religious critics of the religious right to be found among the baton-charged demonstrators for justice.

In Latin America and in the USA the religious right plays a role in the refeudalization of politics homologous to that of the economy. Like the economy, it seeks to bring political processes under the control of non-political logics of action and actors. Formal procedures are observed and the appearance of democratic political processes is preserved. The content with which political processes are overdetermined is however not political, but economic or religious. On account of the media power of these people, voters can be made to believe that the best "deal" or God's manifest will is the most important thing in politics. Refeudalization is moreover further pushed forward by breaking down systematically the boundaries between the differentiated fields of modern societies. Functional differentiation is undermined by economics and religion. The Alliance Defense Fund in the USA in the 1990s had the goal of giving the 10 Commandments constitutional status; similar efforts are underway in some countries in Latin America. As propagated by Seven Mountain Dominionism, the Dominion doctrine aims at the conquest of all social systems by religious authorities. It is tempting to think that certain religious actors have the return to the Middle Ages on their agenda.

Even if this return is for many reasons unlikely to come about, it is quite obvious that the connection between modern religiosity and democratic politics has been terminated by the actors of the religious right, especially those of the MANAGEMENT formation – notwithstanding its constant talk of democracy. A look back at church history shows the following. The political claim to power of the Catholic Church in the Middle Ages was based on religion. This claim finds its strongest expression in the so-called "two sword theory" (bull *Unam Sanctam*, 1302), a far-fetched theory which Pope Boniface VIII derived from Bible verse Luke 22:38.[102] One sword

---

102 For those interested in the Bible: the verse cited comes in the context of an announcement of his suffering by Jesus. True, Jesus recommends his disciples to buy a sword. But apart from that, he tells them that his end is near. When they answer that they have two swords already, Jesus rejects their offer to use them, employing however these words: "You do not understand me." It is possible that Pope Boniface VIII also did not quite understand Jesus' words.

was to be wielded *by* the Church, a second by the political authorities *for* the Church. The Church therefore claimed total dominion for itself in a feudal order. The Lutheran Reformation did away with this, much to the delight of the urban bourgeoisie and early capitalist economic subjects who had become self-confident. While authoritarian structures were still acknowledged at first, different models of democracy developed within the church in classic Protestantism, whether of the congregational, presbyterial or synodal order. This creates a fundamental openness to political contract theories and the development of political democracy. In the European and North American developments, parallels can be observed throughout between the organizational methods of Historical Protestantism and those of democratic constitutions. Moreover, it is not only the organizational structure but also the legal-rational mode of legitimation that is similar. The democracy-like structures are also largely maintained in the Evangelicalism of the USA and Latin America. But its fundamentalist splinter groups usually replace them by doctrinaire authoritarianism. In addition, Evangelical missionary societies developed that functioned according to the model of trading companies. Since they were financed by donations, they must, like an industrial enterprise, show quantitative success, in their case in the number of converts. Thus, the basis was created for the organizational form of the free "ministry," a salvation enterprise – following Weber's Lutheran "institution of salvation" – under the direction of an owner who was responsible for the success of the product and could siphon off the profit gained, whether this was the symbolic capital of a successful missionary or simply money. With Dwight Moody and especially Billy Sunday it was both.

A special phenomenon occurred in the groups of the early Pentecostal movement, namely the charismatic form of legitimation. The claim made there was to direct legitimation through revelation – not through writing, legal or rational argument. This can be understood as an attempt by people who were discriminated against in ethnic, economic and/or religious ways to gain self-worth and a new competence to act in their situation, without having this self-worth questioned by the wealthy and well-educated. As long as this dynamic plays out in small congregations with face-to-face relationships and in trips to preach in the streets, it has an emancipatory and *practical* democratic character; the revelations of the sister in faith can be questioned or overcome at the next opportunity by your own revelations of different content. So far, so good. But the treacherous thing about social life is the unintended effects. To the extent that religious event companies and media actors adopt the charismatic mode of legitimation, it becomes an instrument of religious authoritarianism. This is precisely what has been happening in the USA and Latin America since the 1970s when the Neopentecostal movement established itself successfully in the market of the salvation industry. The mutual relativization of claims to revelation in small communities was now taken over by the authority of mass preachers on television, in campaigns in sports stadiums or in megachurches. Speaking experts and hearing masses met each other without entering into dialogue. It was the preachers who now claimed for themselves the authority of divine revelation, first exercised over the masses of their listeners and then extended to other contexts such as politics. The religious claim to absolute authority was thus based on nothing but their own opinions, which were developed out of a shrewd populist intuition and a few verses from the Bible. Exactly like Pope Boniface VIII, these preachers could through this manipulation extract claims to power with a global reach from an insignificant verse or merely from their sheer pretension. To lend their claim also similar historical legitimization, they invented for themselves the office of the "apostolate," which put them on the same hierarchical level as the Pope. This however with the subtle difference that according to the First Vatican Council (1870) the Pope is infallible only in *ex cathedra* statements on faith, whereas Neopentecostal apostles enjoy infallibility also in political or private affairs – in short, everything they are interested in. We have already remarked that Pat Robertson had a revelation that the Venezuelan President Chavez was to be assassinated by the CIA. Such programs are hardly compatible with democratic participation, but very much so with refeudalization and post-democracy.

The stars of religious events function like PR experts who have a silent mass of people in front of them that only react to their signals; and like lobbyists who in their own interest feed the reactions of the masses into politics that are conducted behind closed doors. This puts the people of the masses into a state of religious fixation, of disinterest in political argument, and cheap manipulability, "returning voluntarily to the position they were forced to occupy in pre-democracy" (Crouch 2004, 23).

So far, so bad. But this is not the whole story. The logics of colonization of thought and refeudalization are far from determining the practical logic of all Protestantism in the United States and Latin America.

7.3 Panama 2016

Panama is much too hot for a congress where people from temperate latitudes are supposed to work during the day. But the country has had the interoceanic canal since 1914 and is therefore in a much more convenient location than the more moderate San José in Costa Rica. The canal construction in the then still Colombian province of Panama was started in the 19th century by a French company, which however never completed the project. An attempt by the USA to negotiate a contract with Colombia for the canal construction under US direction failed in 1903. The USA therefore supported the independence movement of the province and was able to recognize the young Republic of Panama as early as 1904 and went on to start construction of the canal. The "big stick" created a new state with "open doors" for the US economy. The canal became an emblem of the US-dominated world trade. For the population of Panama it was to become also an emblem of ethnic segregation. For the construction of the canal, black workers from the Antilles were forced to work under poor working conditions. After construction ended in 1914, most of them remained in Panama as a marginal population group. To this day, it has been above all the Episcopal Church of Panama that is dogged by segregation into white and black members, as I know from my own work with this church. As always, everything depends on how you look at things.

In Panama, as I have mentioned, there were two meetings in 2016, which owing to their different perspectives took quite different views of the canal and Protestant politics in Latin America.

Polycentrism: World Evangelical Alliance

The World Assembly of the World Evangelical Alliance (3-7 October 2016), which dates back to Billy Graham's initiative of 1974, has as its logo the image of a merchant ship in the canal against a background of an embroidery by the Cuna *Indígenas* from the Caribbean coast of Panama. The ship dominates the image and is moved towards the viewer by the technical equipment of the locks. In the background is the indigenous weaving piece, colorful and motionless like the firmament. How is the picture to be understood as the emblem of a missionary congress in such a historical place as Panama? Is the mission to be identified with the merchant ship and indigenous Panama as no more than a location or, perhaps better, a gateway for the global trade with salvation goods? Be that as it may, it is clear that the canal and the mission affirm each other, just as they did in the fading 19th century.[103] Nothing else can be found in the "brief historical overview" by Timothy Halls, who in the "geopolitical context" takes a nostalgic look back at the opening of the Canal Zone with the beautiful Hotel Tivoli and the visit by Teddy Roosevelt. I could not find a critical examination of the various positions at the 1916 conference in the documents of the 2016 conference. But what has actually changed?

---

103 https://www.worldea.org/news/4723/wea-mission-commission-highlights-polycentric-mission-during-panama-global-consultation (accessed 29 October 2019), https://weamc.global/category/conferences/panama/ (accessed 29 October 2019).

The mission has become "polycentric." The theme of the consultations is "Polycentric Mission – from all nations to all nations." "The fast changing world scenario" – as it says in the introduction to the conference[104] – requires "partnership solutions." There are by now in the world well-positioned Christians in widely different places. What could be more obvious for a global organization than to make a formal adaptation of its working concept to this structural given? This change would then correspond to the changes of the Evangelical movement in the global periphery. In Latin America in the 1980s the above mentioned CONELA was founded, which for its part initiated the foundation of the Congreso Misionero Iberoamericano (COMIBAM, 1987), which assembles national Evangelical mission initiatives and orientates them in an international and ethnic direction.[105] The World Evangelical Alliance can thus fall back on different regional Evangelical initiatives worldwide in different degrees and bundle them. As the newly appointed head of the Mission Commission David Ruiz (2016) expressed it in Panama, the view of the regions remains oriented towards quantitative growth, but now against a background of coordinated activities of the world mission. This may also lead to former sending countries becoming receiving countries which ask for mission from the South. Whether this is the USA or Europe remains an open question.

In the hope of finding something really new, let me take up two presentations from the conference. The one looks like a discussion of the 1916 meeting, which is the promise made by the title of his lecture by the exegete Samuel Pagán (2016) from the Florida Center for Theological Studies in Miami. But he does little more than give a description of the use of the Bible at the 1916 Congress and then thematizes the exegetical challenges for the present. To be sure, the complexity of societies and the necessity of contextual Bible interpretation are *mentioned*, but this is not followed up with a proposal

---

104 https://www.comibam.org/es/ (accessed 29 November 2018). Its motto: "Iberoamérica llevando todo el evangelio a todas las etnias".

105 … with growing tolerance of Catholics.

for a contextual hermeneutics. Instead, we are only given a reference to the blessings of the computer, which allows us to find more details in the text of the Bible. This procedure marks a position that belongs to a period even decades before Liberation Theology appeared. Problem acknowledged – and skirted around.

Samuel Escobar, the author of the other presentation, "Mission from the Periphery," promises salvation. We learn for a start that mission is always a risk – a widespread self-assessment among US missionaries. Then Escobar references Orlando Costas' interesting idea of applying the center-periphery rhetoric of dependency theory to mission. This, he says, would level criticisms against the mission of the center. Moreover, he goes on to say, a look at conversion figures shows that growth in the South is currently almost 20 times higher than in the North. This is paralleled by a missionary movement from the periphery and – in Muslim countries – "from below." The missionaries in the South are more self-critical and return to biblical models informed by "historical awareness." But what that means in practical terms remains in the dark here too.

The central concern of the conference, the "polycentric mission," is described more precisely in the closing statement by other, "closely related concepts":

> This would include a polyphonic mission conversation, poly-directional mission, poly-generational, cruci-centric or Christo-centric mission, and unity in mission. (WEA Mission Commission 2016)

It is certainly the case that US missionaries no longer are in sole command of the mission ship. But the goals – quantitative church growth at the expense of non-Evangelical denominations and religions – remain the same just like the contents – a conservative, Evangelical, cruci-centered theology of sacrifice and conversion individualism.

From a decolonial perspective it is impossible to get rid of the impression that the program of polycentric mission is a successful attempt to colonize the religious dispositions of religious actors from the global South using the central concepts of the US mission tradition in such a way that the actors themselves, and entirely of their own free will, are likely to think and act like the colonizers, and by means of the South-North mission even in the direction of the colonizers themselves. It would be a successful operation of "symbolic violence" (Bourdieu) if this was indeed the case.

From a theological perspective, there are several things to be said for this view, as becomes clear by a contrast with other Latin American models of action and corresponding theological criticism. It is the very theology of sacrifice propagated by the WEA (and favored by traditional US fundamentalism) that is sharply criticized by Pentecostal theologians from Latin America, for example by the Brazilian theologian Paulo Ayres Mattos at the 2016 conference of the Red Latinoamericana de Estudios Pentecostales (RELEP).

Red Latinoamericana de Estudios Pentecostales (RELEP)

This Latin American network for Pentecostal studies originated from various meetings of theological training institutes[106] between 1995 and 2000, at which a group of ecumenically trained Pentecostal academics decided to build up a network. It began in Mexico in 1998 with a meeting of four activists from Mexico, Brazil, Peru and Chile. The first major meeting was held in Santiago de Chile in 1999 with 20 Pentecostal academics from eight countries. A second meeting was organized in 2002 in Costa Rica with the support of the Universidad Bíblica Latinoamericana, and others followed in Santiago de Chile (2008, 2009) in Quito (2011) and finally in Panama (2016). The conference contributions were published.[107] Most importantly, regional groups were set up over time. Currently, the Brazilian group has about 40 members and the Hispanic Latin Ameri-

---

106 *Comunidad de Educación Teológica Ecuménica Latinoamericana y Caribe* (CETELA) and *Asociación de Teólogos del Tercer Mundo* (ASETT).

107 Chiquete und Orellana 2003; 2009a; 2009b; Mesquiati de Oliveira and Freire de Alencar 2017.

can group about 100. The network unites disciplines from theology, history, anthropology, architecture, pedagogy to the sociology of religion. Its objective is to reflect Pentecostal church praxis in the social context of Latin America and to support it within a theologically responsible framework. In contrast to the rigorous separation of normative theology from descriptive social sciences in North Atlantic countries, here these sciences are brought together in a problem-oriented, interdisciplinary dialogue. The members of the Association are for the most part employed in universities, theological seminaries or NGOs and are usually very well versed in the religious field of their respective countries.

The 2016 meeting in Panama had the aim to critically review the 1916 Congress and was held in cooperation with the Foro Pentecostal Latinoamericano y Caribeño (FPLC). This forum is a loose association of churches and people interested in ecumenical dialogue in the broadest sense. It was established between 2007 and 2010 as a regional expression of the work of the Global Christian Forum.[108] This global institution was founded in 1998 on the initiative of the World Council of Churches to offer an ecumenical communication channel also to those churches for which an institutional membership would mean too close a link with the Council's program. The Forum has by now become institutionally completely independent of the World Council and establishes a dialogue between churches of the most diverse traditions.

Numerous members of RELEP are also involved in Foro Pentecostal. Between 21 and 26 November 2016, two back-to-back meetings were held at the same venue in Panama with almost the same participants and a strong influence of RELEP among them. With few exceptions, all participants belonged to the Latin American Pentecostal Movement. Their view of the situation of Christianity in Latin America differed profoundly from that of the polycentric missionaries, not least with regard to the Canal.

---

108 http://www.globalchristianforum.org/ (accessed 29 October 2019).

Pentecostal Conference 2016

The Canal was also a reference point for several speakers at the FPLC and RELEP conferences. In marked contrast to the World Evangelical Alliance Congress, most of them situated the 1916 Congress as well as the Canal within the framework of the Monroe Doctrine and the ideology of manifest destiny. These and various further positions of the Latin American Pentecostals that will be outlined in what follows highlight again the difference we have already seen in the misunderstanding between the theologians of the Society for Pentecostal Studies and those of the Iglesia Apostólica de la Fe en Cristo Jesús.

At the meeting of the FPLC there was again such a systematic misunderstanding. The veteran US-American Pentecostal theologian and long-standing Fuller Professor Mel Roebeck was invited to the FPLC meeting as a member of the Committee of the Global Christian Forum. He spoke – in English – at the end of the second day to the assembled Latin American academics. The North, he said, was interested in a dialogue with strong voices from the South. In addition, a process of mutual (!) forgiveness should be sought. In the Pentecostal movement in the USA it was theology that was taught, not sociology, which latter was obviously the case in Latin America. But the questions of the Latin Americans should be answered spiritually, in the same way as Jesus referred his disciples to the leaves of a tree if they wanted to learn what season it was, and as John in the Apocalypse had received the circular letters to seven churches in a vision. It was crucial for "all of us" to hear what the Spirit tells us. Then he emphasized the importance of interconfessional and interreligious dialogue, saying that the great advantage of Pentecostalism was that it was a form of spirituality that could establish links with many denominations. The Brazilian historian Gideon Freire de Aléncar responded – feeling the Brazilian religious right breathing down his neck – that it was usual among the conservative Protestants and Catholics in Latin America to cooperate interdenominationally on topics like homosexuality and abortion; and he went on to ask whether it would not be better to cooperate on issues like violence, war or emancipation. In reply, Roebeck referred to the experiences he had gained in the dialogue with the Catholic Church, especially with Pope John Paul II, and said that one could talk about many topics, such as human dignity or even education. The Chilean historian Luis Orellana then asked about the political responsibility of the churches. He learned from Roebeck that the main thing was to keep the church together and to be a-political; but, alright, let the churches of the South urge those of the North to talk more about politics. Perhaps Roebeck's concession was the result of his politeness.

Politics, social conditions and cultural discrimination were recurrent topics of the Latin American conferences which saw them as concrete contexts of the work of their churches. There was a consensus that the social context played a decisive role in interconfessional dialogue. Again the difference to the USA becomes evident. The majority of the Latin American Christians present no longer accepted that theology was to be pursued as an academic glass bead game and that church unity was understood as verbal agreement on theological dogmas. This became clear in most of the contributions to the topics of the conferences.

The 1916 Congress

Four of the 18 lectures of the FPLC and 12 out of the 22 lectures at the RELEP dealt with the Mission Congress of 1916. Assessments ranged from an appreciation of the missionary efforts for a Pan-American democratization in Latin America (Tomás Gutiérrez) via reflections on the modernization of the continent against the background of the Monroe Doctrine (Daniel Oviedo) to a clear critical positioning of the 1916 congress in the context of geopolitical power strategies (Freire de Aléncar and David Mesquiati).

Freire de Aléncar (2016) saw the Canal and the 1916 Congress in the context of geopolitics. In 1914, the First World War began (and in the USA the debate about whether to enter it) and the Canal was completed. Aléncar underlined that the 1916 Congress for Christian Work in Latin America was attended as guests by Panamanian ministers, foreign ambassadors, and envoys from the US State Department and the head of the canal, a US colonel. He also emphasized that of the 230 US religious delegates, only 145 also lived in Latin America and that only 21 native Latin Americans were present. And he was not alone at the 2016 Congress in his view that these were important factors for a contextual understanding of the Congress. From the point of view of a modern Brazilian Pentecostal, Aléncar thought one of the problems of the 1916 Congress to be that it threw Protestantism into relief as an anti-Catholic cultural model and that this orientation also influenced the nascent Pentecostal movement in Latin America (Freire de Alencar 2016).[109] But above all he thought that the Congress took a colonialist perspective on Latin America enriched with racist and intellectualist prejudices. A major problem – here he quoted Arturo Piedra's fundamental study (1993) – was that the Congress was oriented toward the interests of the Latin American middle and upper classes.

Aléncar made a point of illustrating this not with the discourse of the US missionaries, but with that of the three Brazilian representatives at the Congress. The Congress was preceded by a schism in 1903 in the Brazilian Presbyterian Church: the pro-US American Igreja Presbiteriana do Brasil, equipped with missionaries and close to Freemasonry, as opposed to the nationalist project of Brazilian pastors, the Igreja Presbiteriana Independente. Representatives of the former traveled to Panama. This explained, according to Alencar, that they – each to a greater or lesser extent – presented the USA and its Protestantism as white (which was perceived as a value in itself), educated and capitalist, while Latin America was presented as base, racially mixed and sick. Given such a setting, he continued, the Pentecostal movement – although already present in the USA, Brazil and other countries – did not receive a mention because its members were, and still are, poor and black.

109 Freire de Alencar 2016; recording of an oral presentation of 21 November 2016.

A similar view was held by David Mesquiati, a professor of theology. Since 1916 mission and capitalism had been identified with each other. There was an urgent need to focus the concept of evangelism on human rights, social justice and peace.

The pastor and theologian Daniel Chiquete used an analysis of the media to show how in the 19th century a *leyenda negra* was woven over Latin American Catholicism and how justification metaphors like "modernization," "freedom" and "ethics" were legitimizing mission still today.

Others stressed the fact that the North-dominated Pan-Americanism had by no means brought only democracy – what did that word actually mean? – to Latin America, but dictatorships, torture, lack of freedom and marginalization. It was of course true that many missionaries had also criticized imperialist policies, but the mission was a very ambivalent enterprise and had also – as the indigenous peoples claimed from their perspective – sometimes not shied away from genocide. The Brazilian professor of theology Paulo Ayres Mattos suggested for the North-South missionary relationship the metaphor of "cultural man-eating" (*antropofagia cultural*), since it was a case of the dominated culture being devoured by the dominant one. In evidence of his view he cited the militarization of Pentecostal songs by American missionaries, where there is constant talk of *blood* and "Christ's battalions" are sent into the fight for cities.

Pastoral Challenges

Many of the presentations and discussions at the RELEP conference were directly or indirectly related to pastoral challenges for the Pentecostal movement. In this context it is important to note that, to the best of my knowledge, none of the Pentecostal academics present belonged to a megachurch and all were familiar with Pentecostal church life of the lower middle and even the lower classes. For many small congregations, especially in marginal quarters, street mission in the neighborhood was clearly more important than the world mission. So the question of legitimate proselytism certainly came up and was answered by Bernardo Campos, a Peruvian pastor and theological author, who pointed out that evangelization and the integration into church congregations must have as their goal the realization of being human in a holistic sense, but not the quantitative realization of mission goals. The innumerable small congregations of the poor, informal sector workers were usually composed of 20 to 30 members, often headed by a woman, where practically all members had the role of activists and experts. One of the particular challenges for daily pastoral work in these neighborhoods was the youth gangs, which were often involved in drug trafficking. Many of these churches provided, and served as, an exit option.

The look at pastoral praxis was admittedly taken not only for documentary purposes, but was certainly self-critical. David Mesquiati emphasized that violence was by no means a new challenge, but that the Pentecostal movement had simply taken no note of it in the past. Many Pentecostals continued to be uncritical and adapted to the prevailing conditions and power structures. They were often ecclesiocentric and interested only in services and evangelization campaigns, thus betraying the obligation that Reformed churches had for social responsibility. Instead, they clung to US American concepts of religious conservatism, and left civil rights activists to fend for themselves. The Pentecostal movement, however, was challenged to become critically involved in culture and society, to decolonize itself, to learn to read the Bible with a hermeneutic approach and establish a good relationship with Catholics.

Put in somewhat more abstract terms, the demands mentioned can be expressed pointedly as social justice, peace and ecology, which all played in fact an important role in the most various contributions as a demand for a new ethics. Instead of the visa for heaven, what was at stake was the values mentioned.

Theology: Management and Sacrifice

All this, of course, does not apply to the Neopentecostal megachurches. The actors of the MANAGEMENT formation were clearly identified as opponents in the religious field, although not much speaking time was spent on it.[110] Widespread criticism emphasized the fact that the Neopentecostals in Latin America conducted themselves like "viceroys" of the USA and followed the neo-liberal logic of victim blaming, which both caused the victims additional psychological damage and provided a cheap legitimation of wealth.

Another target for sharp criticism was the victim terminology of the US-American Evangelical movement, whose majority was organized in the LAW formation. Paulo Ayres Mattos claimed that the theology of sacrifice and atonement together with the idea of reparation through punishment distorted the Christian doctrine of salvation by a juridical interpretation. This paved the way, he asserted, for an even more far-reaching distortion by the Neopentecostal and, at the same time, neo-liberal prosperity program, which attributed to the bloody sacrifice of Christ an equal value with the money sacrifice at the time of donation. This belief was the source, as in a credit transaction, from which an obligation of God was derived, and money ended up as a form of salvation. Thus neo-liberal capitalism was legitimized, the victims of the system were blamed and consumption was staged as the Promised Land.

Indigenous Pentecostals

The tension between the US American mission and Latin American religious praxis shows itself in a very special way in relation to indigenous Pentecostals. Entanglement often occurs here with a strong dose of indigenous culture. Bernardo Campos from Peru has pointed out that there is a "syntony" between Pentecostalism and indigenous culture which finds expression for instance in the fact that Pentecostal pastors take a role similar to that of the indigenous priest. Beyond this functional analogy, ongoing work centers on the pro-

110 Neopentecostals were praised only once, and that on account of their knowledge of the media. They could be invited, it was said, to help with the strategies of the speakers' own churches.

grammatic entanglement of enculturated Pentecostal praxis and indigenous identity. This current, particularly strong in the Andes, but also in Guatemala, was represented at the conference by Jacobo Tancara from Bolivia, who is Aymara and holds a doctorate[111] in theology. Tancara has profound and reflective experience of everyday indigenous life, also as a pastor in indigenous congregations in marginal quarters of Bolivia[112] and possesses broad academic knowledge of Liberation Theology and philosophy. Working at a theological college in the Andes, Tancara designs an indigenous program that counters that of the mission and the conservative white Pentecostal movement.

For this he uses on the one hand such indigenous religious practices that are mediated with Pentecostal ones, as for example the assumption of a nature animated by spirits[113] and a high valuation of the community as opposed to the individual. On the other hand, he succeeds in discovering elements of decolonization in Pentecostal praxis and supports his findings with academic references to the literature on decolonization (from Mariátegui to Quijano and Enrique Dussel). If the Pentecostal churches see themselves as innovative, which they undoubtedly do, Tancara challenges them to push innovation in the direction of society. Just as Trotsky spoke of permanent revolution, so it is now necessary to speak of permanent reformation.[114] Lastly, what can be learned from Liberation Theology is that you can only do theology and church praxis if you take seriously both the conflict between the social classes and its translation into an ethnic conflict as a basis of theological and pastoral praxis.

111 Doctorate from the University of Bielefeld, his thesis advisor being the present author.

112 On this cf. Tancara Chambe 2011.

113 As far as European systematic theology is concerned, there are undoubted possibilities of reaching an understanding via an all-encompassing pneumatology.

114 … which has already been established anyway in Reformed Protestantism.

Viewed from the indigenous perspective, the vanishing point of such a theology and pastoral praxis is decolonization, understood as a farewell to a harmful entanglement with the North, and the prospects for a new attempt from the South – maybe one day.

For the time being, disentanglement seems to many people to be the best form of entanglement.

Epilogue: Dynamics of Entanglement

> But when the rafts, junks, and dinghies got closer,
> and the people aboard became clearer,
> the ship's passengers saw
> that they were not coming empty-handed.
> They had no food, and they had little water,
> but in each of these tiny vessels,
> there were the distinctive orange-covered books
> that had once lined the bridge of the *Glory*.
> (Dave Eggers: *The Captain and the Glory*)

Entanglement of practices, habitūs and social institutions occurs in the most diverse forms. In this book, only one easily delimited field has been examined, namely that of the Protestant mission from the USA in Latin America and its repercussions. This look has revealed a dynamic of entanglement that discloses not only asymmetry but also a certain dialectic. The US-American mission (thesis) produces in its entanglement with Latin America a special Protestantism (antithesis), which in its turn becomes active in the USA and leads to a synthesis. Now, wouldn't that be nice! The processes are much more complicated than that, although they are considered in this book only with reference to two collective actors. At this point, we cannot do more than to present some practical forms of entanglement.

Dominance: Objective entanglement occurs through the establishment of agents of control at the subaltern pole. Classic US mission pursued the goal of cultural dominance in Latin America and administered Protestant praxis through US missionaries. A cognitive-emotional dominance arises when perception and evaluation schemata are transferred and incorporated through long-term, obligatory praxis. This can be assumed for mission schools and even more so for the training of Latin American preachers.

Subalternity: This is the complementary form to dominance. The subaltern actors accept their subalternity, identify with the dominant form and develop corresponding practices. Right-wing Hispanic Protestantism seems to follow this dynamic, as does the "polycentric mission from the South."

Subversion: This also operates in conditions of dominance, but recognizes them and works on its own emancipation using elements of the dominant praxis. This is probably the case in the practices of the indigenous Protestants, as also, in a similar way, in Liberation Theology. A drastic form of the subversion of Catholicism is the cult of *Santa Muerte*.

Cooperation: The ideal form of entanglement occurs when objective and perceived synergies are generated. This happened in the case of the first liberal missionaries in Latin America and the (economically) liberal Criollo elites. It can in addition be observed between indigenous Protestants in Latin America and the ecumenical aid agencies of the North, and also between conservative Evangelicals in the USA and CONELA in Latin America.

Merging: This takes place when, due to an objective alignment of social positions, concurrent (religious) habitūs develop over time and a more or less immediate understanding becomes possible. This is likely to be the case with the "transnational religious class" (after Sklair) that has emerged in the last, say, five to six decades. In individual cases it can be assumed that positions of individual dissident missionaries grow closer to those of Latin American Christians, this is especially the case where long-lasting family ties are entered into.

Misunderstanding: This can be described as failure to establish cooperation. It occurs when the dispositions of perception and evaluation are so different that identical concepts are understood in a completely different way. We have observed this happening between US American and Latin American theologians.

Renunciation: The renunciation of promised advantages of entanglement and their rejection demonstrates the self-confident conviction of being able to manage one's own situation better than with interference from outside. This strategy can be observed among indigenous peoples in the rejection of mission initiatives.

Termination: Termination is an active variant of renunciation in already existing relationships, such as in dominance. An emblematic instance of this is represented by the nationalization of many classic US missions in 1960s Latin America.

Counter: Counteraction is very likely the only form of entanglement that can be described as dialectical. It occurs in the conscious, explicit criticism of the positions of others. Instances of this are the uprisings of the young Evangelicals at the CLADE Congress in Bogotá in 1969 and at the World Missionary Congress in Lausanne in 1974. On the level of everyday religious praxis, counteraction is found in the action of religious migrants in the USA in the role of religious expatriates who assume to themselves the divine task to bring the right faith to the consumerist *gabachos* (gringos).

Works cited

Alarcon, Rafael, Luis Escala, and Olga Odgers. 2016. *Making Los Angeles Home. The Integration of Mexican Immigrants in the United States*. Berkeley: University of California Press.

Alba, Richard D., Albert J. Raboteau, and Josh DeWind. 2009. *Immigration and Religion in America: Comparative and Historical Perspectives*. New York: New York University Press.

Arbeitskreis ILV. 1979. *Die Frohe Botschaft unserer Zivilisation: evangelikale Indianermission in Lateinamerika: eine Dokumentation über den Einfluss protestantisch fundamentalistischer Mission am Beispiel des Summer Institute of Linguistics (ILV/ SIL/WBT)*. Göttingen, Wien: Gesellschaft für bedrohte Völker.

Banks, Adelle. 2018. "Trump to Sign Executive Order Creating New White House Faith-Based Initiative." National Catholic Reporter. May 3rd 2018. Accessed October 11, 2019. https://www.ncronline.org/news/politics/trump-sign-executive-order-creating-new-white-house-faith-based-initiative.

Barreto Jr., Raimundo. 2010. "O Movimento Ecumênico e o Surgimento da Responsabilidade Social no Protestantismo Brasileiro." *Numen: revista de estudos e pesquisa da religião* 13 (1 & 2): 273-323.

Beecher, Lyman. 1835. *A plea for the West*. Cincinnati: Truman & Smith.

Bellah, Robert N. 1967. "Civil Religion in America." *Daedalus* 96 (1): 1-21.

Blanke, Svenja. 2003. "Civic Foreign Policy. U.S. Religious Interest Groups and Central America." Dissertation, Berlin: Freie Universität.

Bourdieu, Pierre. 1991. "Genesis and Structure of the Religious Field," ed. Craig Calhoun. *Comparative Social Research* 13: 1-44.

Boyd, Gregory A. 2005. *Myth of a Christian Nation. How the quest for political power is destroying the church.* Grand Rapids: Zondervan. Epub retrieved from https://www.amazon.de.

Brinkley, Douglas. 2007. "Reagan, Unscripted." *Vanity Fair*, May 1, 2007. Accessed October 1, 2019. https://www.vanityfair.com/news/2007/06/reagan200706.

Bubeck, Mark I. 1975. *The Adversary: The Christian versus Demon Activity*. Chicago: Moody Press.

———. 1984. *Overcoming the Adversary: Warfare Praying Against Demon Activity*. Chicago: Moody Press.

Buitrago Valencia, Clara. 2021. *Missionaries: Migrants or Expatriates? Guatemalan Pentecostal Leaders in Los Angeles*. Trier, New Orleans: Wissenschaftlicher Verlag Trier, University of New Orleans Press.

Bustillos Almendáriz, Daniel. 2014. "Hasta lo último de la tierra". In *Cien años de Pentecostés*, ed. Domingo Torres Alvarado, 461-537. Mexico: Iglesia Apostólica de la Fe en Cristo Jesús.

Caballeros, Harold. 1999. *De victoria en victoria: conceptos, experiencias y tecnicas sobre la guerra espiritual*. Nashville, TN: Caribe/Betania.

Calvani, Carlos Eduardo B. 2015. "Protestantismo liberal, ecumênico, revolucionário e pluralista no Brasil – um projeto que ainda não se extinguiu". *Horizonte* 13 (40): 1896-1929.

Cambridge Tribune. 1911. "Pageant of Darkness and Light," May 6, 1911. Accessed October 11, 2019. https://cambridge.dlconsulting.com/?a=d&d=Tribune19110506-01.2.88&srpos=3&e=-------en-20--1--txt-txIN-Pageant+of+Darkness+and+Light------.

Capitol Ministries. n.d. Capitol Ministries. Accessed October 11, 2019. https://capmin.org/.

Capitol Ministries. 2019. "Nicaragua President to CM: Come Establish Bible Studies to National Leaders!" Capitol Ministries. Accessed July 13, 2019. https://capmin.org/nicaragua-president-to-cm-come-establish-bible-studies-to-national-leaders/.

Carbonelli, Marcos A. 2014. "Evangélicos, globalización y política en Argentina. Intervenciones públicas y misión divina." *Civitas Revista de Ciências Sociais* 14 (3): 507-522.

Casaús Arzú, Marta Elena. 2007. *Guatemala: Linaje y racismo*. Guatemala: F&G Editores.

Castillo Hernández, Juan Carlos. 2014. "Escenarios socioculturales de la IAFCJ en México (1914-2014)." In *Cien años de Pentecostés*, ed. Domingo Torres Alvarado, 37-93. Mexico D.F.: Iglesia Apostólica de la Fe en Cristo Jesús.

Catholic Institute for International Relations. 1989. *The Road to Damascus: Kairos and conversion: a document signed by Third World Christians from El Salvador, Guatemala, Korea, Namibia, Nicaragua, Philippines, South Africa.* London, Washington, D.C.: Catholic Institute for International Relations, Center of Concern.

CEH. 1999. *Guatemala: Memoria del silencio*. Guatemala: UNOPS.

Cesar, Waldo. 2007. "Sociólogo relembra a abertura dos evangélicos para a realidade social brasileira nos anos 60." *Ultimato*, 2007. Accessed May 2, 2019. https://www.ultimato.com.br/revista/artigos/305/sociologo-relembra-a-abertura-dos-evangelicos-para-a-realidade-social-brasileira-nos-anos-60#extras.

Chiquete Beltrán, Daniel. 2014. "La arquitectura apostólica." In *Cien años de Pentecostés*, ed. Domingo Torres Alvarado, 339-385. Mexico D.F.: Iglesia Apostólica de la Fe en Cristo Jesús.

Chiquete, Daniel, and Luis Orellana, ed. 2003. *Voces del pentecostalismo Latinoamericano*. Concepción: RELEP.

———, ed. 2009a. *Voces del pentecostalismo Latinoamericano II. Identidad, teología, historia.* Concepción: RELEP.

———, ed. 2009b. *Voces del pentecostalismo Latinoamericano III. Identidad, teología, historia.* Concepción: RELEP.

Clawson, Michael. 2012. "Misión Integral and Progressive Evangelicalism: The Latin American Influence on the North American Emerging Church." *Religions* 3: 790-807.

Committee on Co-operation in Latin America. 1915. "Change of name of the conference." *Congress on Christian Work in Latin America Bulletin* 4 (August). Accessed December 12, 2018. http://hdl.handle.net/2027/nnc2.ark:/13960/t5k99p97n.

———. 1916. *Christian work in Latin America. Message and method. Education. Report of commission II.* Vol. 2. New York N.Y.: Committee on Co-operation in Latin America. Accessed

December 12, 2018. http://hdl.handle.net/2027/nnc2.ark:/13960/t9z08j32x.

———. 1917. *Christian work in Latin America. Survey and occupation. Message and method. Education. Reports of commissions I, II and III*. Vols. 1-3. New York: Missionary Education Movement.

Conrado, Flávio. 2008. "Igreja e sociedade em meio às rápidas transformações sociais." Revista Ultimato. Accessed April 4, 2019. https://www.ultimato.com.br/revista/artigos/ 310/igreja-e-sociedade-em-meio-as-rapidas-transformacoes-sociais.

Crouch, Colin. 2004. *Post-Democracy*. Malden, MA: Polity.

Damboriena, Prudencio. 1963. *El Protestantismo en América Latina. Vol. I*. Fribourg: FERES.

D'Antonio, William V., and Fredrick B. Pike. 1964. *Religion, Revolution, and Reform: New Forces for Change in Latin America*. New York: Praeger.

Dawson, John. 1989. *Taking Our Cities for God: How to Break Spiritual Strongholds*. Lake Mary: Creation House.

De Sanctis, Fausto Martin. 2015. *Churches, Temples, and Financial Crimes: A Judicial Perspective of the Abuse of Faith*. Cham: Springer.

Department of the Army Headquarters. 1971. *Operaciones de contraguerrilla. FM 31-16*. Buenos Aires: Editorial Rioplatense.

Diamond, Sara. 1989. *Spiritual Warfare. The Politics of the Christian Right*. Boston: South End Press.

Dickason, C. Fred. 1987. *Demon Possession and the Christian*. Chicago: Moody Press.

Drollinger, Ralph. 2019. *Dr. Ralph Drollinger transmite mensaje de Paz en el 40/19*. Managua, July 19, 2019. Youtube. Accessed October 11, 2019. https://www.youtube.com/watch?v=bur_HW_j1MI&app=desktp.

Duchrow, Ulrich, Gerd Eisenbürger, and Jochen Hippler, ed. 1989. *Totaler Krieg gegen die Armen. Geheime Strategiepapiere der amerikanischen Militärs*. München: Kaiser.

Durkheim, Émile. 1995. *The Elementary Forms of the Religious Life*. New York: The Free Press.

Ehrenreich, Barbara. 2010. *Smile or Die.* London: Granta Books.

Escobar, J. Samuel. 1994. "Conflict of Interpretations of Popular Protestantism." In *New Face of the Church in Latin America: Between Tradition and Change*, ed. Guillermo Cook, 112-134. Maryknoll: Orbis Books.

Ezcurra, Ana María. 1982. *The Neoconservative Offensive: U.S. Churches and the Ideological Struggle for Latin America*. New York: CIRCUS Publications.

———. 1983. "Neoconservative and ideological struggle toward Central-America in the USA." *Social Compass* 30 (2-3): 349-362.

Fea, John. 2020. *Believe Me. The Evangelical Road to Donald Trump*. Grand Rapids, MI: Eerdmans.

Ferreira Vilela, Márcio Ananias. n.d. "Cristo e o Processo Revolucionário Brasileiro:" a Conferência do Nordeste e a responsabilidade social da Igreja Presbiteriana do Brasil." Accessed May 2, 2019. https://www.encontro2012.historiaoral.org.br/resources/anais/3/1338502095_ARQUIVO_CristoeProcessoRevolucionarioBrasileiro-aConferenciadoNordesteearesponsabilidadedesocialdaIPB.pdf.

Flores, Antonio. 2017a. "Facts on U.S. Latinos, 2015. Statistical Portrait of Hispanics in the United States." *Pew Research Center* (blog). Accessed September 18, 2017. https://www.pewresearch.org/hispanic/2017/09/18/2015-statistical-information-on-hispanics-in-united-states/#growth-sources.

———. 2017b. "How the U.S. Hispanic Population Is Changing." *Pew Research Center* (blog). Accessed September 18, 2017. https://www.pewresearch.org/fact-tank/2017/09/18/how-the-u-s-hispanic-population-is-changing/.

Freire de Alencar, Gedeon. 2016. "El ethos anticatólico del protestantismo brasileño: evangelización y geopolítica." Contribution to the RELEP conference, 24-27 November, 2016, Panama.

Fuerstenberg, Georg. 1984. "Kreuzzug gegen den Kommunismus. Die Vereinigungskirche in Lateinamerika." *Evangelische Kommentare* 17 (8): 430-432.

Fuller, Robert C. 1995. *Naming the Antichrist: The history of an American obsession*. New York: Oxford University Press.

García Canclini, Néstor. 1999. *La globalización imaginada*. Buenos Aires: Paidós.

———. 2001. *Consumers and Citizens. Globalization and Multicultural Conflicts*. Minneapolis/London: University of Minnesota Press.

Garrard-Burnett, Virginia. 2010. *Terror in the Land of the Holy Spirit. Guatemala under General Efraín Ríos Montt, 1982-1983*. Oxford, New York: Oxford University Press.

Goff, Fred. 1966. "Some Reflections on the Role of the Churches in the Formulation of Foreign Policy." *NACLA*, December.

Gutiérrez Sánchez, Tomás. 2015a. "Perspectivas y desafíos para establecer una cultura de valores y justicia desde las ideas y las prácticas del cristianismo evangélico." Contribution to the conference: *45 años FTL y las fronteras teológicas de la contemporaneidad*. 4-6 June, 2015, São Paulo.

———. 2015b. "La teología pública en América Latina." Contribution to the conference: *45 años FTL y las fronteras teológicas de la contemporaneidad*. 4-6 June, 2015, São Paulo.

———. 2017. "Protestantismo y política en América Latina una interpretación desde las ideologías políticas. Siglo XX." Dissertation, Lima: Universidad Nacional Mayor de San Marcos.

Habermas, Jürgen. 2004. "Faith and Knowledge." Acceptance speech. Peace Prize of the German Book Trade 2001. Frankfurt a. M., October 14. Accessed January 5, 2007. https://www.friedenspreis-des-deutschen-buchhandels.de/sixcms/media.php/1290/2001%20Acceptance%20Speech%20Juergen%20Habermas.pdf.

Hochgeschwender, Michael. 2007. *Amerikanische Religion*. Frankfurt: Verlag der Weltreligionen.

Holland, Clifton L. 2011. "Encyclopedia of Religious Groups in Latin America and the Caribbean: Religion in Guatemala." Accessed August 31, 2020. http://www.prolades.com/cra/regions/cam/gte/gte-rd.htm.

Howell, Leon. 2003. *United Methodism @ risk: A wake-up call.* Kingston N.Y.: Information Project for United Methodists.

Huntington, Samuel P. 1982. *American Politics: The Promise of Disharmony*. Cambridge: The Belknap Press of Harvard University Press.

Hvalkof, Søren, and Peter Aaby. 1980. *Is God an American?* Kopenhagen: IWGIA.

Jefferson, Thomas. 1998. "Jefferson's Letter to the Danbury Baptists, sent on Jan. 1, 1802." The Library of Congress. 1998. Accessed October 10, 2019. https://www.loc.gov/loc/lcib/9806/danpre.html.

———. 2006. "First Inaugural Address. 4.3.1801." In *The papers of Thomas Jefferson. 17 February to 30 April 1801*, 33: 148-152. Princeton N.J.: Princeton University Press. Accessed April 1, 2019. https://avalon.law.yale.edu/19th_century/jefinau1.asp.

Jones, Robert P., and Daniel Cox. 2017. *America's changing religious identity. Findings from the 2016 American Values Atlas*. Washington D.C.: Public Religion Research Institute (PRRI). Accessed June 5, 2018. https://www.prri.org/research/american-religious-landscape-christian-religiously-unaffiliated/.

Jones, Robert P., Daniel Cox, E.J. Dionne, William A. Galston, Betsy Cooper, and Rachel Lienesch. 2016. "How immigration and concerns about cultural changes are shaping the 2016 election. Findings from the 2016 PRRI/Brookings Immigration Survey." Washington D.C.: Public Religion Research Institute / Brookings.

Juergensmeyer, Mark, ed. 2005. *Religion in global civil society*. Oxford, New York: Oxford University Press.

Kaltmeier, Olaf. 2016. *Konjunkturen der (De-)Kolonialisierung: Indigene Gemeinschaften, Hacienda und Staat in den ecuadori-*

anischen Anden von der Kolonialzeit bis heute. Bielefeld: Transcript.

———. 2019. *Refeudalización*. Bielefeld: Transcript.

Kirkpatrick, David. 2019. "Reforming Fundamentalism in Latin America: The Evangelical Left and Universidad Bíblica Latinoamericana." *Journal of the American Academy of Religion* 87 (1): 122-155.

Krumwiede, Heinrich-W. 2002. *Soziale Ungleichheit und Massenarmut in Lateinamerika*. Berlin: Dt. Inst. für Internat. Politik und Sicherheit.

Lalive d'Epinay, Christian. 1969. *Haven of the Masses. A Study of the Pentecostal Movement in Chile*. London: Lutterworth.

———. 1975. *Religion, dynamique sociale et dependance. Les mouvements protestants en argentine et au Chili*. Paris: Mouton.

Lienemann-Perrin, Christine, and Wolfgang Lienemann, ed. 2006. *Kirche und Öffentlichkeit in Transformationsgesellschaften*. Stuttgart: Kohlhammer.

Lint Sagarena, Roberto. 2009. "Migration and Mexican American Religious Life, 1848-2000." In *Immigration and Religion in America: Comparative and Historical Perspectives*, ed. Richard Alba, Albert J. Raboteau, and Josh DeWind, 56-70. New York, London: New York University Press.

López Torres, Samuel. 1999. *Historia de la Iglesia Apostólica de la Fe en Cristo Jesús*. Tijuana: Iglesia Apostólica de la Fe en Cristo Jesús.

———. 2014. "Historia, cotidianidad y testimonio." In *Cien años de Pentecostés*, ed. Domingo Torres Alvarado, 387-427. Mexico D.F.: Iglesia Apostólica de la Fe en Cristo Jesús.

Luque, Elias. 2014. "La doctrina apostólica." In *Cien años de Pentecostés*, ed. Domingo Torres Alvarado, 153-196. Mexico D.F.: Iglesia Apostólica de la Fe en Cristo Jesús.

Martin, David. 1990. *Tongues of Fire. The Explosion of Protestantism in Latin America*. Oxford: Blackwell.

———. 2001. *Pentecostalism. The World Their Parish*. Oxford: Blackwell.

Martín-Baró, Ignacio. 1984. "Guerra y salud mental." *Estudios Centroamericanos*, Nr. 429-430: 503-514.

Melander, Veronica. 1999. *The Hour of God. People in Guatemala Confronting Political Evangelicalism and Counterinsurgency (1976-1990)*. Studia Missionalia Upsaliensia 71. Uppsala: Swedish Institute of Missionary Research.

Mesquiati de Oliveira, David, and Gedeon Freire de Alencar. 2017. "Research Note: The Contribution of the Rede Latino-Americana de Estudos Pentecostais." *International Journal of Latin American Religions* 1 (1): 156-165.

Míguez Bonino, José. 1995. *Rostros del protestantismo Latinoamericano*. Buenos Aires, Grand Rapids: Nueva Creacion, W.B. Eerdmans Pub. Co.

Montejo, Victor. 2008. *Voices from Exile. Violence and Survival in Modern Maya History*. Norman, OK: University of Oklahoma Press.

Montero, Paula. 2006. "Religião, pluralismo e esfera pública no Brasil." *Novos estudos* 74: 47-65.

National Archives and Records Administration, ed. 1789. "George Washington's Inaugural Address of 1789." Accessed November 1, 2018. https://www.archives.gov/exhibits/american_originals/inaugura.html.

Neckel, Sighard. 2010. "Refeudalisierung der Ökonomie. Zum Strukturwandel kapitalistischer Wirtschaft. MPIfG Working Paper 10/6." Max-Planck-Institut für Gesellschaftsforschung, Köln.

Noll, Mark. 2008. *God and race in American politics*. Princeton: Princeton University Press.

O'Sullivan, John. 1845. "Annexation." *United States Magazine and Democratic Review* 17 (1): 5-10.

Pagán, Samuel. 2016. "Congreso misionero en Panamá (1916): Realidades, desafíos y posibilidades." World Evangelical Alliance: Misión Policéntrica, Panama.

Pally, Marcia. 2008. *Warnung vor dem Freunde. Tradition und Zukunft US-amerikanischer Außenpolitik*. Berlin: Parthas.

Pareto, Vilfredo. 1916. *Trattato di sociologia generale*. Firenze: G. Barbèra.

Pew Research Center. 2014. "The Shifting Religious Identity of Latinos in the United States. Nearly One-in-Four Latinos Are Former Catholics." Washington, D.C.: Pew Research Center.

Piedra Solano, Arturo. 1993. "Latin American Protestantism from the neglected continent to the continent of opportunity: An assessment of the justification for Protestant expansion in Latin America, 1894-1960." Dissertation. Edinburgh: University of Edinburgh.

Prätorius, Rainer. 2003. *In God we Trust: Religion und Politik in den U.S.A.* München: C.H. Beck.

Prien, Hans-Jürgen. 1978. *Die Geschichte des Christentums in Lateinamerika*. Göttingen: Vandenhoeck & Ruprecht.

Ramírez, Daniel. 2015. *Migrating Faith: Pentecostalism in the United States and Mexico in the Twentieth Century*. Chapel Hill: University of North Carolina Press.

Roberts, W. Dayton, and John A. Siewert. 1989. *Mission Handbook*. Monrovia: MARC.

Rosenberg, Emily S. 1999. *Spreading the American Dream: American Economic and Cultural Expansion, 1890-1945*. New York: Hill and Wang.

Ruiz, David. 2016. "Asuntos misionológicos de América Latina en el protestantismo latinoamericano de la segunda mitad del siglo XX." World Evangelical Alliance: Misión Policéntrica, Panama.

Rushdooney, Rousas. 1986. "Back to the future." *New Wine* (November): 24.

Salinas, Daniel. 2009. *Latin American Evangelical Theology in the 1970's: The Golden Decade*. Leiden, Boston: Brill.

———. 2017. *Taking up the Mantle: Latin American Evangelical Theology in the 20th Century*. Carlisle: Langham Global Library.

Schäfer, Heinrich Wilhelm. 1990. "'...und erlöse uns von dem Bösen.' Zur politischen Funktion des Fundamentalismus in Mittelamerika." In *"Gottes einzige Antwort." Christlicher Fundamentalismus als Herausforderung an Kirche und Gesellschaft*, ed. Uwe Birnstein, 118-139. Wuppertal: P. Hammer Verlag.

———. 1992a. "Lìbranos del mal! Estructuras simbólicas y funciones políticas en el protestantismo centroamericano." In *Protestantismo y crisis social en América Central*, ed. Heinrich Wilhelm Schäfer, 189-214. San José: Departamento Ecuménico de Investigaciones.

———. 1992b. *Protestantismo y crisis social en América Central.* San José: Departamento Ecuménico de Investigaciones.

———. 1992c. *Protestantismus in Zentralamerika. Christliches Zeugnis im Spannungsfeld von US-amerikanischem Fundamentalismus, Unterdrückung und Wiederbelebung "indianischer" Kultur*. Studien zur interkulturellen Geschichte des Christentums 84. Frankfurt a.M.: Lang.

———. 2008. *Kampf der Fundamentalismen. Radikales Christentum, radikaler Islam und Europas zweite Moderne*. Frankfurt a.M.: Verlag der Weltreligionen (Suhrkamp).

———. 2009. "Pfingstbewegung – sozialer Wandel und religiöser Habitus." In *Woran glaubt die Welt? Analysen und Kommentare zum Religionsmonitor 2008*, ed. Bertelsmann Stiftung, 553-608. Gütersloh: Verlag Bertelsmann Stiftung.

———. 2013. "Notizen zu religiöser Transnationalisierung Lateinamerika." In *Transnationale Vergesellschaftungen. Verhandlungen des 35. Kongresses der Deutschen Gesellschaft für Soziologie in Frankfurt am Main 2010*, ed. Hans-Georg Soeffner. Wiesbaden: VS Verlag für Sozialwissenschaften, CD-ROM. https://pub.uni-bielefeld.de/record/2580832.

———. 2015. *Identität als Netzwerk. Habitus, Sozialstruktur und religiöse Mobilisierung*. Wiesbaden: Springer VS.

———. 2016. "Mission inverted: Inter-American Religious Flows and how to capture them." In *Entangled and Mobile Americas*, ed. Maryemma Graham and Wilfried Raussert. Farnham: Ashgate: 203-244.

———. 2019. *Friedenspotenzial von Freikirchen in den USA und Lateinamerika: Potenziale und Hindernisse für die internationale Zusammenarbeit.* ifa-Edition Kultur und Außenpolitik. Stuttgart: ifa – Institut für Auslandsbeziehungen.

———. 2020. *HabitusAnalysis, Vol. 2. Praxeology and meaning.* Wiesbaden: Springer VS.

Schäfer, Heinrich Wilhelm, Tobias Reu, and Adrián Tovar Simoncic. 2013. "Cambios en el campo religioso de Guatemala y Nicaragua: 1985 a 2013." *Sendas. Revista Semestral del Instituto de Investigaciones del Hecho Religioso* 1 (1): 11-32.

Schäfer, Heinrich Wilhelm, Leif Hagen Seibert, Adrián Tovar Simoncic, and Jens Köhrsen. 2015a. "Towards a Praxeology of Religious Life 1: Modes of Observation." In *Making Religion: Theory and Practice in the Discursive Study of Religion*, ed. Frans Wijsen and Kocku von Stuckrad, 147-171. Leiden: Brill.

———. 2015b. "Towards a Praxeology of Religious Life 2: Tools of Observation." In *Making Religion: Theory and Practice in the Discursive Study of Religion*, ed. Frans Wijsen and Kocku von Stuckrad, 175-202. Leiden: Brill.

Schilling, Annegreth. 2016. *Revolution, Exil und Befreiung. Der Boom des lateinamerikanischen Protestantismus in der internationalen Ökumene in den 1960er und 1970er Jahren.* Göttingen: Vandenhoeck & Rupprecht.

Segnini, Giannina, and Mónica Cordero. 2019. "Líderes evangélicos amparados por la Casa Blanca exportan agenda fundamentalista a América Latina." Centro Latinoamericano de Investigación Periodística. August 2019. Accessed August 14, 2019. https://www.elclip.org/?s=L%C3%ADderes+evangélicos+amparados+por+la+Casa+Blanca+exportan+agenda+fundamentalista+a+América+Latina.

Sherman, Amy L. 1997. *The soul of development: biblical Christianity and economic transformation in Guatemala.* Religion in America series. New York: Oxford University Press.

Silva, Elizete. 2017. "Protestantes no Brasil: entre a omissão e o engajamento político." *Esboços: histórias em contextos globais* 24 (37): 126-148.

Sinner, Rudolf von. 2012. *The Churches and Democracy in Brazil: Towards a Public Theology Focused on Citizenship*. Eugene: Wipf and Stock Publishers.

Sklair, Leslie. 2001. *The Transnational Capital Class*. Oxford, MA: Blackwell Publishers.

Smith, Brian H. 1998. *Religious politics in Latin America. Pentecostal vs. Catholic*. Notre Dame: University of Notre Dame Press.

Smith, Samuel. 2018. "California's Sanctuary Cities 'a Little Picture of Hell,' Franklin Graham Says." *The Christian Post* (blog). 30. Mai 2018. Accessed January 14, 2019. https://www.christianpost.com/news/california-sanctuary-cities-little-picture-of-hell-franklin-graham.html.

Sombart, Werner. 1976. *Why Is There No Socialism in the United States?* White Plains: M.E. Sharpe.

Stoll, David. 1990. *Is Latin America turning Protestant? The politics of Evangelical growth*. Berkeley: University of California Press.

Strong, Josiah. 1900. *Expansion. Under new World-Conditions*. New York: The Baker and Taylor Company.

Swartz, David R. 2012. "Samuel Escobar and the Global Reflex". In *Moral Minority: The Evangelical Left in an Age of Conservatism*, 113-134. Philadelphia, Pennsylvania: University of Pennsylvania Press.

Tancara Chambe, Juan Jacobo. 2011. *Teología pentecostal popular*. La Paz, Bolivia: Instituto Superior Ecuménico Andino de Teología.

The Interhemispheric Education Resource Center. 1988. *Honduras. Private Organizations with U.S.-Connections. Directory and Analysis*. Albuquerque, NM: IHERC.

Torres Alvarado, Domingo, ed. 2014. *Cien años de Pentecostés: desde la vivencia de la Iglesia Apostólica.* Mexico D.F.: Iglesia Apostólica de la Fe en Cristo Jesús.

Trump, Donald J. 2018. “Executive Order on the Establishment of a White House Faith and Opportunity Initiative.” The White House. Accessed October 28, 2019. https://www.whitehouse.gov/presidential-actions/executive-order-establishment-white-house-faith-opportunity-initiative/.

United States. 1969. *Rockefeller Report on Latin America: hearings before the United States Senate Committee on Foreign Relations, Subcommittee on Western Hemisphere Affairs, Ninety-First Congress, first session, on Nov. 20, 1969.* Washington: U.S. G.P.O.

United States Senate, ed. 1791. “Constitution of the United States.” Accessed November 1, 2018. https://www.senate.gov/civics/constitution_item/constitution.htm#amdt_1_(1791).

———. 1976. *Supplementary Detailed Staff Reports on Foreign and Military Intelligence. Book IV, Final Report.* Washington D.C.: U.S. Government Printing Office. https://www.intelligence.senate.gov/sites/default/files/94755_IV.pdf.

Valcárcel, Luis. 1972. *Tempestad en los Andes.* 2nd ed. Lima: Ed. Universo.

Vasquez, Manuel A., and Marie F. Marquardt. 2003. *Globalizing the Sacred: Religion across the Americas.* New Brunswick, N.J.: Rutgers University Press.

Volkan, Vamik D. 2018. *Psychoanalysis, international relations, and diplomacy: A sourcebook on large-group psychology.* London, New York: Routledge.

WEA Mission Commission. 2016. “WEA Mission Commission highlights Polycentric Mission during Panama Global Consultation.” World Evangelical Alliance: Misión Policéntrica. Panama. Accessed December 12, 2016. https://weamc.global/wea-mission-commission-highlights-polycentric-mission-during-panama-global-consultation/.

Weber, Max. 1946a. "The Protestant Sects and the Spirit of Capitalism." In *From Max Weber: Essays in Sociology*, ed. Hans H. Gerth and C. Wright Mills, 302-322. New York: Oxford University Press.

———. 1946b. "Religious Rejections of the World and Their Directions." In *From Max Weber: Essays in Sociology*, ed. Hans H. Gerth and C. Wright Mills, 323-359. New York: Oxford University Press.

———. 1978. *Economy and Society: An Outline of Interpretive Sociology*. Berkeley: University of California Press.

———. 2001. *The Protestant ethic and the spirit of capitalism.* London, New York: Routledge.

Weiß, Anja, and Peter A. Berger. 2008. "Logik der Differenz – Logik des Austausches: Beiträge zur Transnationalisierung sozialer Ungleichheiten." In *Transnationalisierung sozialer Ungleichheit*, ed. Peter A. Berger and Anja Weiß, 7-13. Wiesbaden: VS Verlag für Sozialwissenschaften / GWV Fachverlage.

Werner, Michael, and Bénédicte Zimmermann. 2002. "Vergleich, Transfer, Verflechtung. Der Ansatz der Histoire croisée und die Herausforderung des Transnationalen." *Geschichte und Gesellschaft* 28 (4): 607-636.

Willems, Emílio. 1967. *Followers of the New Faith. Culture Change and the Rise of Protestantism in Brazil and Chile.* Nashville: Vanderbilt University Press.

Williams, William Appleman. 1980. *Empire as a Way of Life*. New York: Oxford University Press.

Wisdom, Alan. n. y. "Discernment Needed: What Mainstream Christians Know and Don't Know about Possible War with Iraq." IRD. Accessed October, 10, 2019 (not available anymore by March 28, 2020). http://www.theird.org/Document.Doc?id=11.

Wong, Janelle. 2018. *Immigrants, Evangelicals, and Politics in an Era of Demographic Change*. New York, N.Y: Russell Sage Foundation.

World Evangelical Fellowship. 1974. "The Lausanne Covenant." Lausanne Movement. *1974 International Congress on World Evangelization (ICOWE)*, August 1, 1974. Accessed March 18, 2020. https://www.lausanne.org/content/covenant/lausanne-covenant.

Virtual Interview

1. Why a book on this subject?

The "sects" of the USA, as Max Weber called them, have become an influential variant of Christianity, both religiously as well as politically, and not only in Latin America. The centenary of Weber's death and the anniversary of the 1916 missionary congress in Panama recall the roots of this development. But its specific dynamic is revealed by looking at the history of the entanglements (*histoire croisée*). Protestantism changes as it takes root in Latin America; and this new religious praxis has an effect on the United States.

2. Which new perspectives does your book open up?

What is new is the combination of history of entanglements with the social science of praxis. The analysis of interrelationships (*histoire croisée*) presents the US mission in Latin America, the churches there and Latin American migration to the USA in their mutual interactions. The praxeological approach (Weber, Bourdieu) makes it possible, beyond culturalism (of the type "betterment for Latin America"), to describe those entanglements through the analysis of religious and political discourses, practices and social structures.

3. What significance does the topic have in current research debates?

In the regional sciences, Protestantism in Latin America and the USA is at present increasingly debated. The history of entanglements lends historical depth to the interpretation of these developments (1916 to 2016) and their social conjunctures (e.g. planning of the US mission, Central American wars, US religious policy, migration). The praxeological approach illustrates how the religious processes merge with the socio-structural ones, such as refeudalization and Neopentecostal religiosity.

4. Who would you most like to discuss your book with?

With Max Weber and Pierre Bourdieu! The book should be of interest to organizations of international cooperation and their partners in Latin America. Thanks to the editions in Spanish and English, debates with colleagues in social sciences and theology from Latin America and the USA should also be of interest.

5. Your book in one sentence?

A praxeological essay on the entanglements of religion, power and resistance between Latin America and the USA.

INTER-AMERICAN STUDIES
Cultures – Societies – History

ESTUDIOS INTERAMERICANOS
Culturas – Sociedades – Historia

This interdisciplinary series examines national and transnational issues in the cultures, societies, and histories of the Americas. It creates a forum for a critical academic dialogue between North and South, promoting an inter-American paradigm that shifts the scholarly focus from methodological nationalism to the wider context of the Western Hemisphere.

Vol. 1
Raab, Josef, Sebastian Thies, and Daniela Noll-Opitz, eds. *Screening the Americas: Narration of Nation in Documentary Film / Proyectando las Américas: Narración de la nación en el cine documental*. 2011. 470 pp.

WVT Wissenschaftlicher Verlag Trier	ISBN 978-3-86821-331-7	€ 29,50
Bilingual Press / Editorial Bilingüe	ISBN 978-1-931010-83-2	$ 29.50

Vol. 2
Raussert, Wilfried, and Michelle Habell-Pallán, eds. *Cornbread and Cuchifritos: Ethnic Identity Politics, Transnationalization, and Transculturation in American Urban Popular Music*. 2011. 292 pp.

WVT Wissenschaftlicher Verlag Trier	ISBN 978-3-86821-265-5	€ 29,50
Bilingual Press / Editorial Bilingüe	ISBN 978- 1-931010-80-1	$ 29.50

Vol. 3
Butler, Martin, Jens Martin Gurr, and Olaf Kaltmeier, eds. *EthniCities: Metropolitan Cultures and Ethnic Identities in the Americas*. 2011. 268 pp.

WVT Wissenschaftlicher Verlag Trier	ISBN 978-3-86821-310-2	€ 29,50
Bilingual Press / Editorial Bilingüe	ISBN 978-1-931010-81-8	$ 29.50

Vol. 4
Gurr, Jens Martin, and Wilfried Raussert, eds. *Cityscapes in the Americas and Beyond: Representations of Urban Complexity in Literature and Film*. 2011. 300 pp.

WVT Wissenschaftlicher Verlag Trier	ISBN 978-3-86821-324-9	€ 29,50
Bilingual Press / Editorial Bilingüe	ISBN 978-1-931010-82-5	$ 29.50

Vol. 5
Kirschner, Luz Angélica, ed. *Expanding* Latinidad*: An Inter-American Perspective.* 2012. 292 pp.

WVT Wissenschaftlicher Verlag Trier	ISBN 978-3-86821-309-6	€ 29,50
Bilingual Press / Editorial Bilingüe	ISBN 978-1-931010-84-9	$ 29.50

Vol. 6
Raussert, Wilfried, and Graciela Martínez-Zalce, eds. *(Re)Discovering 'America': Road Movies and Other Travel Narratives in North America / (Re)Descubriendo 'América': Road movie y otras narrativas de viaje en América del Norte*. 2012. 252 pp.

WVT Wissenschaftlicher Verlag Trier	ISBN 978-3-86821-384-3	€ 29,50
Bilingual Press / Editorial Bilingüe	ISBN 978-1-931010-91-7	$ 29.50

Vol. 7
Kaltmeier, Olaf, ed. *Transnational Americas: Envisioning Inter-American Area Studies in Globalization Processes*. 2013. 278 pp.

WVT Wissenschaftlicher Verlag Trier	ISBN 978-3-86821-415-4	€ 29,50
Bilingual Press / Editorial Bilingüe	ISBN 978-1-931010-92-4	$ 29.50

Vol. 8
Raab, Josef, and Alexander Greiffenstern, eds. *Interculturalism in North America: Canada, the United States, Mexico, and Beyond*. 2013. 312 pp.

WVT Wissenschaftlicher Verlag Trier	ISBN 978-3-86821-460-4	€ 29,50
Bilingual Press / Editorial Bilingüe	ISBN 978-1-931010-99-3	$ 29.50

Vol. 9
Raab, Josef, ed. *New World Colors: Ethnicity, Belonging, and Difference in the Americas*. 2014. 418 pp.

WVT Wissenschaftlicher Verlag Trier	ISBN 978-3-86821-461-1	€ 29,50
Bilingual Press / Editorial Bilingüe	ISBN 978-1-939743-00-8	$ 39.50

Vol. 10
Roth, Julia. *Occidental Readings, Decolonial Practices: A Selection on Gender, Genre, and Coloniality in the Americas*. 2014. 284 pp.

WVT Wissenschaftlicher Verlag Trier	ISBN 978-3-86821-446-8	€ 26,50
Bilingual Press / Editorial Bilingüe	ISBN 978-1-939743-07-7	$ 32.50

Vol. 11
Thies, Sebastian, Gabriele Pisarz-Ramirez, and Luzelena Gutiérrez de Velasco, eds. *Of Fatherlands and Motherlands: Gender and Nation in the Americas / De Patrias y Matrias: Género y nación en las Américas*. 2015. 344 pp.

WVT Wissenschaftlicher Verlag Trier	ISBN 978-3-86821-528-1	€ 29,50
Bilingual Press / Editorial Bilingüe	ISBN 978-1-939743-08-4	$ 39.50

Vol. 12

Fuchs, Rebecca. *Caribbeanness as a Global Phenomenon: Junot Díaz, Edwidge Danticat, and Cristina García*. 2014. 298 pp.

WVT Wissenschaftlicher Verlag Trier	ISBN 978-3-86821-533-5	€ 26,50
Bilingual Press / Editorial Bilingüe	ISBN 978-1-939743-09-1	$ 32.50

Vol. 13

Andres, Julia. *¡Cuéntame algo! – Chicana Narrative Beyond the Borderlands*. 2015. 202 pp.

WVT Wissenschaftlicher Verlag Trier	ISBN 978-3-86821-569-4	€ 25,00
Bilingual Press / Editorial Bilingüe	ISBN 978-1-939743-11-4	$ 28.50

Vol. 14

Hertlein, Saskia. *Tales of Transformation: Emerging Adulthood, Migration, and Ethnicity in Contemporary American Literature*. 2014. 228 pp.

WVT Wissenschaftlicher Verlag Trier	ISBN 978-3-86821-570-0	€ 25,00
Bilingual Press / Editorial Bilingüe	ISBN 978-1-939743-10-7	$ 31.50

Vol. 15

Raab, Josef, and Saskia Hertlein, eds. *Spaces – Communities – Discourses: Charting Identity and Belonging in the Americas*. 2016. 382 pp.

WVT Wissenschaftlicher Verlag Trier	ISBN 978-3-86821-590-8	€ 29,50
Bilingual Press / Editorial Bilingüe	ISBN 978-1-939743-13-8	$ 39.50

Vol. 16

Mehring, Frank, ed. *The Mexico Diary: Winold Reiss between Vogue Mexico and Harlem Renaissance. An Illustrated Trilingual Edition with Commentary and Musical Interpretation* (includes color plates and audio CD). 2016. 244 pp.

WVT Wissenschaftlicher Verlag Trier	ISBN 978-3-86821-594-6	€ 29,50
Bilingual Press / Editorial Bilingüe	ISBN 978-1-939743-14-5	$ 39.50

Vol. 17

Raussert, Wilfried, Brian Rozema, Yolanda Campos, and Marius Littschwager, eds. *Key Tropes in Inter-American Studies: Perspectives from the* forum for inter-american research (fiar). 2015. 374 pp.

WVT Wissenschaftlicher Verlag Trier	ISBN 978-3-86821-627-1	€ 29,50
Bilingual Press / Editorial Bilingüe	ISBN 978-1-939743-16-9	$ 39.50

Vol. 19

Rehm, Lukas, Jochen Kemner, and Olaf Kaltmeier, eds. *Politics of Entanglement in the Americas: Connecting Transnational Flows and Local Perspectives*. 2017. 226 pp.

WVT Wissenschaftlicher Verlag Trier	ISBN 978-3-86821-675-2	€ 27,50
Bilingual Press / Editorial Bilingüe	ISBN 978-1-939743-17-6	$ 32.50

Vol. 20
Britt Arredondo, Christopher. *Imperial Idiocy: A Reflection on Forced Displacement in the Americas*. 2017. 194 pp.

WVT Wissenschaftlicher Verlag Trier	ISBN 978-3-86821-706-3	€ 26,50
Bilingual Press / Editorial Bilingüe	ISBN 978-1-939743-20-6	$ 30.00

Vol. 21
Schemien, Alexia. *Of Virgins, Curanderas, and Wrestler Saints: Un/Doing Religion in Contemporary Mexican American Literature*. 2018. 218 pp.

WVT Wissenschaftlicher Verlag Trier	ISBN 978-3-86821-724-7	€ 27,50
Bilingual Press / Editorial Bilingüe	ISBN 978-1-939743-22-0	$ 32.50

Vol. 22
Fulger, Maria Diana. *The Cuban Post-Socialist Exotic: Contemporary U.S. American Travel Narratives about Cuba*. 2020. 266 pp.

WVT Wissenschaftlicher Verlag Trier	ISBN 978-3-86821-769-8	€ 32,50
Bilingual Press / Editorial Bilingüe	ISBN 978-1-939743-27-5	$ 36.00

Vol. 24
Kaltmeier, Olaf, Mirko Petersen, Wilfried Raussert, and Julia Roth, eds. *Cherishing the Past, Envisioning the Future. Entangled Practises of Heritage and Utopia in the Americas*. 2021. 176 pp.

WVT Wissenschaftlicher Verlag Trier	ISBN 978-3-86821-804-6	€ 23,50
UNO University of New Orleans Press	ISBN 978-1-60801-206-0	$ 27.50

Vol. 26
Raussert, Wilfried. *'What's Going On': How Music Shapes the Social*. 2021. 224 pp.

WVT Wissenschaftlicher Verlag Trier	ISBN 978-3-86821-811-4	€ 28,50
UNO University of New Orleans Press	ISBN 978-1-60801-199-5	$ 34.00

Vol. 27
Frank-Job, Barbara. *Immigration as a Process: Temporality Concepts in Blogs of Latin American Immigrants to Québec*. 2021. 138 pp.

WVT Wissenschaftlicher Verlag Trier	ISBN 978-3-86821-820-6	€ 20,00
UNO University of New Orleans Press	ISBN 978-1-60801-215-2	$ 24.00

Vol. 28
Roth, Julia. *Can Feminism Trump Populism? Right-Wing Trends and Intersectional Contestations in the Americas*. 2021. 166 pp.

WVT Wissenschaftlicher Verlag Trier	ISBN 978-3-86821-821-3	€ 23,00
UNO University of New Orleans Press	ISBN 978-1-60801-205-3	$ 26.00

Vol. 30

Buitrago Valencia, Clara. *Missionaries: Migrants or Expatriates? Guatemalan Pentecostal Leaders in Los Angeles.* 2021. 236 pp.

WVT Wissenschaftlicher Verlag Trier	ISBN 978-3-86821-818-3	€ 28,50
UNO University of New Orleans Press	ISBN 978-1-60801-210-7	$ 34.50

Vol. 31

Schwabe, Nicole. *De-Centering History Education: Creating Knowledge of Global Entanglements.* 2021. 92 pp.

WVT Wissenschaftlicher Verlag Trier	ISBN 978-3-86821-828-2	€ 18,00
UNO University of New Orleans Press	ISBN 978-1-60801-214-5	$ 21.00

Vol. 32

Manke, Albert. *Coping with Discrimination and Exclusion. Experiences of Free Chinese Migrants in the Americas in a Transregional and Diachronic Perspective.* 2021. 162 pp.

WVT Wissenschaftlicher Verlag Trier	ISBN 978-3-86821-829-9	€ 23,00
UNO University of New Orleans Press	ISBN 978-1-60801-207-7	$ 27.00

Vol. 33

Rohland, Eleonora. *Entangled Histories and the Environment? Socio-Environmental Transformations in the Caribbean, 1492-1800.* 2021. 92 pp.

WVT Wissenschaftlicher Verlag Trier	ISBN 978-3-86821-833-6	€ 18,00
UNO University of New Orleans Press	ISBN 978-1-60801-208-4	$ 21.00

Vol. 34

Kaltmeier, Olaf. *National Parks from North to South. An Entangled History of Conservation and Colonization in Argentina.* 2021. 210 pp.

WVT Wissenschaftlicher Verlag Trier	ISBN 978-3-86821-834-3	€ 27,50
UNO University of New Orleans Press	ISBN 978-1-60801-204-6	$ 32.50

Vol. 35

Raussert, Wilfried. *Off the Grid. Art Practices and Public Space.* 2021. 232 pp.

WVT Wissenschaftlicher Verlag Trier	ISBN 978-3-86821-835-0	€ 29,50
UNO University of New Orleans Press	ISBN 978-1-60801-213-8	$ 34.50

Vol. 36

Ravasio, Paola. *This Train Is Not Bound to Glory. A Study of Literary Trainscapes.* 2021. 114 pp.

WVT Wissenschaftlicher Verlag Trier	ISBN 978-3-86821-836-7	€ 18,00
UNO University of New Orleans Press	ISBN 978-1-60801-216-9	$ 21.00

Vol. 37

Schäfer, Heinrich Wilhelm. *Protestant 'Sects' and the Spirit of (Anti-)Imperialism. Religious Entanglements in the Americas.* 2021. 242 pp.

WVT Wissenschaftlicher Verlag Trier	ISBN 978-3-86821-855-9	€ 29,50
UNO University of New Orleans Press	ISBN 978-1-60801-209-1	$ 34.50